THE
WORKS

Of the REVEREND

WILLIAM LAW, M.A.,

Sometime Fellow of *Emmanuel*
College, *Cambridge*.

In Nine Volumes.

Volume II.

I. Remarks upon a late Book, entitled,
  '*The Fable of the Bees*,' &c.
  Page 3.

II. The Case of Reason, or Natural Religion, fairly and fully stated, &c.
  Page 55.

III. The absolute Unlawfulness of Stage-Entertainments fully demonstrated.
  Page 139.

Wipf and Stock Publishers
150 West Broadway • Eugene OR 97401
2001

Volume II-Remarks upon 'The Fable of the Bees'; The Case of Reason; The Absolute Unlawfulness of the Stage-Entertainment...

By Law, William

ISBN: 1-57910-616-1

Reprinted by **Wipf and Stock Publishers**
150 West Broadway • Eugene OR 97401

Previously published by G. Moreton, Setley, 1892.

Prefatory Advertisement.

I. Remarks upon '*The Fable of the Bees.*'

WILLIAM LAW'S second publication was, like his first, of a controversial nature, although his opponent was a very different personage from Doctor *Hoadly*, Bishop of *Bangor ;* of whom a few very general particulars should have been given in the previous volume ; which omission is now supplied, by way of brief digression, here. *Benjamin Hoadly* was born in the year 1676 ; educated at *Catherine* College, *Cambridge ;* Bishop of *Bangor* in 1715, which See he held at the breaking out of the Bangorian Controversy, to which *William Law's* three Letters —written between the years 1717-1719, when he was about thirty-one years of age—are considered to have been the most important contribution. His Lordship was translated successively to the Sees of *Hereford, Salisbury* and *Winchester ;* and of the last See he was Diocesan for above twenty-six years. He died in the year 1761, aged 85 years, and was buried in *Winchester* Cathedral.

BERNARD DE MANDEVILLE, who was *William Law's* second opponent, was of Dutch extraction, a Native of *Holland* and an Author of a very temporary and unenviable kind of celebrity. Having graduated in Medicine at one of the Continental Universities he came to *London*, where he practised his profession ; but does not appear to have been held in much repute by medical men. He therefore wrote a Satire upon them, which appears to have passed unnoticed. In the year 1714, when he was about forty-four years of age, he published a Poem entitled ' The Grumbling Hive ; or Knaves turned Honest,' setting forth a Hive of Bees who having by dishonest practices acquired wealth and luxury agreed to abandon them and to 'turn honest,' which reduced them to poverty; and occasioned their grumbling —in prose and verse of a very lame and doggerel kind. In this effusion, Mandeville not only ridicules the expediency of being Honest as the best Policy—a treatment perhaps which that time-honoured but most worldly-wise maxim well merits—but entirely rejects 'virtue' and 'reason;' affirming that man like the brutes, is governed by mere instincts and passions. He enlarged and republished this work in the year 1723, with the Title of 'The Fable of the Bees; or Private Vices, Public 'Benefits'—when it achieved the notoriety of being 'presented' by the Grand Jury of *Middlesex*, as dangerous to Religion and Order. *William Law* also 'presented' the book in a very masterly manner in his 'Remarks' upon it; which he wrote the same year and published early in the year 1724. *Mandeville* attempted to vindicate his 'philosophy' in the *London* Journal in *August*, 1723; when *William Law* had written, ready for the press, as far as page 45 of this volume; and this 'Vindication' occasioned further strictures from that Writer.

Of *Mandeville's* later life, little is known. He is said to have resided in obscure lodgings; and to have written in the *London* Journal as a Medical Man, in favour of the use of spirituous liquors—for which he was well paid by the Distillers. He died in *January*, 1733, aged 63 years.

The French Writer, PIERRE BAYLE, upon whose works *William Law* in a Postscript makes 'an Observation or two,' is probably known to some readers as the Compiler of the 'Critical Dictionary' and otherwise, as a voluminous and rather unedifying writer. He died 'of a decay of the lungs, after he had been 'writing the greatest part of the day'—wrote himself to death, poor man!—in the year 1706.

The 'Remarks upon the Fable of the Bees' is *Law's* earliest work which has been republished in later times. This was done in the year 1844 under the Editorship of MR. MAURICE upon the suggestion of JOHN STERLING, who described *Law's* 'Re-'marks' as one of the most remarkable philosophical Essays he had ever seen in English: of which the first Section 'has all the 'highest beauty of' *Law's* 'polemical compositions, and a weight 'of pithy right reason such as fills one's heart with joy. I have 'never seen in our language the elementary ground of a rational 'ideal philosophy as opposed to empiricism, stated in nearly the 'same clearness, simplicity and force.' In MR. MAURICE'S reissue *Mandeville's* Fable is also partly included—a course almost as impracticable here, as it would be to recite all the arguments of the Bangorian Controversy. Readers of *William Law's* Works scarcely need to be reminded that he always renders full justice to his opponents; and generally quotes whole paragraphs from their writings, so that both sides of the question are fairly and comprehensively stated; which is of great assistance to the modern reader. At the time of writing the 'Remarks,' *William Law* was about 37 years of age.

II. *The Case of Reason ; or Natural Religion fairly and fully stated.*

ALTHOUGH 'The Case of Reason' appears as *William Law's* third publication in the collected edition of his works issued after his decease, and is here, for convenience, so retained ; yet it is not the third, but the sixth, in the order of publication. It was not published until the year 1731, after the excellent Pamphlet respecting the 'Unlawfulness of the Stage-Entertainment'; the 'Practical Treatise on Christian Perfection' and the 'Serious Call' had appeared : and when *William Law* was forty-five years of age and well known.

The Case of Reason was written in reply to DR. TINDAL, 'the 'Christian Deist's' work entitled 'Christianity as old as the 'Creation'; which was published in the year 1730 and excited much controversy at the time.

WILLIAM LAW had a curious variety of opponents to contend with. BISHOP HOADLY with his Invisible Church, disregard for outward and visible Ordinances, and Salvation by Sincerity: BERNARD MANDEVILLE with his rejection of anything of the moral nature beyond mere brute instinct ; and DR. TINDAL with his supreme dependence upon Reason or Natural Religion: against each of whom *William Law* most effectually turned their own weapons.

MATTHEW TINDAL is said to have been born in the year 1657. He was a Doctor of Laws and wrote various books of which the most important was that replied to by *William Law*. His 'Defence of the Rights of the Christian Church'—incorrectly reprinted as 'Rites' in the Bangorian Letters—was burnt by Order of the House of Commons. His other works, of a nature sufficiently indicated by the subjects of which they treat, 'Jacobitism, Perjury, Popery, Law of Nations, Rights of 'Sovereigns,' &c., appear to have long since passed with their Author—who died in the year 1733—into Oblivion.

III. The Absolute Unlawfulness of the Stage-Entertainment fully demonstrated.

THIS Pamphlet is WILLIAM LAW'S third work in the order of publication; published in the year 1726, when he was about forty years of age. It has been severely censured by *Law's* so-called Admirers; and a late writer describes it as written with greater zeal than knowledge of the facts—a description which is more epigrammatic than just. Even CANON OVERTON gravely considers it his duty as 'a faithful Biographer not to shrink from 'admitting the weaknesses of his Subject'—very gratuitously and unnecessarily we think in this case; which reveals to us how little real insight he had into the *life* of *William Law*. JOHN DENNIS a kind of 'Critic' and an ex-Playwright, replied to it in 'The Stage Defended from Scripture, Reason, Experience and 'the Common Sense of Mankind for 2,000 years'—by which he is usually misrepresented as having completely vanquished poor *Law*. Two thousand years ago takes him back to classical times—and he naturally refers to the Grecian stage; as if the London Play-house of *Law's* time, could possibly be compared with the Athenian or Corinthian stages. His Scriptural Authorities, according to CANON OVERTON, appear to be quite negative—*e.g.*, St. *Paul* did not condemn the Athenian stage of his time. From Reason no less than from Experience, *William Law* sufficiently condemns such Entertainments; and the 'Common Sense of Mankind for the last 2,000 years' can scarcely be received as an authority upon any important subject. Disregarding all Criticism: is it possible for any truly piousminded man to answer the following interrogatory respecting the Stage-Entertainment, which *William Law* puts at page 156, in the affirmative?

'Is it conformable to that Heavenly Affection, that Love of 'God, that Purity of Heart, that Wisdom of Mind, that Per'fection of Holiness, that Contempt of the World, that Watch'fulness and Self-denial, that Humility and Fear of Sin, which 'Religion requires?'

G. B. M.

REMARKS upon
'The Fable of the Bees.'

REMARKS

UPON

A BOOK,

ENTITLED

The Fable of the Bees,

OR

Private Vices, Publick Benefits.

IN A

LETTER to the AUTHOR.

To which is added,

A POSTSCRIPT, containing an Observation or two upon Mr. *Bayle.*

By *WILLIAM LAW*, M. A.

LONDON:

Printed for J. RICHARDSON, in *Pater-noster-row.*

1723.

Remarks
upon a Book entitled
'The Fable of the Bees.'

Sir,

I HAVE read your several Compositions in favour of the Vices and Corruptions of Mankind; and hope I need make no Apology, for presuming to offer a Word or two on the Side of Virtue and Religion.

I shall spend no Time in Preface, or general Reflections, but proceed directly to the Examination of such Passages as expose *moral Virtue*, as a Fraud and imposition, and render all Pretences to it, as odious and contemptible.

Though I direct myself to you, I hope it will be no Offence, if I sometimes speak, as if I was speaking to a Christian, or show some ways of thinking, that may be owing to that kind of worship which is professed amongst us. Ways of thinking derived from revealed Religion are much more suitable to our low Capacities, than any arrogant Pretences to be wise, by our own Light.

Moral Virtue, however disregarded in Practice, has hitherto had a speculative Esteem amongst Men; her Praises have been celebrated by Authors of all kinds, as the confessed Beauty, Ornament, and Perfection of Human Nature.

On the contrary, *Immorality* has been looked upon as the greatest Reproach and Torment of Mankind; no Satire has been thought severe enough upon its natural Baseness and Deformity, nor any Wit able to express the Evils it occasions in private Life, and public Societies.

Your Goodness would not suffer you to see this part of Christendom, deluded with such false Notions, of I know not what *Excellence* in Virtue, or *Evil* in Vice, but obliged you immediately to compose a *System* (as you call it) wherein you do these three things.

1*st*. You consider Man, *merely* as an *Animal*, having, like other Animals, nothing to do but to follow his Appetites.

2*dly*. You consider Man as cheated and flattered out of his natural State, by the Craft of Moralists, and pretend to be very sure, that the '*moral Virtues are the political offspring which 'Flattery begot upon Pride.*'

So that Man and Morality are here both destroyed together; Man is declared to be only an *Animal*, and Morality an Imposture.

According to this Doctrine, to say that a Man is dishonest, is making him just such a Criminal, as a Horse that does not dance.

But this is not all, for you dare further affirm in praise of immorality, '*That Evil, as well moral, as natural, is the solid 'Basis, the Life and Support of all Trades and Employments 'without exception; that there we must look for the true Origin of 'all Arts and Sciences; and that the Moment Evil ceases, the 'Society must be spoiled, if not dissolved.*'*

These are the principal Doctrines, which with more than Fanatic Zeal you recommend to your Readers; and if lewd Stories, profane Observations, loose Jests, and haughty Assertions, might pass for Arguments, few People would be able to dispute with you.

I shall begin with your Definition of Man. '*As for my part, 'say you, without any Compliment to the courteous Reader, or 'myself, I believe, Man (besides Skin, Flesh, Bones, &c., that are 'obvious to the Eye) to be a Compound of various Passions, that 'all of them as they are provoked, and come uppermost, govern him 'by turns whether he will or no.*'†

Surely this Definition is too General, because it seems to suit a *Wolf*, or a *Bear*, as exactly as yourself, or a *Grecian Philosopher*.

You say, '*you believe Man to be,*' &c., now I cannot understand to what part of you, this believing Faculty is to be ascribed; for your Definition of Man makes him incapable of believing anything, unless believing can be said to be a *Passion*, or some Faculty of *Skin* or *Bones*.

But supposing such a Belief as yours, because of its blindness, might justly be called a Passion, yet surely there are greater things conceived by some Men, than can be ascribed to mere Passions, or Skin and Flesh.

That Reach of Thought, and strong Penetration which has carried Sir *Isaac Newton* through such Regions of Science, must truly be owing to some higher Principle. Or will you say, that all his Demonstrations, are only so many blind Sallies of Passion?

---

* Page 428. † Introduction.

Fable of the Bees.

If Man had nothing but *Instincts* and *Passions*, he could not *dispute* about them; for to *dispute* is no more an *Instinct*, or a *Passion*, than it is a *Leg*, or an *Arm*.

If therefore you would prove yourself to be no more than a *Brute*, or an *Animal*, how much of your Life you need alter I cannot tell, but you must at least forbear writing against Virtue, for no *mere Animal* ever hated it.

But however, since you desire to be thought only *Skin* and *Flesh*, and *a Compound of Passions*, I will forget your better part, as much as you have done, and consider you in your own way. You tell us, '*that the moral Virtues are the political Offspring, 'which Flattery begot upon Pride.*'*

You therefore, who are an Advocate for moral Vices, should by the Rule of Contraries, be supposed to be acted by *Humility;* but that being (as I think) not of the number of the Passions, you have no Claim to be guided by it.

The prevailing Passions, which you say have the sole Government of Man in their turns, are Pride, Shame, Fear, Lust, and Anger; you have appropriated the moral Virtues to *Pride*, so that your own Conduct must be ascribed either to Fear, Shame, Anger, or Lust, or else to a beautiful Union and Concurrence of them all.

I doubt not, but you are already angry, that I consider you only as an Animal, that acts as Anger, or Lust, or any other Passion moves it, although it is your own Assertion that you are no better.

But to proceed, '*Sagacious Moralists*, say you, *draw Men 'like Angels, in hopes, that the Pride at least of some, will put 'them upon copying after the beautiful Originals, which they are 'represented to be.*'†

I am loath to charge you with Sagacity, because I would not accuse you falsely; but if this Remark is well made, I can help you to another full as just; viz., '*That Sagacious Advocates for 'Immorality, draw Men like Brutes, in hopes, that the Depravity 'at least of some, will put them upon copying after the base Originals, 'which they are represented to be.*'

The Province you have chosen for yourself, is to deliver Man from the *Sagacity* of Moralists, the Encroachments of Virtue, and to replace him in the Rights and Privileges of Brutality; to recall him from the giddy Heights of rational Dignity, and Angelic likeness, to go to Grass, or wallow in the Mire.

Had the Excellence of Man's Nature, been only a false Insinua-

---

* Page 37. † Page 38.

tion of crafty Politicians, the very falseness of the thing, had made some Men at Peace with it; but this Doctrine coming from Heaven, its being a principle of Religion, and a foundation of solid Virtue, has roused up all this Zeal against it.

And God said, *Let us make Man in our own Image, after our Likeness.*

This was a Declaration of the Dignity of Man's Nature, made long before any of your Sagacious Moralists had a Meeting. As this Doctrine came thus early from Heaven, so in the several Ages of the World, God has had his *Oracles*, and *Prophets*, to raise Men's Thoughts to their first Original; to preserve a Sense of their Relation to God, and Angelic Natures, and encourage them to expect a State of Greatness suitable to that Image after which they were created. To assure *them*, that *they that sleep in the Dust of the Earth shall awake, some to Everlasting Life, and some to shame and everlasting Contempt. And they that be wise shall shine as the brightness of the Firmament*, and *they that turn many to Righteousness, as the Stars for ever and ever.**

The last Revelation which God has made to the World, by his Son Jesus Christ, is greatly Glorious in this respect, that it has more perfectly brought Life and Immortality to light; that it turns our Thoughts from the low satisfactions of Flesh and Sense, to press and aspire after that deathless State of Greatness, where we shall be *as the Angels of God.*

It is not therefore the Sagacity and Cunning of any Philosophers that has tricked Men into Notions of Morality, as a thing suitable to a pretended Dignity of Nature within them.

But it is God himself, who first declared the Excellence of human Nature, and has made so many Revelations since, to fill Men's Minds with high and noble Desires suitable to it.

Before I proceed to consider your *Inquiry into your Origin of moral Virtue*, I shall take Notice of the Apology that you make to Jews and Christians.

You are sensible that what you have said is inconsistent, both with the Old and New Testament, and therefore thus excuse yourself to your scrupulous Reader.

That in '*your Inquiry into the Origin of moral Virtue, you speak* '*neither of Jews nor Christians, but Man in his State of Nature* '*and Ignorance of the true Deity.*'†

The Absurdity of this Apology will appear from hence; Let us suppose that you had been making an *Inquiry into the Origin of the World*, and should declare that it arose from a *casual Concourse of Atoms*, and then tell your scrupulous Reader, by way of

---

* Dan. xii, 2, 3. † Page 35.

Excuse, that you did not mean the World, which *Jews* and *Christians* dwell upon, but that which is inhabited *by Man in his State of Nature and Ignorance of the true Deity* : Could anything be more weak or senseless than such an Apology? yet it is exactly the same as that which you have here made.

For the difference of *Jew* or *Heathen*, no more supposes or allows of two different *Origins of Morality*, than it supposes or allows of two different Origins of the World.

For as the Creation of the World was over, and owing to its true Cause, before the Existence of either *Jew* or *Heathen*, so Morality was in being, and sprung from its proper Source, before either Jew or Heathen came into the World. And consequently, neither the Origin of the one or the other admits of any different Account, because in the after Ages of the World, some People were called *Jews*, and others *Heathens*. Besides, if you contradict the Religion of Jews and Christians, in your Account of Morality, is it less a Contradiction, or less false, because you pretend that your Face was turned towards *Pagans* ?

If you were to assert that there was no God, or true Religion, could it be any Excuse, to say that you were speaking to a *Mahometan* ?

2*dly*. To defend your Account of the Origin of Morality, you suppose Man in a State of Nature, savage and brutal, without any Notions of Morality or Ideas of Religion.

Now this very Supposition, is so far from being any Apology for you, that it enhances your Accusation : For you suppose such a State of Nature (as you call it) as the Scripture makes it morally impossible, that Men should ever have been in.

When *Noah's* Family came out of the Ark, we presume, they were as well educated in the Principles of Virtue and moral Wisdom, as any People were ever since ; at least we are sure they were well instructed in the true Religion.

There was therefore a Time, when all the People in the World were well versed in moral Virtue, and worshipped God according to the true Religion.

He therefore that gives a *later* Account of the Origin of moral Virtue, gives a *false* Account of it.

Now as all Parts of the World were by degrees inhabited, by the Descendants of such Ancestors, as were well instructed both in Religion and Morality, it is morally impossible that there should be any Nation of the World, amongst whom there were no Remains of Morality, no Instances of Virtue, no Principles of Religion derived from their Ancestors.

At least it is absolutely impossible for you to show that there was any such Nation, free from all Impressions of Religion, and

Morality. This you can no more do, than you can show that all the World are not descended from *Adam*.

So that your *Origin of moral Virtue* supposes a State of Man, which the Scriptures make it morally impossible ever to happen, and which it is absolutely impossible for you to show, that it really did ever happen.

But supposing some of the Posterity of *Noah*, in some Corner of the World, should have become so degenerate, as to have not the least Remains of Virtue or Religion left among them; and suppose some Philosophers should get among them, and wheedle and flatter them into some Notions of Morality; could that be called an Account of the *Origin* of moral Virtue, when moral Virtue from the beginning of the World had been practised and taught, by the virtuous Ancestors of such a depraved Offspring?

To make the taming of some such supposed Savage Creatures the *Origin of Morality*, is as just a way of thinking, as to make the History of the curing People in *Bedlam*, a true Account of the *Origin of Reason*.

3*dly*. Your Apology to your scrupulous Reader, as if your Origin of Morality related not to Jews or Christians, is false and absurd.

Because, the Observations which you have made upon human Nature, on which your Origin of moral Virtue is founded, are only so many Observations upon the Manners of *all Orders* of *Christians*. 'Tis their Falseness, Hypocrisy, Pride, and Passion, that have induced you to consider Morality, as having no rational Foundation in Man's Nature, but as the *political offspring which Flattery begot upon Pride*.

And yet you, *good Man*, are not talking about *Christians*, or *Jews*.

But every Page of your Book confutes that Excuse, and indeed needs must; for how should your Observations relate to any but to those People, whose Natures and Practices have furnished you with them?

'*I have*, say you, *searched through every Degree and Station of* '*Men;*' at last, you tell us, you went to the *Convents*, but even there you found that all was *Farce* and *Hypocrisy*.*

You tell us also, that whoever searches thus deep into *human Nature* will find, *that moral Virtue is the political offspring which Flattery begot upon Pride*. Yet this searching into all Orders of Men, into Convents, and from thence making this Discovery,

---

* Page 263.

that Morality is all owing to *Pride* and *Policy*, is not pronouncing anything upon Christians.

Nothing can be more weak than to form your Opinion of human Nature, upon the Tempers and Practices of all Orders of Christians, and then pretend you are only treating of Man in such a State of Nature, as you never saw one in, in your Life.

For how can your Observations upon Men, under the Power of Education, Custom, Laws, and Religion, tell you what Man is, in a supposed State, where all these are wanting?

Or will you say that you are acquainted, and intimately acquainted with Men, so entirely divested of all the Ideas of Religion, Morality, and Virtue, that you can make their Natures a true Specimen of Man in his most savage, brutal Condition?

Though your Knowledge of human Nature was great, yet you were forced, it seems, to visit the *Convents*, before you could pronounce anything of them. It seems therefore necessary, in order to know what Creatures Men are in a State of brutality, destitute of all Sense of God and Virtue, that you should know where to visit them.

Again, this *Apology* of yours, happens to be inconsistent with the first and main Principle upon which your fine Discourse is founded. I mean your Definition of *Man*, whom you define to be, besides *Skin*, *Flesh*, and *Bones, &c.*, *a compound of various Passions*. This is the vile, abominable, false, proud *Animal*, that you treat of under the Name of Man. In your Excuse you tell us, this is Man only in a State *of Nature*, but in your Introduction, you tell us, that to forbear complimenting, that Definition belongs both to *yourself, and the courteous Reader*.

So that you must either allow, that you and your courteous Readers are all Savages, in an unenlightened State of Nature, or else that the Man you have described, belongs to all Orders of Christians.

Having shown the weakness and folly of your Apology, I proceed now to your more particular Account of the *Origin of moral Virtue*.

You are pleased to impute its Origin to *Pride* alone, that having the same Cause as fine Clothes, we may wear as much, or as little, or as we please, without incurring any greater Offence, than a little variation in Dress.

If *Pride* be the only foundation of Virtue, then the more vicious anyone is, the more humble he ought to be esteemed; and he who is the most humble is at the greatest distance he can be placed from moral Virtue. And a perfect Humility (which by most Moralists has been reckoned a Virtue) must according to this Account, render anyone incapable of any Virtue; for such a one not only wants that which you make the only Cause of Virtue, but is possessed of the contrary Quality.

Having carefully considered human Nature, you have at last discovered, that '*the moral Virtues are the political offspring* '*which Flattery begot upon Pride*.'

You are so fond of this Discovery, that you cannot help showing us how you made it.

The first Moralists or Philosophers, say you, '*thoroughly* '*examined all the Strength and Frailty of our Nature*, and '*observing that none were either so savage*, as not to be charmed 'with Praise, *or so despicable, as patiently to bear Contempt, justly* '*concluded, that Flattery must be the powerful Argument that could* '*be used to human Creatures*.'

What a Graphical Description is here! One would think that you had been an Eye witness to all that passed, and that you had held the Candle to those first Philosophers, when they were so carefully peeping into human Nature. You do not love to dwell upon little Matters, or else you could have told us the Philosopher's Name, who first discovered this *Flattery;* how long he looked before he found it; how he proved it to be agreeable to Pride; what Disputes happened upon the Occasion; and how many Ages of the World had passed, before this Consultation of the Philosophers.

But however, you pass on to more material Points : '*They*, say 'you, (that is the Philosophers) *making use of this bewitching* '*Engine, extolled the Excellence of our Nature above other Animals*. '*Having by this artful way of Flattery, insinuated themselves into* '*the Hearts of Men, they begun to instruct them in the Notions of* '*Honour and Shame ;—they laid before them how unbecoming it* '*was the Dignity of such sublime Creatures, to be solicitous about* '*gratifying those Appetites, which they had in common with* '*Brutes, &c*.'

This you take to be a sufficient Proof, '*that the moral Virtues* '*are the political offspring which Flattery begot upon Pride.*'

I can go no further, till I present you with a fine Speculation of an *Abstract-thinker*, upon the *Origin of the erect posture of Mankind*.

'It was his Opinion, that the nearer we search into human 'Nature, the more we shall be convinced, that walking upon our 'Feet with our Body erect, was the *political offspring which* '*Flattery begot upon Pride*.

'The first Legislators, says he, having examined the Strength 'and Weakness of Man's Body, they discovered, that he was not 'so top heavy, but that he might stand upright on his Feet; but 'the Difficulty was how to raise him up.

Fable of the Bees.

'Some Philosopher more sagacious than the rest found out, 'that though Man crept on the Ground, yet he was made up of 'Pride, and that if Flattery took hold of that, he might easily be 'set on his Legs.

'Making use of this bewitching Engine, they extolled the 'excellence of his Shape above other Animals, and told him 'what a grovelling thing it was, to creep on all fours like the 'meanest Animals.

'Thus did these first Philosophers shame poor Man out of his 'natural State of creeping, and wheedled him into the Dignity 'and Honour of walking upright, to serve their own ambitious 'Ends, and that they might have his Hands to be employed in 'their Drudgery.'

This Gentleman being deeply learned in the Knowledge of human Nature, has much the same Curiosities concerning the Origin of Speech, and the first Invention of Truth, which he thinks upon a strict Research into Nature, may very justly be ascribed to Pride and Flattery.

But to return to your History. The next Thing your Philosophers did, was this:

'*In order to introduce an Emulation amongst Men, they divided* '*the whole Species into two Classes, vastly different from one* '*another. The one consisted of vile grovelling Wretches, which* '*they said were the Dross of their Kind, and having only the* '*Shape of Men, differed from Brutes only in their outward Figure;* '*but the other Class of Men were made up of high Spirited lofty* '*Creatures.*'*

Chronology, and Geography, I presume, are Studies not polite enough for your Attention, or else I suppose you would have told us the Time when, and the Place where all this happened.

For it is material to know what the World was doing before these Philosophers made this Division; whether before this, there was any Fear of God, any Belief of a Providence, any Duty to Parents, any Sense of Equity, any Notions of Faith, or any Regard to Truth.

For if the Inquiry was about the Origin of *Seeing*, or *Hearing*, and you should be ever so exact in telling me the manner how some cunning Philosophers first brought that Matter to bear, I should be very scrupulous about it, unless you told me the Time when, and the Place where they met, what they were doing before, how they came thither, and how they knew when they were there.

* Page 30.

Now there is just this same Difficulty in your Account of the *Origin of moral Virtue*.

For let me tell you, Sir, *moral Virtue* came amongst Men, in the same manner, as *Seeing* and *Hearing* came amongst them.

Had there ever been a Time, when there was nothing of it in the World, it could no more have been introduced, than the Faculties of *Seeing* and *Hearing* could have been contrived by Men who were *blind* and *deaf*.

Were not the first Principles and Reasons of Morality connatural to us, and essential to our Minds, there would have been nothing for the moral Philosophers to have improved upon.

Nor indeed can any Art or Science be formed, but in such Matters, as where Nature has taken the first Steps herself, and shown certain Principles to proceed upon.

Perspective supposes an agreement in the different Appearances of Objects.

Music supposes a confessed Perception of various Sounds; and *moral Philosophy* supposes an acknowledged difference of Good and Evil.

Were we not all naturally *Mathematicians* and *Logicians*, there would be no such Sciences; for Science is only an improvement of those first Principles or Ways of thinking, which Nature has given us.

Take away the Mathematicians' *Postulata*, or those first Elements and Principles of Reason, which are allowed by the common Sense of Mankind, and were Philosophers even as cunning as yourself, they must give up all the Science.

Do but suppose *all* to be invented, and then it will follow that *nothing* could be invented in any Science.

It is thus in all Sciences; the rationality of our Nature contains the first Rules, or Principles, and it is the Speculation of Man that builds and enlarges upon them.

As the Mathematician, seeing the acknowledged Differences and Proportions of Lines and Figures, proceeded upon them to enlarge Men's Knowledge in such matters; so the moral Philosophers, seeing the acknowledged Difference between Right and Wrong, Good and Evil, which the common Reason of Man consented to, they proceeded to enlarge and improve upon them.

So that their Labours are but Speculations and Harangues upon those common Principles of Morality, which were as connatural to the Reason of Man, as the first Principles of any other Science.

Fable of the Bees.

Moral Philosophy may be compared to *Eloquence*; it is an Improvement upon the common Reason of Man, as Eloquence is an Improvement upon Speech.

Now should some *Connoisseur* take it into his Head to inquire into the *Origin of Speech*, and tell the World, 'That once upon a 'time, some *Orators* seeing that Man had something in his Mouth, 'by the Movement of which, he could make a particular Sound, 'they told him of the Dignity and Honour of uttering such 'Sounds, and so through the pride of his Nature taught the '*Animal* to speak, though in reality, it was neither natural to 'him, nor any true Excellence; but ambitious Men flattered 'him into it, that he might be the fitter to go on their 'Errands.'

Should any profound Thinker give this Account of the *Origin of Speech*, you would have a Right to say, that he had stole the Discovery from you, who have given us just the same false and ridiculous Account of the *Origin* of Morality.

For it is full as reasonable, to make Eloquence the *Origin* of forming *articulate Sounds*, as to make the Harangues or Labours of moral Philosophers, *the Origin of moral Virtue*.

Could it be supposed, that an Understanding so *fine* as yours, could be conveyed to your *Descendants*, and that you should ever have a *Grandson* as *wise* as yourself, it may be expected that he will be able to teach that Generation of Men, that *Seeing*, was first introduced into the World, by Sir *Isaac Newton's* Treatise upon *Optics*.

To inquire into the Origin of moral Virtue, is to inquire into the Origin of *Reason*, *Truth*, and the *Relations* of Things.

And to fancy that some Politicians contrived moral Virtue, is to fancy that some Politician contrived *Reason* and Truth, and invented the Difference between one Action and another.

There is nothing that began to be, but what may be destroyed or cease to be; but as Truth and Reason can never cease to be, so it implies a Contradiction in Terms, for Truth and Reason ever to have had a Beginning.

It is the same in moral Virtue, which is *Truth* and *Reason*, considered in relation to Actions; and the Difference between one Action and another, is as immutable and eternal, as the Difference between one Line and another, and can no more be destroyed.

As *things* are different by their own proper Natures, independent of our Wills, so *Actions* have their own peculiar Qualities from themselves, and not from our Thoughts about them. In these immutable Qualities of Actions, is founded the fitness and reasonableness of them, which we can no more alter, than we can change the Proportions or Relations of Lines and Figures.

And it is no more the *Pride* of Man, that has made this Difference between *Actions*, than it is the *Pride* of Man, that makes the Difference between a *Circle* and a *Square*.

Moral Virtue therefore, if considered in itself, as the Rule or Law of intelligent Beings, had *no Origin;* that is, there never was a time when it began to be; but it is as much without Beginning as Truth and Goodness, which are in their Natures as Eternal as God.

But moral Virtue, if considered as the Object of Man's Knowledge, begun with the first Man, and is as natural to him, as it is natural to Man to think and perceive, or feel the Difference between Pleasure and Pain.

For his rational Nature, as much implies a fitness to perceive a Difference in Actions, as to Right and Wrong, as it implies a fitness to perceive a Difference in things as to great and small, pleasing or painful.

It may now be inquired, whether this moral Virtue be our *Law*, and how it appears, that we are under any Obligations to behave ourselves, according to this Difference of *Right* and *Wrong* that appears in Actions?

Now the reasonableness and fitness of Actions themselves is a Law to rational Beings, and the sight of that reasonableness carries an Obligation.

The different Magnitude of things, is a Reason to us, to acknowledge such Difference; and he that affirms anything contrary to the sight of his Mind, offends against the Law of his Nature.

The different nature of *Actions*, is a Reason for us to act according to such Differences, and he who does anything contrary to the sight of his Mind in that respect, sins against the Law of his Nature.

Now that this is not an imaginary Obligation, or a Law fancied by Moralists, may appear from hence; that this is a Law to which even the Divine Nature is subject; for God is necessarily Just and Good, not from any external Force, but from the Excellence of Justice and Goodness. *Reason* is his Law because it is *Reason*. That therefore which is a Law to God because of its Excellence, must surely be a *Law* to all Beings whom he has created capable of discerning that Excellence. For if the Reason or Excellence of the thing, be of sufficient Force to determine the Action of God, certainly it ought not to be thought too little to determine us in our Actions.

Nor can that be said to be an imaginary speculative Law to

intelligent Beings, which is an inviolable Law to the most perfect, intelligent Nature.

2*dly.* It is the Will of God, that makes moral Virtue our Law, and obliges us to act reasonably.

If you ask how this Will of God appears, I must beg leave at present, only to suppose, that God is of infinite Justice, and Goodness, and Truth ; and then the Thing proves itself : For such a God must necessarily Will, that all his Creatures in their several Proportions, be Just, and Good, and True.

Few mathematical Demonstrations conclude stronger than this. There is only one Objection to be made against it, which is to suppose, that God is neither Just nor True.

If rather than yield, you will put the *Epicurean* upon me, and say that God may disregard us, and neither Will one Way, nor the other. It may be answered, that this is inconsistent with the Idea of God just laid down ; for a God of infinite Goodness and Truth, can no more fail to Will Goodness and Truth in *every Instance,* than an infinite Being can fail to be present in every Place, or an omnipotent Being be deficient in any Acts of Power. So that it is absolutely necessary to say, either that God, is not of infinite Goodness and Truth, or to allow that He requires all his Creatures in their several Capacities, to be Just, and True, and Good.

Here, Sir, is the noble and divine Origin of moral Virtue, it is founded in the immutable Relations of Things, in the Perfections and Attributes of God, and not in the *Pride* of Man, or the Craft of cunning Politicians.

As the Reasons and Obligations to moral Virtue have always been in being, so has Mankind always had Sight of them : It being as essential and natural, for a rational Being to perceive these Differences of Actions, as it is for an extended Being to occupy Space.

And the Creation of a rational Nature, as much implies a Sight of the reasonableness of things, as the Creation of an extended Being, implies its Possession of so much Space.

Matter of Fact also supports this Observation : For History tells us of no Age or Country, where Men have not agreed to ascribe Justice, Goodness, and Truth, to the Supreme Being.

Now this shows, that they always not only knew, what Goodness, Justice, and Truth were, but also that they took them to be such excellent Qualities, as ought to be ascribed to the highest and best Being.

How monstrous is it therefore, to impute these fine moral Virtues to the Contrivance of Politicians, when all Ages of the

World have agreed to ascribe them to God, and number them amongst his glorious Attributes!

God is Just, therefore there is such a thing as Justice, independent of the Will and Contrivance of Man, is a way of reasoning that cannot be refuted.

It is in vain to say, that there may be a Divine Justice and Goodness, and yet what we call Goodness and Justice amongst Men, may be only a human Contrivance.

For to this it may be answered, that we cannot ascribe anything to God, of which we have not some Conception ourselves. Did we not perceive some degrees of Wisdom, we could not call him *All-wise;* did we not feel Power, and understand what it is, we could not ascribe *Omnipotence* to God. For our Idea of God is only formed by adding *Infinite* to every Perfection that we have any Knowledge of.

So that had we not from the rationality of our Nature, as plain a Sight of Justice, Goodness, and Truth, as we have of *Power, Existence,* or anything else, we could not attribute them to God.

That we are rational Beings, is as plain, as that we have Bodies, and bodily Senses. As there is no Man so refined and elevated, but gives frequent Proof, that he is subject also to Instincts and Passions; so there is no one so addicted to an Animal Life, as to show no Signs of an higher Principle within him.

It is this rationality of our Nature, that makes us both capable of, and obliged to practise moral Virtue, and brings us into a kind of Society with God and all other intelligent Beings.

For our Reason gives us a share in that common Light, which all intelligent Beings enjoy, and by making us Partakers of the same Things, so far makes us of one Society.

By our Reason we know some Truths, which God, and all intelligent Beings know; and apprehend some Perfections, and different Qualities in Things and Actions, which all intelligent Beings apprehend.

Now by being let into this Region of Truth, by being able to see some Truths which God also sees, and to know some Perfections which he also knows, we are as plainly declared to be rational Beings, and that Reason is one Law of our Nature, as the Principles of Flesh and Blood show us to be Animals, and subject to the Instincts of an Animal Life.

For how weak is it to suppose, that the *Animal* Life should be the Foundation of Laws of Nature, so as to make it fit for us to act agreeable to its Wants and Desires; and that the *Rationality* of our *Beings,* which is, in some degree, a Likeness to God, should be the Foundation of no Laws of Nature, so as to make it fit for us to act suitable to its Perfection and Happiness.

The short is this. *Truth* and *Reason* is the Law by which God acts; Man is, in some degree, made a Partaker of that Truth and Reason; therefore it is a Law to him also. The more we act according to Order, Truth and Reason, the more we make ourselves like to God, who is Truth and Reason itself.

This is the strong and immovable Foundation of *moral Virtue*, having the same Certainty as the Attributes of God.

Away then, I beseech you, with your idle and profane Fancies about the *Origin of moral Virtue*. For once turn your Eyes towards Heaven, and dare but own a just and good God, and then you have owned the true Origin of Religion and moral Virtue.

Thus much will, I presume, be thought sufficient to vindicate the Excellence and Obligations of *moral Virtue*, from the false and impious Accounts you have given of its Origin.

I proceed to consider in the next place, some other Methods that are made use of to render *moral Virtue* odious and contemptible.

Section II.

THE most boasted Objection against the Reality of Virtue which is urged by Men, who appropriate the Knowledge of human Nature to themselves, is this, that no Action is performed by us through a *Love of Goodness*, or upon a rational Principle of Virtue, but that it is *Complexion, natural Temper, Education, Pride, Shame*, or some other blind Impulse, that moves us in all our Actions that have the Appearance of Virtue. Thus a man who relieves an Object of Compassion, only gratifies his *commiserating Temper;* he is subject to *Pity*, ' *which is a Frailty of our Natures, and of* ' *which the weakest Minds have generally the greatest Share, as* ' *may be seen in Women and Children.*'* Again, ' *The humblest* ' *Man alive*, say you, *must confess, that the Reward of a virtuous* ' *Action, which is the Satisfaction that ensues upon it, consists in a* ' *certain Pleasure he procures to himself in contemplating his own* ' *Worth ; which Pleasure, together with the Occasion of it, are as* ' *certain Signs of Pride, as looking pale and trembling at any im-* ' *minent Danger are the Symptoms of Fear.*'†

---

* Page 42. † Page 43.

Now, Sir, if this be a true Account of the *humblest Man alive*, then by the Rule of Contraries, this must be a true Account of the *proudest Man alive ; that the Satisfaction he enjoys in being so, consists in a certain Pleasure he procures to himself by contemplating his own Vileness.*

This accurate Description you have given us of the *Pleasure of the humblest Man alive*, must be owing to such a feeling Sense as the *blind Man* had of *Light*, who being asked what it was like, answered that it was like the *Sound of a Trumpet.*

But to consider this Charge against human Virtue, that it is nothing but Education, natural Temper, or Complexion ; this being so laboured a Point, I shall state the whole Matter as clearly as I can.

1*st*. It is granted, that an Action is only then virtuous when it is performed, because it is agreeable to Reason, and those Laws which God requires us to observe.

Now this Virtue is Man's Duty, not as a Task that is imposed upon him, but as it is the only Practice, that is the natural Pleasure and proper Good of his being.

Virtue having that natural Fitness to a rational Soul, that fine Sights have to the Eye, or harmonious Sounds to the Ear.

A rational Being is in order, in its right State and Frame, when it is acting reasonably.

The infinite Goodness of God makes him infinitely happy ; and the Perfection of every Being is its Happiness ; and the greater and more perfect the Virtue of anyone is, the more perfect is his Happiness.

Now it is here to be observed, that an Action is not less virtuous, or loses any of its Excellence, because the Soul is delighted and made happy by it ; for it is the very Nature of Virtue to produce such Effects, and it shows the Rectitude of the Soul, when it can act virtuously with Delight, and feel its Happiness in so doing.

This is being virtuous upon Principle, and through a *Love of Goodness ;* for Goodness is loved for itself, when it is loved for what it is, the true Good and proper Delight of a rational Being.

Now will anyone say that there is no Excellence in Virtue, that it is mere *Nature* and *Temper*, because it is so agreeable, so proper to our rational Natures; Then let him say there is no Excellence in the Goodness and Justice of God, because they are so suitable to his Nature, and constitute his Happiness.

Granting therefore that Virtue was its own Reward, as it elevates and perfects the Soul, and keeps it in a State of right enjoyment, it would not be the less reasonable, on that Account.

For Happiness is the only reasonable *End* of every Being.

An action is not good, or virtuous, because it is *Self-denial*, but because it is according to Duty ; and he who through long habits of Goodness, has made the Practice of Virtue to have less of Self-denial in it, is the most virtuous Man.

Now, it is no Objection against the *Reality* of Goodness, that as rational Beings, we are *naturally* and *complexionally* disposed to practise and delight in it ; or that this natural Disposition, may by Exercise, Meditation and Habits, be heightened and increased.

For Custom, Habit, and natural Temper, are proper Assistances of our most virtuous Actions, and cannot be said to make them less reasonable, unless it be a Fault or Imperfection, to be habitually and strongly disposed to Goodness.

Thus much therefore is true of us considered only as *rational Beings ;* that we must even in that State be by Nature and Temper formed to perceive Pleasure, from some particular ways of acting ; and that the very excellence of our Natures, consists in a Fitness and Disposition for virtuous Actions, which the more we improve and strengthen by Meditation and Habit, the more reasonable we make ourselves.

It has pleased God in the Formation of Man, so to unite this rational Nature to a Body of Flesh and blood, that they shall generally act together ; and that the Soul shall as well be influenced by bodily Instincts, and Motions of the Blood and Spirits, as by its own Thoughts and reflections.

Thus, a delightful Thought conceived ever so secretly in the Mind, shall, at its first Conception, have the Blood and Spirits join in the Pleasure.

So that every right Judgment of the Mind, every proper Aversion, or regular Love, has as much the Concurrence of the Blood and Spirits, as if they were the only Agents.

The Body being thus visible an Agent in all that we do, has made some weak Heads imagine, that we are nothing else but Body ; as from the same want of Thought some have concluded, that there is nothing besides the material World, because nothing else is obvious to their Eyes.

The Soul being thus united to the Body, no Act of the Man is less reasonable, or virtuous, because it has the Concurrence of the Blood and Spirits : For this was the Intention of the Union, that a Creature of such a Form, should exert its Instincts and Passions in conformity to Reason.

For Instance, suppose anyone should meditate upon the Attributes and Perfections of God, till the great Idea had raised and warmed his Spirits; though the Reflection is then supported by the Agitation of bodily Spirits, yet the Meditation is not less religious, or less devout, or reasonable, because the Heat of bodily Spirits assisted in it.

Suppose anyone should so often reflect upon an eternal state of Darkness, and Separation from God, till his Blood and Spirits join in increasing the Horror; such an Horror would not be less reasonable, because the Body joined in keeping it up.

The mechanical Influence which our Spirits and Temperament have upon our Actions, does not take away from the reasonableness of them, any more than the rational Frame of our Minds, which is naturally disposed to acquiesce in the Reason of things, destroys the reasonableness of Actions.

As it would be no Excellence in a pure thinking Being, to be equally inclined to Truth or Falsehood, so it would add no Merit to such a mixt Nature as ours is, if our bodily Temperaments were neither more or less inclined to, or delighted with one sort of Actions than another.

Let us only suppose, that a rational Soul and an animal Nature, were united to act in a State of Personality.

It cannot be, that the Reasonableness of its Actions should be impaired by the Body's appearing to have a Share in them, because it does not act according to its Nature, unless the Body does concur; and in such a mixt Being, it is no more required that its Actions should be performed abstractly by pure Reason, than it is allowed that its Motions should be merely Animal.

Yet this is the false Judgment, which Men who are not the greatest Friends of Virtue make, because the Influence of the animal Nature is visible in the best of Men; and because such Enquirers generally converse intimately only with the worst, they rashly conclude against *all Force* of Principle, and deny Reason to have *any* Share in our Actions.

From what has been said, we may easily support the *Reality* of Virtue, from all the Objections of these *Critics* upon human Nature.

For granting the Force of Education, the Power of Custom, and the Influence of our bodily Instincts and Tempers; yet nothing can thence be concluded against the Share that Reason and Principle are required to have in our Actions.

For both Reason and Religion direct us to use the Influence and Assistance of all these Helps; and consequently they no more lessen or take from the Reality of virtuous Actions, when we are assisted by them, than *Fasting* or *Prayer* make our Piety less excellent, because it was assisted by them.

And it is as suitable to our Natures to strengthen and establish our Virtue, by Education, Custom, Complexion, and bodily Instincts, as it is suitable to Religion, to improve and heighten it by Fasting and Prayer.

And he who says, that such or such Actions have no Principle of Virtue or Religion in them, because they are made easy by Education, Temper, and Practice, thinks as weakly, as if he should affirm, that such Actions have no Reality of Principle in them, because they are the Effects of Meditation, and Habits of Attention; for good Habits of Body no more lessen the Excellence of Virtue, than good Habits of Mind.

An Action is virtuous, because it is an Obedience to Reason, and the Laws of God; and does not cease to be so, because the Body is either formed by Use, or created by Disposition, easy and ready for the Performance of it.

A good Education would be a Sin, if the Benefit that is received from it, or the Facility of performing good Actions, took away from their Goodness.

Nay, all Habits of Virtue would, upon this foot, be blamable, because such Habits must be supposed to have rendered both Body and Mind more ready and exact in Goodness.

All these Absurdities necessarily follow from this Argument, that there is no virtuous Principle in our good Actions, because Custom, Education, Temper, and Complexion, have their Share in them.

2dly. This Objection against the Reality of Virtue, is rather a Calumny, than any just Charge against it.

For as it is as certain, that we think and reason, as that we are subject to bodily Instincts and Habits; nothing can prove that our Reason and Reflection do not principally concur in any Action, but the Impossibility of it. He therefore that would prove that my Mind does not act upon a Principle of Reason, where he thinks that Temper or Complexion may carry me through it, can never prove it, till he can show that there was no Principle of Reason, no proper Motive, no Precept of Duty to move me to it: For if there be a plain Reason in the Thing, if there be a Precept of Duty to excite my Mind, as well as a natural Disposition in my Temper to perform the Action, it is impossible for the most penetrating Genius to prove, that my Temperament had a greater Share in the Action, than the Reason of my Mind; and consequently this Objection is a mere Calumny, and an ill-natured Suspicion, which can never prove itself to be justly made.

Now, that Reason is the Chief Principle in the Performance of good Actions, may, in some Degree, be learnt from hence; that reasonable and wise Actions never occasion any Sorrow or Repentance in the Mind; but, on the contrary, in violent Actions, where the Fermentation of the Blood and Spirits may be supposed to have blindly hurried on the Action, that Fermentation is no sooner abated, but there arises a Pain in the Mind, and Reason condemns the Action; which Condemnation chiefly consists in this, that Reason had not the Guidance of it; which is a plain Confession, that it is the way of our Nature to have Reason govern the Instincts and Motions of the Spirits, and that she shrinks, and is uneasy at those Actions, where she was not the principal Agent.

If therefore Actions only satisfy and content us, by being approved by our Reason, it is a manifest Proof, that our Reason is the principal Agent in our good Actions.

Nor will it be any Objection to this, to say, that many People are satisfied with false Notions of Virtue and Religion; for this only shows that the Principle of Reason may be weak, and of very little discerning Force in some People; but still it is their Faculty of Reason, such as it is, that gives them Peace, when it presides; and it is living contrary to Reason, that gives them Pain, as it gives Pain to others who enjoy a more enlightened Mind.

If the religious *Turk* abhors the Abomination of Wine, it cannot be said, that such Abhorrence is only the Effect of Temper, bodily Instincts, and Custom, unless it could be shown that he would equally abhor it, though he was fully persuaded that *Mahomet* was a Cheat.

From this Account of human Nature, we may be able to reject all those Reproaches which are cast upon Virtue and Religion, as if they were never founded upon any rational Principle, but were the casual blind Effects of Custom, Education, Temper, or Complexion.

1*st*. As it appears, that in our rational Natures, we are naturally and complexionally formed to practise and delight in reasonable Actions, and that such a Tendency of Temper or Nature towards Virtue, no more lessens the Excellence of it, than the Rectitude of God's Nature, takes away the Excellence of his Actions.

2*dly*. That Actions are not less virtuous for being suitable to any Disposition, whether natural or acquired, than for being suitable to the Reason of the Mind.

3*dly*. That *Education, Custom, Habits, Complexion, &c.*, are so far from taking away the Reasonableness of our Actions, that we could not be said to act reasonably, unless we endeavoured to make a greater Progress in Virtue by their Assistance.

4thly. That it is impossible, even in those Actions, where *Custom, Education, Complexion,* and *Habit* seem to be in full Power, for anyone to prove that Reason and Principle have not the greatest Share in them.

5thly. That Peace of Mind, which attends our good Actions, is a plain Proof of the Power which our Reason had in the Performance of them.

To come now to a particular Instance or two.

1st. Philo's Charity and *Compassion* is no Virtue, you say, because it is mere Complexion and Temper; he gratifies his *Pity*, and acts in Conformity to his Blood and Spirits.

Now this is so far from proving that he has not the Virtue of Charity, that it might be urged as a Proof of his having it.

For his Body is in that Disposition that it should be, supposing that his Mind had been long exercised and indued with Habits of Charity; it gives that further Pleasure in charitable Acts, which the right Turn of the Instincts, and Blood and Spirits, should give to the Mind in every virtuous Action.

For as I have observed, Man is then in his best State, when the Course of the Blood and Spirits act in Concurrence with his Reason; so that when my Body with its *Instincts* and *Motions*, joins with the right Judgments of my Mind, what I so perform has all the Perfection that an human Creature is able to exert.

This Complexion therefore, or bodily Disposition towards charitable Acts, is so far from implying that therefore the Mind has no Share in the Action, that were the Mind in its best State, and in its full Power (as at first created) it would use a greater and more constant Concurrence of all bodily Tempers in the Performance of its Duty.

So that when Complexion, or bodily Temperament readily joins in the Performance of good Actions, this is so far from implying any Defect of Principle, or want of rational Motive, that it shows, in some degree, the Remains of that primitive Rectitude of Body and Mind before the *Fall*.

2dly. To say that *Philo's* Charity is mere Complexion, is a Calumny, and groundless Accusation; it is a Suspicion as ill-grounded, as if I were to suspect that a Man had no Pride in his Mind, because there appeared an Haughtiness in his Carriage; or no Humility within, because of a natural Lowliness without: It is a Suspicion thus founded against all the Appearances of Truth, and is forced to make those the Proofs of the Absence of a Thing, which are the natural Signs of its Presence.

And as it is thus unreasonable, so is it utterly impossible that it should ever justify itself.

For seeing it is not only possible, but natural for this complexional Disposition to act in Conformity to the internal Principle of the Mind, it can never be proved that it does not.

It can never be proved, that Reason and Religion have not a greater Share in *Philo's* Charity, than his Complexion. How far some Precept of Religion, some Principle of Reason may influence his Mind, cannot be known by the most sagacious Philosopher; therefore the Charge against his Charity, as the mere Effect of Complexion, must be always ill-natured, unjust, and groundless.

Further, granting that *Philo* was complexionally disposed to Pity and Compassion, even before he could be supposed to act upon a Principle of Virtue and Religion, yet even this Supposition will make nothing against it afterwards.

For will anyone argue, that a Man can never fear, love, or hate, upon Principles of Reason, because Children fear, love, and hate, before Reason is of any Force to direct them?

Yet this is as wise, as to suppose that a Man's Complexion is never made to concur with a Principle of Reason, because such Complexion appeared, before Reason could be supposed of sufficient Power to guide it.

As to what you say, 'That *Pity is as much a Frailty of our 'Nature*, as *Anger, Pride, &c., That the weakest Minds have 'generally the greatest Share of it, for which Reason none are more 'compassionate than Women and Children.*'*

Two Things may be observed. First, The Inconsistency of this Assertion with the rest of your Book.

Here you derive the Compassion of Women, from a supposed *Weakness of Mind*, which supposes, that their *Tempers* depend upon their Minds, and are subject to them, and influenced by them, though in this very Page, you make *Pity* to be only an *Impulse* of *Nature*, and it is your chief Design throughout your Book to show, that all our Tempers and Passions are mere Mechanism, and *Constitution*, founded only in the Temper and Tone of our bodily Spirits.

So that according to your deep Philosophy, *Pity* is only an Impulse of Nature, and bodily Temper; yet Women are more pitiful than Men, because they have (as you suppose) *weaker Minds*.

That is, their Minds, because *weak*, have a Power over their Tempers, and form their Dispositions; but Men's Minds being *strong*, have no such Power.

To what Temper of Mind such Philosophy as this, is to be imputed, need not be observed.

---

* Page 2.

2dly. To say that Women have the *weakest Minds*, is saying more than you are able to prove. If they are more inclined to Compassion, through a Tenderness of Nature, it is so far from being a *Weakness of their Minds*, that it is a right Judgment, assisted, or made more easy, by a happy Tenderness of their Constitutions.

And it is owing, perhaps, to this *Make* of their Spirits, that they are commonly more affected with the Truths of Religion, than the Generality of Men are.

When our Minds are once softened, by whatever Cause it is, we are generally in the best Disposition for the Impressions of Religion; so that *Pity* is so far from being *as much a Frailty*, as *Pride* and *Anger*, that they are as different in their Effects, as a *Heart of Flesh* and a *Heart of Stone*, which Holy Scripture makes as different as a *Blessing* and a *Curse*.

But to return (if this be a Digression) to my Subject.

Let us now further suppose, that *Philo's* Charity is greatly owing to his Nature and Complexion; that the quality of his Spirits began the Disposition, and helped to recommend this Virtue to the Mind; yet may such a Virtue be as truly rational and religious, as if it had been let into the Mind any other way.

Sickness, Poverty, and *Distress,* have a natural Tendency to correct our Follies, and convert our Minds towards our true Good. These Conditions of Life may make it as easy for a Man to be *humble* and *compassionate*, as any bodily Complexion whatever; yet are such *Humility* and *Compassion* not to be esteemed void of Principle or Reason, because such Causes contributed towards them, and led the Mind into them.

For the Mind is acting according to the truest Principles of Reason and Religion, when it makes Advantage of these external Helps, and turns *Ease* and *Pain, Sickness* and *Health*, into occasional Causes of greater Piety.

Nor is it any more a Diminution of the Reality of *Philo's* Charity, to say, that bodily Temper first prepared and inclined his Mind towards it, than it is a Diminution of the Reality of anyone's *Repentance*, to say, that it was some Misfortune or cross Accident that first disposed and fitted his Mind for it.

David said (without fear of destroying the Reality of his Piety) *It is good for me, that I have been afflicted.*

Now if Actions, or Ways of Life may be good, though Afflictions contributed towards them, surely they may be equally good, though some Bodily Tempers proved in some degree the Occasions of them.

And it is as consistent with true and real Virtue, to owe its Rise to some bodily Constitution or Temper, as it is consistent with solid and substantial Piety, to owe its Beginning to some particular Calamity or Action of God's Providence.

But to proceed: It is further objected, that *Philo's* Charity must be *mere Complexion*, and not Virtue, for if it were Virtue he would not allow himself in the Neglect of other Duties.

This, again, is a false Conclusion; for a Man may perform one Duty upon a Principle of Virtue, and Sense of Duty, and yet through Mistake, or Negligence, be deficient in others.

Such great Judges of human Nature, should consider, that even in worldly Affairs, a Man does not always act up to the same Principle in everything he does.

Will anyone say, that *Avarus* does not consider Gain, when he is making Bargains, because at some other Times he seems not to value Expense?

If not, why then must *Philo* be looked upon as not *at all* influenced by a Sense of Duty in his Acts of Charity, because at some other Times and Occasions, he seems not to be governed by it.

Our present State, is a State of great Weakness and Imperfection, and our Reason, weak as it is, has a Thousand Impediments to hinder and divert its Force. In the Affairs of Civil Life, we are neither perfectly wise, nor wholly foolish; and we are almost the same Men in the Things that relate to God. In some Instances, Reason and Religion get more Power over us, and guide us under a Sense of Duty; whilst in other Parts of our Life, it may be very apparent, that Reason has a less Share in our Actions.

But to conclude that Reason, or a Principle of Virtue, does not influence us in any Part of our Behaviour, because it does not act equally and constantly in every other Part of our Lives, is as absurd, as to affirm, that we do not *think* at all in any Thing that we do, because we do not *think* with the same Exactness or Attention in every Thing that is done by us.

If *Philo* lives in the Neglect of Violation of some Duties, this shows that he is a weak, imperfect Man; but it does not show that he is the *same* weak and imperfect Man, and as devoid of any Principle of Virtue, when he does his Duty, as when he neglects it: For it is as possible for him to be charitable upon a Principle of Duty, and yet fail in some other Respects, as it is possible for a Man to use his Reason in some Things, and not in others; or to reason right in some Points, and yield to Folly in others.

So that to impute Actions seemingly virtuous, solely to natural *Temper* or *Complexion*, or some other blind Motive, because the Man is not uniform in his Life, is groundless and absurd; all that can with any Truth be affirmed of such a Man, is this, that he is not uniform in his Actions, and that through some Mistake, or Negligence, he is not so careful of his Duty in some Respects as in others.

Our *Understanding* and *Reason*, even in Matters of mere Speculation, are well nigh as weak and inconstant, as in Points of Duty and Conscience.

Few Systems of Philosophy, but obtrude some Errors upon us with as much Assurance, as they affirm the Truth: *Descartes* asserted a *Plenum;* Sir *Isaac Newton* has proved a *Vacuum.*

Now will anyone say, that it was not the *Reason* or *Understanding* of *Descartes* that demonstrated so many solid Truths, because he yielded to Falsity and Error in the Doctrine of a *Plenum?* Yet it would be much more reasonable to affirm this, in Matters of mere Speculation, than to affirm, that in Points of Practice and Duty, a Man is *in no Actions* governed by *Reason* and *Principle*, because in *some* Instances he acts weakly, and not according to Reason.

For, produce but the true Reason why a Philosopher may be said to proceed in some Speculations according to strict Reason and Truth, and yet hold some Tenets contrary to them, and then you will show that it is possible, nay, highly probable, that a Man may, in some Points of Duty, act upon a Principle of Reason and Virtue, though in some Things he may swerve from them.

There is, I acknowledge, a great Difference in bodily Temperaments, so that one Man may be born with better Dispositions for the Practice of some Virtues than others, yet it is Reason within, that is the chief Principle that actuates all of them; for the *finest Spirits* are things as blind and senseless of themselves, as the *Hands* and *Feet*, or the grosser Parts of the Body.

Wit and *Understanding* depend much upon bodily Temperaments; yet who is so weak as to imagine, that therefore the Reason of the Mind has no Share in Arts and Sciences.

It is the same in *Virtue*, or at least, as to some particular Virtues; there may be a kind Disposition in the animal Spirits to produce them, but it is great Weakness to suppose that Reason and Judgment have no Part in them.

It is impossible for our stinted Capacities to explain or calculate the *exact* Powers, that are to be attributed to our Souls and Bodies in the performance of Actions, because we have no clear ideas of them; but we know enough, to affirm the united Operation of both, and to show that he reasons falsely, who would ascribe an Action wholly to the Body, because it appears to have some Share in it; because, supposing it to take its Rise wholly from *Reason*, the Union of the Soul and Body requires, that the Body should appear to have the same Part in the Production of the Action.

There are nothing more various, imperceptible, or more out of our Sight, than the Motives of human Actions. We know no more how *Arguments* and *Opinions*, act upon the Mind, or how far they contribute to our *Choice*, than we can tell how far the *Air*, and how far the *Sun*, operates in the Growth of Plants.

When a Free-Thinker asserts, that our *religious Belief and Persuasions are not at all the Causes of human Actions*, he proceeds upon as good Grounds, as if he had said, that *Air is not at all* the Cause of the Circulation of the Blood.

For it is as easy to show that *Air* has no Influence upon our Bodies, as that *Reason* and *Opinions* have no Power over our Minds.

And it is more possible to tell how far the *Fluids*, and how far the *Solids* in an human Body, contribute to bodily Action, than it is to affirm how far *Opinions* and *Judgments*, and how far *Temper* and Complexion, operate in human Actions.

Nay, these Gentlemen themselves, to make their Philosophy still more ridiculous, are frequently wondering at the strange and monstrous *Contradictions*, which they think they discover in human Nature.

As if they should say, That finding human Nature to be *unaccountable*, they therefore take upon them to give *certain* and *positive* Accounts of its manner of acting.

I shall be pardoned for insisting so long upon this Article, because it is that on which some celebrated *Wits* have spent so much Pains, to the Prejudice of Religion and Morality. It is not easy to imagine the fatal Effects that Mr. *Bayle's* and *Esprit's* Writings have had upon People's Minds, by denying the Power of *Reason* and *Religion*, and ascribing all human Actions to *Complexion, natural Temper, &c.*

It is an easy Thing to be a *Wit*, and a *Philosopher*, if you will but write against Religion and Virtue; for I need not say all Arguments, but all Fancies, are admired as Demonstrations on that Side; and the bolder Steps you take, the surer you are of being esteemed a *Genius*.

Had Mr. *Bayle* filled his Books with the most useful, noble Truths, he had not had half so many Admirers, as for one single Sentence, which the most thoughtless Rake might have said through the mere Assurance of his own Extravagancies.

Speaking of *Fornication, I question*, says he, *whether one Man in a Hundred is clear of the Guilt.*

Could he have said a more extravagant Thing, that had reflected more upon Morality, and the Power of Religion, he had still been more admired. It is thus that Mr. *Bayle* and *Esprit* have purchased the Esteem, and increased the Numbers, of Infidels and Libertines.

These Gentlemen are dead, and their Ashes safe, if the Death of Men implies no more than the Fall of Leaves.

What Reasons you have to appear in the same Cause of Immorality, or what Security you have against the Power of God, is, I dare say, not known to yourself.

Infidelity and Irreligion have few Topics for Reflection; they have not so much as one Argument on their Side.

You can no more show that you are not immortal, than you can show what was doing before the Creation of the World.

To fancy that all expires with the Body, is as well supported, as if you were to fancy that there are no Beings but what are visible to your Eyes. To suppose that Man will never be called to an Account, is as much to be depended upon, as if you supposed, that there will be nothing in Being a Thousand Years hence.

Yet these are the *strong Foundations* of Infidelity and Profaneness; these are the *solid Principles* upon which great *Philosophers* establish deluded (or as they call themselves) *Free-thinkers.*

A Revelation from God, that justifies itself from the Creation of the World; that tells you every Truth that a wise Man would be glad to hear; that is supported with all the Authority that an omnipotent God can give; that is confirmed with all the Assurance that human Testimony can afford; is of no Weight against a few bold Assertions of weak Mortals, who exceed their Fellow-Creatures only in Arrogance and Presumption.

Section III.

ONE would imagine, by what has already passed, that you had sufficiently vented your Passion upon moral Virtue, and that you had hardly any more Arrows to draw against it; but you proceed to show us, that however you may fail in Argument, you will never be wanting in Inclination to attack it.

You set yourself with an Air of Satisfaction, as if Morality and Religion lay at your Feet, *to examine into the* Pulchrum *and* Honestum *of the Ancients;* that is, ' to inquire whether there be '*any real Excellence or Worth in Things, a Pre-eminence of one 'Thing above another.'**

And to show that there is no such Thing as any real Worth or Excellence in Things or Actions, but that all is mere Whim and Fancy, you proceed thus:

'*In the Works of Nature, Worth and Excellence are as uncertain. 'How whimsical is the Florist! Sometimes the* Tulip, *sometimes 'the* Auricula, *shall engross his Esteem. What Mortal can decide 'which is the handsomest, abstract from the Mode in being, to wear 'great Buttons, or small ones?*†

'*In Morals, say you, there is no greater Certainty.*'‡

So that according to your Philosophy, he who prefers Equity to Injustice, is but like him that chooses a *great Button* rather than a *small* one; and he who prefers Fidelity to Falseness, as whimsical as the *Florist*, who admires the *Auricula* more than the *Tulip*.

Now if there be only this Difference between *Actions*, then there can be no greater Difference between *Agents*, the best of Men can only excel the vilest of their Race, as a *Tulip* may excel an *Auricula*.

Nay, if Truth and Falsehood be no otherwise different from one another, than as one Button differs from another, then it must follow, that there can be no greater Difference between the Author of the one, and the Author of the other.

Now, the Religion of our Country tells us, that God is *Truth*, and the Devil the Author of *Lies*.

This, Sir, you see is the direct, immediate Blasphemy of your Notions, and not drawn from them by any distant or remote Consequences.

And if I should ask you, why one should be worshipped rather than the other? I should puzzle your profound Philosophy, as much as if I asked you which was the finest Flower? for you cannot tell me that one of these Beings is really good, and the other really evil, and yet maintain, that there is no real Goodness in Truth, nor any real Evil in Lies and Falsehood.

It is utterly impossible to answer this Question, without giving up your *Uncertainty in Morals*, and allowing that there is something certain and immutable in the Worth and Excellence of Things and Actions.

Should anyone charge you with the grossest Villanies, and most flagrant Immoralities that were ever committed by Man, you could have no more Pretence to be angry at the Imputation, than if he had said, you were particularly fond of little Buttons.

---

* Page 373.   † Page 377.   ‡ Page 379.

To proceed: '*Which is the best Religion,* say you, *is a Question that has caused more Mischief, than all other Questions together.*'*

Religion never comes in your way, but it puts you in a Passion; though I daresay, you never had any harm by it in your Life. This is a heavy Charge upon Religion, and upon the best Religion, for that is it which is inquired after. You charge a great deal of Mischief to this Inquiry after the best Religion, on purpose to enhance, I suppose, your own Merit, that you may appear to do a more public Good, who endeavour to destroy the very Idea of it.

But as Mischievous as you reckon this Inquiry to be, I am of another Opinion, taken from him who made the Inquiry necessary, who is God himself.

Thou shalt have no other God besides me, was setting up the best Religion; and *thou shalt not make to thyself any graven Image, &c.,* was a Determination against *Paganism.* Now I look upon the best Religion to be a Matter of great Moment, because God has commanded it; and take the Inquiry after it to be well authorised, because God has forbid all false Worship.

If you like it the worse for having this Authority, and should be better pleased with Religion, if it was some Politician's Invention, I shall only say, that you are fonder of Cheats than I am.

Again; I do not allow myself to be angry at the Inquiry after the best Religion, because I find that our blessed Saviour came into the World to teach Men the best Religion, and with the highest Rewards and Punishments to persuade Men to seek after and embrace it. *This is Life eternal, to know Thee, the only true God, and Jesus Christ whom thou hast sent.* And again, *Go ye and teach all Nations, baptizing them in the Name of the Father, and of the Son, and of the Holy Ghost; and lo, I am with you alway, even unto the End of the World.*

This convinces me, that the Inquiry after the best Religion, is the noblest, the most happy and beneficial of all others, because it is an Inquiry after eternal Happiness: But since you take it to have done more Mischief than all other Inquiries, you know now where to charge it, you know who it was that sent Twelve Apostles, indued with resistless Power, to persuade all the Nations of the World to inquire after, and receive the one best Religion. '*Ask it,* say you (*i.e.,* which is the best Religion), *at* ' Peking, *at* Constantinople, *at* Rome, *and you will receive three* ' *distinct Answers, extremely different from one another, yet all of* ' *them equally positive and peremptory. Christians are well assured* ' *of the Falsity of the Pagan and Mahometan Superstitions; but*

---

* Page 379.

'*inquire of the several Sects they are divided into, which is the true Church of Christ? and all of them will tell you it is theirs.*'*

Then comes your Golden Conclusion. '*It is manifest, then, that the hunting after this* Pulcrum *and* Honestum, *is not much better than a wild Goose Chase,*' &c.

Here I observe, that very consistently indeed with yourself, having rejected all moral Virtue, and natural Religion, you treat Revelation in the same manner. Christianity and Paganism are put upon the same Foot, and the Inquiry which is the best, esteemed no better than a *wild Goose Chase,* &c. Is this Declaration of yours the Effect of a serious Inquiry into the Merits of different Religions? That cannot be, it reflects too much upon so fine an Understanding as yours, to suppose, that you could ever have been seriously *chasing of wild Geese.*

The Acuteness of your Parts, must have always prevented the Inquiry. You knew, I suppose *ab origine,* from your Cradle, that there was no God, or you could not have been always so clear about the Insignificance of any Religion? For if there be a God, it is more than probable that he is to be worshipped, and it is hardly to be supposed that all Ways of Worship are equally acceptable to him.

You represent the Inquiry after the best Religion, as a mere *wild Goose Chase,* because, if the Question is put at *Peking, Constantinople,* or amongst the various Sects of Christians, all of them claim the only true Worship.

Now, Sir, I will remove the Question from the Disciples and Followers, to the *Authors* of these Religions. You shall put the Question thus, Ask *Jesus,* ask *Mahomet,* ask some *Pagan* Impostor, and you will receive three distinct Answers, extremely different from one another, and yet equally positive and peremptory.

Will you stand to your Conclusion here, that therefore it is Madness to concern ourselves more about the one than the other?

Is there any Creature so absurd, as to think this an Argument against *Christ,* or that the Inquiry after Him is Folly, because there was one *Mahomet* called for Disciples?

Yet the Argument is full as just and cogent against Christ himself, as against the Religion which he has instituted; for if the Religion of *Christ* and that of *Mahomet* have nothing to distinguish them, and Christianity is to be ridiculed and despised, because there is such a Religion as *Mahometanism,* then it undeniably follows, that Christ, when on Earth, might be

---

* Page 379.

justly rejected, because there have been other Persons who have pretended to come from God.

This Argument of yours (if it proves anything) proves it impossible that there ever should be any Revelation or Religion from God, which Mankind would be obliged to receive, so long as there were either wicked Spirits, or wicked Men in the World. For evil Spirits and evil Men will have evil Designs, and will oppose the Wisdom and Providence of God, in setting up Ways of Religion suitable to their own Tempers and Designs. But according to your Argument, no Religion has any Pretence to our Regard, when once it is opposed; nor need we trouble our Heads about the Truth of any, because there is more than one that lays Claim to it; which is as good Sense, as if you were to affirm, that a *Lie* was a Demonstration, that there was no such thing as *Truth*.

Whereas, the very Possibility of a false Religion, implies the Possibility of a true one, as much as Falsehood implies the Possibility of Truth, or Wrong supposes Right.

The wisest Speech therefore that you can make to your sagacious Followers, is this:

'Gentlemen, I would not have you to eat or drink, because '*Physicians* differ very much about Diet, and Poisons are 'generally conveyed that way; nor would I have you take any 'Money, because there is counterfeit Coin in the World.

' There are a great many false Accounts of Things, therefore ' you need not, nay, ought not to trouble yourselves about any ' that are true.

'You may laugh at *David*, when he says, *the Heavens declare* ' *the Glory of God, and the Firmament showeth his handiwork;* 'because there is a contrary Opinion; *a Fool that hath said in* ' *his Heart there is no God.*

'You need not regard Christianity, or its divine Institution, 'because there are other Religions at *Peking* and *Constantinople;* 'nor need you worship the true God, because in *Egypt* they 'worshipped *Leeks* and *Onions:* Nay, you need not hold that 'there is any true God, because there are People who have 'invented false Deities.

' When any History is urged upon you, you may answer, That ' of *Robinson Crusoe* is called a *true* Account; or if anyone 'pretends to be *positive* on the side of Virtue, you may confute 'his Arrogance, by saying, It can never be proved that the '*Auricula* exceeds the *Tulip*.

' These are strong and short Maxims, which will support you ' against the Wisdom of all Ages; they confute whole Volumes 'of *Prophets* and *Apostles* with a Word speaking.

'These are Doctrines that require no Study or Application, 'and you may believe them to be proper, by their Fitness for 'use. You may drink, debauch, eat, and sleep as you please, 'without hindering your Progress in these Doctrines. Luxury, 'and Wantonness will improve your Readiness; and your very 'Dulness will make you more acute.

'Nay, the more you sink into Sensuality and the animal Life, 'the more you will feel and relish the Truth of these Sentiments. 'Though you are to fly from all Appearance of Truth, and avoid 'all Concern about any Religion, as you would avoid the Folly 'of *chasing of wild Geese*, yet you must remember, that you are 'my Scholars: For I am an *Abstract-Thinker*, and in these my 'abstract Speculations, you must be my diligent and dutiful 'Scholars. Though Christianity may be despised, because 'other Religions are set up against it, yet you must value me 'the more, for being contrary to the wisest Men of all Ages in 'the World.

'Though there is nothing certain or valuable in religious 'Truths, though moral Virtue is the *Offspring* of Pride, the '*Invention* of Philosophers, and all mere Whim and Fancy; yet 'my Speculations having the utmost Contrariety to all that is 'virtuous, moral, or religious, you may safely put your whole 'Trust and Confidence in them.'

This is the best Speech that you can possibly make to your deluded Followers; and I dare say, if your Principles would allow of greater Stupidity or Dulness, you would not be without a Party, who, to avoid Salvation, would join with an Enemy to Virtue, merely for the Sake of his Cause.

The Infidelity of the present Age is very great, and shows such a Contempt of sacred Things, as was hardly ever heard of before.

If one inquires into the Grounds of it, it seems founded on such an implicit Faith reposed in Men of wanton and sensual Minds, as is looked upon to be mean and slavish, when yielded to the highest Evidence in Matters of the last Moment.

To believe *Moses* and the *Prophets*, is ridiculed, because it is *believing;* but to be a Slave to a wanton Infidel, and blindly swear into his Opinions, is glorious and manly, because it is *Free-thinking*.

Deists and *Free-thinkers* are generally considered as *Unbelievers;* but upon Examination, they will appear to be Men of the most resigned and implicit Faith in the World; they would believe *Transubstantiation*, but that it implies a believing in God; for they never resign their Reason, but when it is to yield to something that opposes Salvation.

For the *Deist's* Creed has as many Articles as the *Christian's*, and requires a much greater Suspension of our Reason to believe them. So that if to believe Things upon no Authority, or without any Reason, be an Argument of Credulity, the *Free-thinker* will appear to be the most easy, credulous Creature alive. In the first place, he is to believe almost all the same Articles to be false, which the Christian believes to be true.

Now, it may easily be shown, that it requires stronger Acts of Faith to believe these Articles to be false, than to believe them to be true.

For, taking Faith to be an Assent of the Mind to some Proposition, of which we have no certain Knowledge, it will appear that the Deist's Faith is much stronger, and has more of Credulity in it than the Christian's. For instance, the Christian believes the *Resurrection* of the Dead, because he finds it supported by such Evidence and Authority, as cannot possibly be higher, supposing the Thing was true; and he does no more Violence to his Reason in believing it, than in supposing that God may intend to do some Things, which the Reason of Man cannot conceive how they will be effected.

On the contrary, the *Deist believes* there will be no Resurrection. And how great is his Faith! for he pretends to no Evidence or Authority to support it; it is a pure, naked Assent of his Mind to what he does not know to be true, and of which no Body has, or can give him any full Assurance.

So that the Difference between a *Christian* and a *Deist*, does not consist in this, that the one assents to Things unknown, and the other does not; but in this, that the Christian assents to Things unknown, on the account of Evidence; the other assents to Things unknown, without any Evidence at all.

Which shows, that the *Christian* is the rational Believer, and the *Deist* the blind Bigot.

Ask a *Deist* or a *Free-thinker*, why he believes Christianity to be an Imposture, you must not expect to have any Arguments offered you; but however, all Arguments aside, he can tell you, that the Inquiry after the best Religion has done *more Mischief*, than all other Inquiries together; that it is, at best, but a *wild Goose Chase;* he will tell you how *Jesus* has been called the *Galilean* by way of Contempt; that there are various Readings in the Scriptures; that Mr. *Whiston* is the most learned and sincere Divine of the Age; that he has called the present Doctrine of the Trinity an *Apostasy;* and says, that the present Text of the *Old Testament*, is not that which was used in our Saviour's Time: He may, perhaps, crack a Jest upon some Text of the

New Testament, and tell you how such a one used to say, that *working a Miracle, was like showing a Trick.*

If you have Strength enough to maintain your Ground against such Attacks as these, the *Deists* can get no Power over you: But it must be confessed, that idle and foolish as these Arts appear in Point of Reason, yet they are very fatal in their Effects upon the Minds of Men.

Religion requires a serious and wise Use of our Reason, and can only recommend itself to us, when we are in a Disposition to reason and think soberly; it preserves its Power over our Minds no longer, than whilst we consider it as the most serious, important, and sacred Thing in the World.

Hence it appears, why we are generally so little affected with Religion, because we are seldom in a State of sober thinking. The Concerns of the World keep our Spirits in a constant Hurry, and prevent our judging rightly of those Things, which are not to be judged of, but by cool Reason.

Every one knows, that Sickness, Adversity, and the Approach of Death, are advantageous Seasons for the Truths of Religion to affect us; whereas they carry no other Advantage, than as they bring a Man into such a State, as disposes him to think seriously. For this Reason, they who only *laugh* at Religion, may be said to have used the strongest Argument against it, for there is no coming at it any other Way; it is only to be attacked by little Jests, lewd flings of Wit, such as may betray the Mind into Levity, and corrupt the Imagination, which so far as it is effected, so far is the Power of Religion lessened.

It is not the Deist's Business to reason soberly, and consider the Weight and Moment of Things with Exactness; for, to reason soberly, is to act against himself, and put his Reader into that State of Mind, in which Religion has its chief Force.

But idle Stories about Gods and Goddesses, and pagan Mysteries, saucy Jests, lewd Innuendoes, and Nick-names given to serious Things, serve the Cause of Infidelity, much better, than any Arguments it has yet found out.

For these not only serve to confound and distract the Mind, and lessen the Difference of Things, but they also gratify and engage the most immoral and wicked Men, as they furnish them with a Confutation of Religion at so cheap a Rate.

How many fine Gentlemen must have been forced to have owned themselves Christians, had not such short Confutations of Christianity been provided to their Hands! But as the Cause is now managed, no one can be too dull, senseless, or debauched, to be a powerful Deist; a poor inflamed Wretch, who never had the Use of his Reason in his Life, may easily call Religion a

Fable of the Bees.

Dulcinea del Tobosa, and all who would procure any regard to it, *Saint Errants ;* and when he has done this, he may reckon himself a *great Genius,* and to have shown as much Learning in favour of Deism, as the first Rate Infidel of the Age.

How many lively *Beaux* had buried their Parts in Swearing and Obscenity, had not all Jests upon Scripture been allowed as true Proofs of *Deism* and Politeness!

And though the *Fraternity* now boasts of its Numbers (as every Vice if it could speak might do the same) yet, if no one was to be allowed to be a *Deist,* till he had examined the Truths and Authority of Religion, as he would examine the *Title* to an Estate, even the present Age, would be able to show more *Squarers* of the Circle, or *Discoverers* of the Longitude, than *Professors* of Deism.

Nay, was one to ask the most philosophical amongst them, to show the *great Danger* of being a good Christian, or the fatal Consequences of living in Expectation of the *Resurrection,* and *Judgment* to come ; was he asked to show the certain Safety of *Infidelity,* or why an Infidel can be no Sufferer for rejecting the Offers of the Gospel ; he could give you as plain an Answer, as if you had asked what State this *Globe* of Earth will be in, five thousand Years hence.

But indeed, it seems needless to observe, that Prudence and common Sense have no Hand in Infidelity. Self-murder does not more directly prove Lunacy, than Infidelity proves the loss of Reason.

There is no one that seems more to depend upon the Folly and Madness of his Readers, than you do.

You tell them, that you are a *mere Animal* governed by Appetites over which you have no Power ; that is, you describe yourself as a *Machine* that would look well in a *Bridle,* and then pretend to talk of God, and Providence, and Religion, and Morality, and to pierce into the inmost nature of Things and Actions, with as much Ease, as if you were some superior Form, that was made up of pure Wisdom and Intelligence.

But the thing is, you knew what side you had chosen, and that if you were not wanting in Impiety, Lewdness, and Reproaches upon Virtue, you might abound in Nonsense as much as you pleased.

And indeed it must be confessed, that as hardly any Authority is sufficient to recommend a Person, that comes from God, to do us good ; so is there scarce any Folly great enough to expose another, that comes a Missioner from the Kingdom of Darkness to do us Harm.

Section IV.

YOU are at last so sensible of the Abilities, which you have discovered, in laying open the Mysteries of human Nature, that you think it but a necessary piece of Civility, to make an Apology to the World, for showing such a superior Knowledge.

Thus say you, '*What Hurt do I do to Man, if I make him more known to himself than he was before?*'

'*But we are so desperately in Love with Flattery, that we can never relish a Truth that is mortifying.*'

To prove the Justice of this Remark, you say, '*I do not believe the Immortality of the Soul would even have found so general a Reception in human Capacities as it has, had it not been a pleasing one, that extolled and was a Compliment to the whole Species.*'*

This Remark supposes that the *Mortality* of the Soul is a *Truth*, for you make our not believing it to be Mortal, a Proof that we cannot relish a Truth that is mortifying. You also impute our Opinion of the Soul's Immortality, to a *desperate love of Flattery;* which is giving it as sure a Mark of an Error, as you could well have thought of.

The reasonableness of this Remark, is founded upon that Advantage and Dignity which arise from Immortality; this is what induces you to think that its Reception in human Capacities is owing to a love of Flattery.

You might have made the same Remark upon the *Belief* of the *Being* and Providence of God, that they had never had so general a Reception in human Capacities, were not Men desperately *in love with Flattery, and not able to relish a Truth that is mortifying.*

For the *Being* and *Providence* of God, are the most pleasing *Truths*, and more extol and elevate Man's Nature and Condition, than anything else; and whilst we assert the Providence of God, we assert our own Happiness, as being the Care and Concern of so great and glorious a Nature.

But how ought that Man to be treated, who should bring the *Belief* of a Divine Being as an Instance of the Power of Flattery over human Nature, or allege the Doctrine of Providence as a Proof, that we cannot relish a Truth that is mortifying.

Yet this would be as well, as to instance, as you have done, in

---

* Page 256.

the Immortality of the Soul. For it is as reasonable to rejoice in the Immortality of our Souls, as in the Being of God ; and it is as impious to say, that we hold its Immortality, because we cannot relish a Truth that is mortifying, as to say that we believe the Providence of God for the same Reason.

What an Aversion must you have to the Force of this Principle, that when you were to show, that we cannot relish a *Truth* that is mortifying, you could like no Instance so well, as the general disbelief of the Soul's Mortality? Can it be supposed that you would have instanced in this Opinion, if you had not wished, that it should lose its Force upon Men's Minds, and be no longer considered as the corner Stone of Religion, but as a *Notion* founded in the Falseness, Pride, and Flattery of Man's Nature?

Was anyone ever so angry as the *Macedonian* Hero's Vanity of being a God, need he have reproached him more, than by imputing it to a *desperate love of Flattery* ?

Yet this is the tender Method, in which you have chosen to expose the Belief of the Soul's Immortality, as owing to a desperate love of Flattery.

You will perhaps say, *Have I denied the Soul's Immortality?*

In express Terms you have not denied it; such a flat denial would have signified much less than what you have said.

You knew very well, that to impute the Belief of it to Falseness and Flattery, was the best Way of denying it.

It is rejected here in a manner that highly suits the Temper of Irreligion, by being considered not only as false, but as arising from the basest Qualities of human Nature, *Pride* and a *desperate* Love of *Flattery*.

These Things serve not only to raise a Disbelief, but to excite an Indignation against a Principle owing to such reproachful Causes ; and what is still a greater Point gained, they teach People to look with Contempt and Dislike on those Persons and that Religion, which teach such a Principle.

Our blessed Saviour saith, *I am the Resurrection and the Life, he that believeth in me shall never die.*

Now, according to your Philosophy, this Speech of our Saviour's, must be reckoned an artful Application to the Weakness and Vanity of Human Nature, an Address to the blind Side of Man, to increase his Love of Flattery, and keep him from a true Knowledge of himself.

For if Man believes the Immortality of his Soul, through a desperate Love of Flattery, certainly he who comes to encourage and establish such a Belief, comes to encourage and establish that Immoderate Love of Flattery.

Nay, this Doctrine of yours, not only serves to expose the

Opinion of the Immortality of the Soul, and reproaches the Christian Religion which teaches it, but it prepares a Man to be Proof against all Doctrines of Religion that have any Happiness in them; for whatever is believed or practised that tends any way to raise or exalt the Condition of Man, is equally subject to this Reproach, that it is *received* through an excessive Fondness of Flattery.

So that your wise Philosophy comes to this, that if there was no Honour or Happiness in Religion, no Greatness to be acquired by our obeying God, it could not be charged upon our Pride and Vanity; but since Religion is in order to Happiness, and since our worshipping of God, implies our having a great and glorious Friend and Benefactor, such a Religion may be owing to a Vice of our Nature, a *desperate Love of Flattery*.

And the same may be said of every virtuous Action, that it is practised through a desperate Love of Flattery, in as much as Virtue is supposed to make us Friends and Favourites of God, and so dignifies and exalts our State.

Nay, this way of arguing proves, that the greater and more glorious the Idea is, which we form of God, the more we may be influenced by an ill Motive; for the greater and more glorious we represent the Nature of God, the more we raise and dignify ourselves, who are related to so great a Being, and are in Covenant with him.

So that to clear ourselves of a desperate Love of Flattery, and to show that we can relish Truths that are mortifying, we should conceive very low and mean Notions of God, and such as would make it neither our Honour nor Happiness to worship him.

Such a Religion as this, that had nothing in it worthy of God or Men, might, according to your Account, be owing to some rational Principle, and not capable of being imputed to the Pride or Vanity of Man's Nature.

For since you impute the Belief of the Soul's Immortality, to a desperate Love of Flattery, because such Belief sets us out to great Advantage, and adds Dignity to our Nature, the same Imputation is equally chargeable upon every Doctrine, or Practice, that promises any Happiness or Honour to us; and no Religion or Opinions can be free from that Charge, but such as are of no Benefit or Advantage to us.

From this therefore we may believe, that had we a Religion which proposed nothing worthy of God, or beneficial to Man, the *Deists* and Wits of your Size, would all of them turn *Priests*, and devoutly wait at its *Altars*.

To speak now a Word or two concerning *Pride*.

Pride is an Error or a Vice, as *Covetousness* is a Vice; it is a notable Desire, ill directed: It is a right Desire, earnestly to desire Happiness; but that Desire is sinful, when it is wholly set upon *Gold*, or any other *false* Good.

So a Desire of Greatness is an excellent Desire, a right Turn of Mind; but when it fixes upon a false Honour, it is a vicious Irregularity. To desire the highest Exaltation of which our Nature is capable, is as right a Disposition, as to desire to be as like to God as we can.

Now, had you said that the Belief of the Soul's Immortality, was assisted and strengthened in us through a Desire of Greatness, you had said as reasonable a Thing, as to say, that Christianity makes a stronger Impression upon the Minds of Men through a Desire of Happiness.

For had we not these Dispositions, neither Religion, nor anything else that was of any Advantage to us, could take any hold of us: For, what would the Happiness or Greatness of any Proposal signify to Beings, whose Natures were not affected with them?

Now, to say that Religion is better received through this Tendency of our Nature, is no more a Reproach, than it is to say that our Understanding and Reason recommend Religion to us.

For these Dispositions or Inclinations constitute the Excellence of our Nature, and give us all the Dignity that we have.

It being as right a Judgment of the Mind, to desire to be as like to God as our Natures will allow, as it is to prefer Truth to Falsehood.

But to impute our Belief of the Immortality of the Soul to *Pride*, is as ridiculous, as to impute our Desire of eternal Happiness to *Avarice*.

For *Pride*, considered as a Vice, is no more the Cause of our Approbation of Immortality, than *Avarice* is the Cause of our setting our Affection on Things above.

Pride is as earthly and down-looking a Vice as Covetousness, and as truly sinks the Soul into a State of Meanness.

A Delight in false Honour as much debases and hinders the Mind from aspiring after its true Greatness, as a Fondness for empty Riches keeps the Soul averse from the Approbation of her true Good. That this is the Effect of Pride, that it debases the Mind, and makes it unable to relish its true Greatness, that it unfits it for the Reception of Doctrines which exalt and raise our Nature, may be also learnt from Him, who came to lead us unto all Truth.

Speaking of vain-glorious Men, says our blessed Saviour, *How can ye believe, which receive Honour one of another, and seek not that Honour, which cometh from God alone?**

But you make the Pride of Man, the Cause of his believing divine Truths, though they are as opposite to one another, as Avarice and Heavenly-mindedness, Light and Darkness. To make some Apology for yourself, you say, '*What Hurt do I do* '*to a Man, if I make him more known to himself than he was* '*before?*'

You should have put the Question thus: What Hurt do I do to a Man, if I make him more vicious than he was before, if I deprave his Understanding, and lead him into a Contempt and Dislike of the strongest Principles of Religion?

For if there is any Danger either to yourself or others, in corrupting their Minds, and destroying the Motives to Religion and Virtue, you are capable of no other Apology, but what that Being may make, *who goeth about as a roaring Lion, seeking whom he may devour.*

The *Arrow that flieth by Day*, and the *Pestilence that walketh in Darkness*, are mere Blessings, if compared to the Man who infuses vicious Opinions into the Mind, which weaken the Power of Religion, and make Men less devoted to the Worship and Service of God.

How can you say, that you have only made Man more known to himself, by teaching him that the general Belief of the Soul's Immortality, is owing to a desperate Love of Flattery?

Have you proved, that he does not know himself, if he thinks it is owing to any other Cause? Have you so much as attempted to show, that it can have no other Foundation? That it is not founded in Reason, Religion, and the Attributes of God?

But proving (I recollect) is no Talent of yours; and if you may be allowed to *shine* in anything, it is in loose Insinuations, positive Assertions, and vain Conjectures.

Section V.

YOU come now to give us a Taste of your Skill in *Phraseology*, or the Force and Propriety of Words. All sorts of Learning seem to be at your Service, and you are so constant to yourself, as to make them all conspire in one and the same Design against Religion. *Hope*, being a Word of great Consolation in the Christian

---

* St. John v. 44.

Religion, you have pitched upon that, as most deserving the kind Assistance of your learned Hand.

'*All hope*, say you, *includes Doubt; a silver Inkhorn may pass*
'*in Speech, because every Body knows what we mean by it; but a*
'*certain Hope cannot; the Epithet destroys the Essence of the Sub-*
'*stantive; it is palpable Nonsense. The Reason therefore why it*
'*is not so shocking to some, to hear a Man speak of* certain Hope,
'*as if he should talk of* hot Ice, *or* liquid Oak, *is not because*
'*there is less Nonsense contained in the first,* than in either of the
'*latter, but because the Word* Hope, I mean the *Essence* of *it, is*
'*not so clearly understood by the Generality of the People, as the*
'*Words and Essences of* Ice *and* Oak *are.*'*

What a Triumph is here over Religion! And with how much Ease do you reject an Article of Faith with a *Noun Substantive!*

In our *Burial* Service we have these Words, *In sure and certain Hope of a Resurrection, &c.*

This it seems cannot pass in Speech, without the Destruction of a *Substantive; it is shocking, and palpable Nonsense.*

Let it first be observed, that *Hope* implies the *Belief, Dependence, or Expectation* of something that shall come to pass. Now I should think that a Thing may as well be expected with Certainty, as Uncertainty; and that its being certain to happen, is no Inconsistency in the Expression. It can hardly be denied, but that a Man may be certain that some Things will never happen; and where is the Contradiction of supposing him as certain that some Things will happen?

But to come to your own Arguments.

All Hope, say you, *includes Doubt.* This as much contradicts my Understanding, as if you had said, that *all Trust* includes *Diffidence;* and I cannot trust a Man, unless I distrust him. The Apostle says, *By Hope we are saved;* according to you, he must mean, by *Doubting* we are saved; for if *Hope* necessarily includes *Doubting,* and *Hope* be necessary to Salvation, it evidently follows, that *Doubting* is necessary to Salvation; and every Exhortation to *hope* in God, is an exhortation to *doubt* of God.

Our blessed Saviour said, *If ye have Faith, and doubt not, &c.* Now had you been present at this saying, you could have shown the Impossibility of what he exhorted them to; that *Faith* or *Hope* implied *Doubting;* and that to talk of *certain Hope* or *Faith,* was as shocking to a fine Understanding, as to talk of *hot Ice,* or *liquid Oak.*

Certain Hope, you say, is *palpable Nonsense,* because the *Epithet* destroys the Essence of the *Substantive.*

---

* Page 149.

So that *Doubting* is the Essence of *Hope*, and consequently whatever else belongs to Hope, is only *accidental;* the Essence of Hope is Doubting.

Now if Doubting is the Essence of Hope, then where there is the most Doubting, there must be the most of Hope; for where there is most of the Essence of a Thing, there must necessarily be most of the Thing itself.

Now it seems to me as ridiculous, to make *Doubting* the Essence of *Hope*, as to make *Fear* the Essence of *Courage*. For Hope, so far as it goes, as much excludes Doubting as Courage, so far as it extends, banishes Fear. There may be a weak Hope which is mixed with Doubt, as there may be a half Courage that is attended with Fear, but a thorough Hope as truly rejects Doubt, as a perfect Courage shakes off all Fear. And it is just such *shocking Nonsense* to talk of a *certain Hope*, as to speak of a *fearless Courage:* And there is just as much Murder of the *Substantive* in one Case, as the other.

Hope, or Expectation, does not imply *Uncertainty*, but *Futurity*, that the things expected, are not in being, but are to come to pass; this is all that is of the Essence of Hope; it is only the *Futurity* of things that makes it.

Let the things come to pass, and the Hope ceases, this is the only way of destroying it. But whether the things to come be with Certainty, or Uncertainty expected, no more destroys that Disposition of Mind, which is called Hope, than the Passion of *Fear* is destroyed, by exerting itself reasonably, or unreasonably.

Hope is uncertain, not because we cannot hope or expect with Certainty, but because the things we hope for are generally not in our Power, so as we can be secure of the Event.

But you ridiculously suppose, that Hope, or Expectation, as a Faculty of the Mind, necessarily includes Uncertainty, as if a Man cannot expect or hope for that, which he is sure will answer his Expectation; or that he must cease to expect things, because he has certain grounds to expect them. These are the Absurdities which you plunge into, rather than allow a *certain* Hope of the *Resurrection* of the Dead.

Hope is as the things hoped for. In uncertain things it is uncertain. But if God is pleased to inform us of things to come, we are with *certain Hope* and Expectation to depend upon them.

Agreeable to this, St *Paul* says, *In hope of eternal Life, which God, that cannot lie, promised before the World began.*

Here we have an Apostle's Authority for a *certain Hope*, made as undeniable as the Veracity of God.

But this must be very shocking to a Gentleman of your refined

Understanding; and must give you a farther uneasiness, to behold the Destruction of a whole Noun *Substantive*, to establish only an Article of Religion.

You compare *certain Hope*, to *hot Ice*, or *liquid Oak*, and say that the Expressions would be equally *shocking*, were the *Nature* of *Hope* as well understood, as the Nature of *Ice* and *Oak*.

Had you not been used to understand everything wrong, you had never made this Observation; for the contrary to this happens to be true, that the Expression is not so shocking in one Case as the other, because the Nature of Hope is well understood, as that of *Ice*, &c.

It is not shocking to say *certain Hope*, because Hope is known to be founded upon some degrees of Assurance.

But does *Ice* suppose some degrees of Heat in order to its Existence? Is *Ice* hotter or colder, as Hope is more or less assured? Hope is stronger and better, the *more* it has of Assurance, and the *less* it is opposed with Doubts; but is *Ice* the stronger and harder, the *more* it has of Heat, or the *less* it is surrounded with Cold?

Your Comparison also of *certain Hope*, to *liquid Oak*, is equally ingenious and worthy of yourself; for it supposes that an *Oak* changes from *solid* to *liquid*, as *Hope* fluctuates from *Doubts* to *Belief*. For were not an *Oak* as various in its Nature, as to *liquid* and *solid*, as *Hope* is various in its Nature, as to *Doubt* and *Assurance*, it must be *shocking* Nonsense, to make a *liquid Oak* the same thing as an *assured Hope*.

I have been the longer upon this Point, because it is levelled at the very Foundation of our Religion, and would teach People to doubt of its greatest Articles, through the mere force of a Word or two, and for the sake of a Noun *Substantive*.

Section VI.

I HAD now taken my Leave of you, if the Letter you published in the *London Journal*, in defence of your Book, had not been just put into my Hands.

Having seen your Talent at Apology, I expected no great Matter from you in that Way; but however I am now convinced, that your Book gives us but a small Essay of your Abilities, and that you can exceed it as much as you please.

For who would imagine that the Author of so poor a Rhapsody, could produce such masterly Strokes as these in the Defence of it.

'*My Vanity*, say you, *I never could conquer, so well as I could
'wish, and I am too proud to commit Crimes.*'

Surely no one after this will venture to lay anything to your
Charge, since great must be your Innocence, if Pride be the
Guardian of it.

But if any one should chance to humble you, you must then
fall into a defenceless State. But if you are not to be proved
guilty, till you can be shown to be deficient in Pride, it may
require some time to effect it.

Since you ground your Vindication so much upon your Pride,
it may not be amiss to recollect the Definition you have given us
of it in your own Book. '*Pride*, say you, *is that natural Faculty,
'by which every Mortal, that has any Understanding, overvalues
'and imagines better things of himself, than any impartial Judge,
'thoroughly acquainted with all his Qualities* and *Circumstances,
'would allow him.*'*

A pretty Qualification indeed, for a Man to found his Innocence upon! Yet you (with a more than ordinary Brightness)
own that you are governed by this *Vice*, to prove yourself to be
Faultless.

Should a *blind* Man who had lost his Way, allege his *Blindness*, as a Proof that he could not lose it, he would show that he
was just as well acquainted with the Advantages of Blindness,
as you are with the Effects of Pride.

The next ingenious Step that you take, is this: '*The Fable of
'the Bees*, say you, *was designed for the Entertainment of People
'of Knowledge and Education;*——it is a *Book of severe and
'exalted Morality, that contains a strict Test of Virtue.*'

Had you said that the Author was a *Seraphim*, and that he
never was any nearer the Earth than the fixed Stars, I should
have thought you in as sober a Way as you now appear to
be in.

That you intended it for the Entertainment of *People of Knowledge and Education*, is what I cannot say is false, for if your
Pride is such as you assert, you may be capable of intending
anything; I know of nothing too monstrous for you to go about.

But if you can believe, that you have wrote a Book of *severe
and exalted Morality*, you must not laugh at those who believed
Stocks and *Stones* to be Objects of Worship, or took a *Leek* or
an *Onion* to be a *Deity*.

You are happy in this, that you have made an Assertion
which an Adversary cannot further expose, because there is no
superior Degree of Extravagance to which it can be compared.

---

* Page 125.

For if a Person will write a Book to prove, that Man is a *mere Animal*, and that *moral Virtue* is the political Offspring which Flattery begot upon Pride, and then call it a Book of *severe* and *exalted Morality*, he has this Satisfaction, that no Skill can aggravate his Nonsense.

'*Such as it is*, you say, *you are satisfied it has diverted Persons* '*of great Probity and Virtue.*'

Pray, Sir, how does this appear? Where do you find these People of *great Virtue*? When you wrote your Book, you knew of no such People. Virtue was then nowhere to be found: For you tell us, that having in vain sought for it in the World, you at last went to the *Convents*, but even there it had no Existence. But now, it seems, rather than want an Apology, you will suppose even what confutes your Book, and what you most hate, that there is such a Being as a Man of *great Virtue*.

'*I lay it down*, you add, *as a first Principle, that in all Societies,* '*great or small, it is the Duty of every Member of it to be good;* '*that Virtue ought to be encouraged, Vice discountenanced, the* '*Laws obeyed, and the Transgressors punished ;* and then, you '*say, there is not a Line in the whole Book that contradicts this* '*Doctrine.*'

This comes so oddly from you, that it need not be exposed to the Reader ; if you had intended it as a *public Recantation* of all that you had delivered before, there had been something in it; but to say, that *there is not a Line in your Book that contradicts this*, is trusting too much to the Weakness of your Readers : For, can you pretend to have a *first Principle*, or to talk of *Duty* or *Virtue*, after you have declared, that the *moral Virtues* are all a Cheat, by making them the *political Offspring which Flattery begot upon Pride*?

Can you recommend *Goodness*, who have compared the *Pulchrum* and *Honestum* in Actions, to the whimsical Distinctions of *Flowers* and made the Difference between Good and Evil as fanciful, as the Difference between a *Tulip* and an *Auricula*.

When therefore you pretend to *lay it down as a first Principle, that it is the Duty of every Man to be good, &c.*

It amounts to as much, as if you had said, Having shown, that there is nothing but Fancy in the Preference of Flowers, *I lay it down as a first Principle, that it is the Duty of every Man to admire the* Tulip *above all other Flowers ; that the Love of* Tulips *ought to be encouraged ; and that of* Auriculas *discountenanced, &c.*

But however, lest any of your Readers should imagine that you meant something more than this, and to clear yourself from all Suspicion of Gravity or Seriousness in your Recommendation of

Virtue and *Goodness*, you immediately add this Explication of yourself.

'Would you banish Fraud and Luxury, prevent Profaneness and
'Irreligion, and make the Generality of the People charitable, good,
'and virtuous; break down the Printing-Presses, melt the Founts,
'and burn all the Books in the Island; knock down Foreign Trade,
'prohibit all Commerce with Strangers, and permit no Ships to go
'to Sea; restore to the Clergy, the King, and the Barons, their
'ancient Privileges, Prerogatives, and Possessions; build new
'Churches, and convert all the Coin you can come at, into sacred
'Utensils; erect Monasteries and Alms-houses in Abundance, and
'let no Parish be without a Charity-School; let the Clergy preach
'Abstinence and Self denial to others, and take what Liberty they
'please for themselves: let no Man be made Lord-Treasurer but a
'Bishop.—By such pious Endeavours, and wholesome Regulations,
'the Scene would soon be altered.—Such a Change would influence
'the Manners of the Nation, and render them temperate, honest,
'and sincere; and from the next Generation we might reasonably
'expect an harmless, innocent, and well meaning People, that would
'never dispute the Doctrine of Passive-Obedience, nor any other
'Orthodox Principles, but be submissive to Superiors, and unanimous
'in Religious Worship.'*

It must be owned, that you never so much exceeded yourself as in this Flight of your Oratory. And had your teeming Imagination been able to have produced one more Evil or Folly, it had been added to the lovely Idea you have formed of a People intending to live like Christians.

He that can now suspect you guilty of one sober Thought in relation to Religion, or Morality, must be acknowledged to be very senseless.

For, mention your Regard to Religion or Virtue as often as you please, you have here taken care to assure us, that you wish their Prosperity as *heartily*, as you wish to see the Kingdom full of *Monasteries*, and all our Money *converted* into *sacred Utensils*.

But I beg pardon for supposing, that what you have so clearly said, to show your Abhorrence of Religion, and Contempt of Virtue, needs any illustration.

But to carry on the *Banter*, you still add, '*If I have shown the
'Way to worldly Greatness, I have always without Hesitation
'preferred the Road that leads to Virtue.*'

Had there been one Instance of this kind in your Book, I suppose you would have referred us to it. But enough has been

---

* Page 253.

Fable of the Bees.

already observed, to show what Virtue implies in your System. I shall however produce one Passage to show, how you *always and without Hesitation prefer the Road that leads to Virtue.*

Speaking of *Lust* you say, ' The *artful Moralists have taught* '*us cheerfully to subdue it.* And then cry out, *Oh! the mighty* ' *Prize we have in view for all our* Self-denial! *Can any Man* ' *be so serious as to abstain from Laughter, when he considers that* ' *for so much Deceit and Insincerity practised upon ourselves as* ' *well as others, we have no other Recompense, than the vain Satis-* '*faction of making our Species appear more exalted, and remote* ' *from that of other Animals than it really is, and we in our own* ' *Consciences know it to be.*'*

Thus it is, that *without Hesitation* you give your Approbation of Virtue; you make the Moderation of our Passions to be even a Sin against our *own Consciences,* as acting *deceitfully,* contrary to what we know becomes us.

You make *Self-denial,* or any Restraints which distinguish us from Brutes, to be so ridiculous a Thing, as ought to excite the Laughter and Contempt of every Creature.

Thus is your prostitute Pen wantonly employed, to put out, as far as you can, the Light of Reason and Religion, and deliver up mankind to Sensuality and Vileness.

Should I now lament the miserable Fruits of *Free-thinking,* which thus tend not only to set us loose from the Regards of Religion, but to destroy whatever is reasonable, decent, or comely in human Nature, though as a Friend of Religion I might be censured by *some,* yet surely as an advocate for the Dignity of Man, I might be pardoned by *all.*

But is it our peculiar Unhappiness as Clergymen, that if we sit loose to the Duties of Religion, we are doubly reproached, and if we firmly assert its Doctrines, we fall under as great Condemnation.

In all other Causes, a Man is better received, because it is his proper Business to appear, yet that which should recommend our Pleadings, happens to make them less regarded: We are worse heard, because God has made it our Duty to speak.

But I wave this Topic; for if, when we assert the common Doctrines of Christianity, we are thought too much interested, we shall hardly be reckoned less selfish, when we plead for common Equity towards ourselves.

You have therefore picked out a right Body of Men to ridicule; and your manner of doing it shows you knew, that no want of Wit would make you less successful.

---

* Page 153.

We often suffer from *Porters* and *Carmen*, who venture to be smart upon us, through an Assurance, that we must lose by replying. A Security like this has encouraged you to be very liberal of your Mirth, and such Mirth as might pass for *Dulness* upon any other Subject.

I will not say how infinite your Wit has been upon our Dress and Habit, or what uncommon *Vivacity* you have shown upon the *Beaver* Hat, whether new or old.

Had you spared our '*Majestic Gait, slick Faces kept constantly 'shaved, handsome Nails diligently pared, and Linen transparently 'curious,*'* nothing of the *Sublime* had been found in your Book. It must be confessed, this is a heavy Charge against the *Priesthood;* but we may see you were loath to enhance it, or you might have mentioned the *black Eyes*, the *high Foreheads*, and the *dimpled Chins*, which may be proved upon several of them, which they show in the Face of the World at Noon-Day.

But since I have charged you with *Wit*, I do not think it fair to leave you under so gross an Accusation, without something to support your Spirits. Read therefore the following Words of the most excellent *Bruyere*.

Have the Libertines, says he, *who value themselves so much upon the Title of* Wits, *have they* Wit *enough to perceive, that they are only called so by Irony?*

You can hardly relish anything of mine, after this taste of so fine a Writer, I shall therefore trouble you but little further.

If you wonder, that I have taken no Notice of the dreadful Evils you charge upon *Charity-Schools,* and the sad Effects which such *catechising Houses* must have upon a Kingdom that is both *Christian* and *Protestant*, I must tell you that I purposely avoided it. Some Things are so plain, that it is yielding too much, to offer to defend them.

Christians, I hope, will have so much common Sense as to know, that no Christian can call such Houses an evil; and as to Complaints from other hands, Who would not wish that the Enemies of Christianity may have every Day more reason to complain?

As to your Part, they will observe, that in these very Writings, where you complain of the Evil of *Charity-Schools*, you make *moral Virtue* a Cheat, the *Offspring* of *Pride*, and the Inquiry after the *best Religion*, but a *wild Goose Chase*. A very worthy Person indeed to talk of either *Good* or *Evil!*

Whilst we can preserve but the very Name of Religion, a charitable Contribution to educate Children in it, must be reckoned amongst our best Works.

---

* Page 137.

Charity-Schools can never need a Defence in a Kingdom, that boasts of having the Scriptures in the *vulgar Tongue.* For if it be our Glory and Happiness to have the Bible in *English*, surely it must be in some Degree glorious, to teach our *Natives* how to read it.

You say, If anyone can show the *least Tittle of Blasphemy* or *Profaneness* in your Book, or *any Thing tending to Immorality, or a Corruption of Manners, you will burn it yourself, at any Time or Place your Adversary shall appoint.* I appoint the first Time, and the most public Place, and if you keep your Word, shall be your humble Servant.

Postscript.

HAVING in my Second Section mentioned Mr. *Bayle*, as the principal Author amongst those, whose Parts have been employed to arraign and expose Virtue and Religion, as being only the blind Effects of *Complexion,* natural *Temper,* and *Custom, &c.* It may not be improper to recommend to his Admirers, the following Instances of that Gentleman's great *Penetration* and *Clearness* on this Subject.

Mr. *Bayle* engaged in a Cause, where he found it necessary to assert, that a *Society of Atheists* might be as virtuous Men, as a Society of other People professing Religion; and to maintain this Opinion, he was further obliged to declare, that religious *Opinions* and *Beliefs*, had no Influence *at all* upon Men's Actions.

This Step was very necessary to be taken; for if religious *Opinions* or *Beliefs* were allowed to have *any* Influence upon our Actions, then it must also have been allowed, that a *Society of Atheists* must have been less virtuous, than a Society of People holding religious Opinions.

Mr. *Bayle* therefore roundly denied, that religious Opinions have any Influence upon us, and set himself to prove, that *Complexion*, natural *Temper, Custom, &c.*, are the *only* Causes of our Actions.

'Thus he says, he *is persuaded that Man is that kind of*
'*Creature, who with all his boasted Reason,* never *acts by the*
'*Principles of his Belief.** Again, *It cannot be denied, that Man*
'*acts* continually *against* Principles. And again, *I pretend to*
'*have demonstrated that Men* never *act by Principle.*'

---

* Miscell. Reflect.

Mr. *Bayle* has often diverted himself with the Unreasonableness of those *Divines*, who first declare the Sublimity and Inconceivableness of the Christian Mysteries, and then pretend to explain them. But they may laugh at him in their Turn, who happens to be as weak and unreasonable even in his *Philosophic Chair.*

For he can give it you out as an undeniable Maxim, '*that the Mind of Man being subject to infinite Caprice and Variety*, no Rule *can be laid down concerning it, not liable to a* thousand *Objections ;*'* and then tell you *he has demonstrated, that Man* never *acts by Principle :* As if he had said, I give you here a *certain* and *infallible Rule* concerning the Mind of Man, not liable to *one* Objection, though I assure you, *that no Rule can be laid down, not liable to a* thousand *Objections.*

Mr. *Bayle*, to show that his *Society* of *Atheists* might be as virtuous as other Men, affirms, 'that a *wicked Inclination neither arises from our Ignorance of God's Existence*, nor *is checked by the Knowledge of a supreme Judge who punishes and rewards. And that an Inclination to Evil, belongs no more to a Heart void of the Sense of God, than one possessed with it,* and *that one is under no looser a Rein than the other.'*†

With how much *Reason* and *Freedom* of Mind Mr. *Bayle* asserts this, may be seen from what he says in other Places. Thus in his *Historical Dictionary* he can tell you, '*that there is nothing so advantageous to Man, if we consider either the Mind or the Heart, as to* know *God rightly.*"‡

He can commend the Saying of *Silius Italicus*, as very *pertinently* spoken of the *Carthaginians*, '*Alas, miserable Mortals! your Ignorance of divine Nature, is the original Cause of your Crimes.* Again, *I will not deny there have been Pagans, who making the utmost Use of their Notion of the divine Nature, have rendered it the Means of abating the Violence of their Passions.'§*

These Contradictions need no Illustration; I shall pass on to show you a few more of the same Kind.

Mr. *Bayle* affirms, *that Man* never *acts by the Principles of his Belief.* Yet see how often he teaches the contrary. Speaking of the strange Opinions and Practices of some *Pagans, who, though persuaded of a Providence, denied nothing to their Lusts* and *Passions ;* he gives this as the Reason of their Conduct, '*Either that they* must *suppose the Gods approved these Ways, or else that one need not trouble one's self whether they did or no.'*‖

See here this elevated Free-Thinker asserting, that *Man* never

---

* Miscell. Reflect., p. 279.   † Ibid., p. 294.   ‡ Vol. iv., p. 2683.
§ Miscell. Reflect., p. 294.   ‖ Ibid., p. 404.

acts by his Belief, and yet making it *necessary*, that the *Pagans* must have had *such* or *such* a *Belief*, or else they could never have acted as they did.

Instances of this Kind are very numerous. In the Article of the *Sadducees*, he says, '*The good Life of the Sadducees might 'have been an Effect* of their believing *a Providence*. Again, the '*Orthodox will feel the Activity of that Impression, as well as the* '*Sadducees, and being moreover* persuaded *of a future State,* '*Religion will have* a greater Influence *upon their Lives.*'*

Here a *Belief* of a Providence in this World, is allowed to be the Cause of a *good Life*, and a *Persuasion* of a future State affirmed to have a still *greater Influence* upon our Lives; and yet the same *great Reasoner demonstrates*, that Men always act without any Regard to their *Beliefs* or *Persuasions*.

To demonstrate that *Beliefs* and *Opinions* have no part in the forming our Lives, Mr. *Bayle* appeals to the Lives of Christians; 'For, *were it otherwise*, says he, *how is it possible that Christians,* '*so clearly instructed from Revelation supported by so many* '*Miracles, that they must renounce their Sins, in order to be* '*eternally happy, and to prevent eternal Misery, should yet live as* '*they do, in the most enormous Ways of Sin and Disobedience?*'

This is Mr. *Bayle's* invincible Demonstration, that *Beliefs* and *Persuasions* have no Effect upon us, and that Man *never* acts by Principle; though you shall see that he can as well demonstrate the contrary to this.

In the Article of *Sommona-codom*, speaking of this Doctrine, *viz.*, '*That an old Sinner who has enjoyed all the Pleasures of Life,* '*will be eternally happy, provided he truly repents on his Death-* '*Bed ;*' he makes this Remark, '*Doubtless, this may be the Reason* '*why the Fear of God's Judgments, or the Hopes of his Rewards,* '*make no great Impressions upon worldly People.*'†

Here you see this learned Philosopher urges the Lives of Christians, as a *Demonstration* that Men never act by *Persuasion;* and yet tells you, as a Thing *past all doubt,* that they live as they do, through a *Persuasion* that a Death-Bed Repentance will set all right.

Take another Instance of the same kind.

Religion and Principle have no Effect upon us: '*This must be* '*the Case,* says Mr. Bayle, *or the ancient Pagans, who were under* '*the Yoke of numberless Superstitions, continually employed in* '*appeasing the Anger of their Idols, awed by infinite Prodigies, and* '*firmly persuaded the Gods dispensed Good or Evil, according to* '*the Life they lead, had been restrained from all the abominable* '*Crimes they committed.*'‡

---

* Hist. Dict.   † Ibid.   ‡ Miscell. Reflect., 275.

This Paragraph is to show, that religious *Persuasions* have no Effect upon us, because if they had, the *Persuasions* of the Pagans must have made them good Men.

But Mr. *Bayle* here forgets, that he himself has affirmed, that the '*Pagan Religion not only taught ridiculous Things, but that it* '*was besides a Religion*, authorising *the most* abominable Crimes.'*
That they were led to their Crimes by their very Religion; that it must have been a Point of Faith *with them, that to make themselves Imitators of God, they ought to be Cheats, Envious, Fornicators, Adulterers.*

So that this Philosopher shows, with great Consistency, that the *Religion* of the *Pagans* engaged them in *abominable Crimes;* and that the *Pagans* did not act by their Religion, *because* they were guilty of *abominable Crimes.*

But I proceed no further at present; this Specimen of Mr. *Bayle's* Absurdities and *Contradictions* on this very Article, where he has been most admired, may suffice to show, that if he has gained upon Men's Minds, it has been by other Arts than those of clear Reasoning. I would not by this insinuate, that he was not a Man of fine Parts; *Bellarmin's* Absurdities, though ever so many, still leave room to acknowledge his great Abilities. This seems to have been Mr. *Bayle's* Case; he was no *Jesuit* or *Papist*, but he was as great a *Zealot* in his way. *Bellarmin* contradicted himself for the sake of *Mother Church;* and Mr. *Bayle* contradicted himself as heartily, for the sake of an *imaginary* Society, a *Society of Atheists.*

I have inserted these few contradictory Passages, for the sake of such as are Proselytes to Mr. *Bayle's* Philosophy; let them here see, that in following him, they only leave Religion, to follow *Blindness* and *Bigotry* in Systems of Profaneness.

When *Clergymen* contradict one another, though it be but upon a Ceremony of Religion, *Infidels* make great Advantage of it; for Irreligion having no Arguments of its own, is forced to catch at every Foreign Objection.

But Mr. *Bayle's Self-contradictions* upon the chief Article of his Philosophy, may perhaps, not lessen his Authority with our Men of *Reason*.

For whether our *Free-Thinkers* are not such *Bigots*, as to adore Mr. *Bayle's Contradictions*, is what I will not presume to say.

I will promise for nothing, but their little Minds, and blind Zeal, to have a Share in every Error that can give Offence to well-minded Men.

Finis.

---

* Miscell. Reflect., 390.

THE CASE OF REASON,

OR

NATURAL RELIGION,

Fairly and Fully Stated.

In ANSWER to a BOOK, entitled, *Christianity as old as the Creation.*

By *WILLIAM LAW*, M. A.

LONDON:
Printed for W. INNYS and J. RICHARDSON, in *Pater-noster-Row.* 1731.

The Contents.

THE Introduction, shewing the state of the controversy, ... Page 57

CHAPTER I.
Enquiring, whether there be anything in the nature and condition of man, to oblige him to think, that he is not to admit of any doctrines, or institutions, as revealed from God, but such as his own reason can prove to be necessary from the nature of things, . . 59

CHAPTER II.
Shewing, from the state and relation between God and man, that human reason cannot possibly be a competent judge of the fitness and reasonableness of God's proceedings with mankind, either as to the time, or matter, or manner, of any external revelation, . 92

CHAPTER III.
Shewing how far human reason is enabled to judge of the reasonableness, truth, and certainty of divine revelation, ... 99

CHAPTER IV.
Of the state and nature of reason, as it is in man; and how its perfection in matters of religion is to be known, 115

CHAPTER V.
Shewing that all the mutability of our tempers, the disorders of our passions, the corruption of our hearts, all the reveries of the imagination, all the contradictions and absurdities that are to be found in human life, and human opinions, are strictly and precisely the mutability, disorders, corruption, and absurdities of human reason, ... 128

The Introduction,

Shewing the

State of the Controversy.

THE Infidelity which is now openly declared for, pretends to support itself upon the *sufficiency, excellency*, and *absolute perfection* of Reason, or Natural Religion.

The author with whom I am here engaged, makes no attempt to disprove or invalidate that *historical evidence* on which Christianity is founded; but by arguments drawn from the nature of God, and natural Religion, pretends to prove, that no Religion can come from God, which teaches anything more than that, which is fully manifest to all mankind by the *mere light* of nature.

His chief principles may be reduced to these following propositions.

1. That human reason, or natural light, is the *only means* of knowing all that God requires of us.

2. That reason, or natural light, is so full, sufficient, plain, and certain a rule or guide in all religious duties, that no external divine revelation can add anything to it, or require us to believe or practise anything, that was not as fully known before. A revelation, if ever made, can only differ from natural religion, in the manner of its being communicated. It can only declare those very *same* things *externally*, which were before equally declared by the *internal* light of nature.

3. That this must be the case of natural and revealed religion, unless God be an arbitrary Being. For if God be not an arbitrary Being, but acts according to the reason and nature of things; then he can require nothing of us by revelation, but what is already required by the nature and reason of things. And therefore, as he expresses it, *reason and revelation must exactly answer one another like two tallies.**

---

* Page 60.

4. That whatever is at any time admitted as matter of religion, that is not manifest from the reason of the thing, and plainly required by the light of nature, is gross superstition.

5. That it is inconsistent with the divine perfections, to suppose, that God can by an external revelation give any religious light or knowledge, at *any time* to *any people*, which was not equally given at *all* times, and to *all* people.

This is the state of the controversy. As to the railing accusations, and scurrilous language, which this author pours out, at all adventures, upon the Christian Clergy, I shall wholly pass them over; my intention being only to appeal to the reason of the Reader, and to add nothing to it, but the safe, unerring light of divine Revelation.

Chapter I.

Enquiring, whether there be anything in the nature *and* condition *of man, to oblige him to think, that he is not to admit of any doctrines or institutions, as revealed from God, but such as his own Reason can prove to be necessary from the nature of things.*

I BEGIN with enquiring what there is to *oblige* a man to hold this opinion, because if there is not some strong and plain proof arising from the *nature* and *condition* of man, to *oblige* him thus to abide by the sole light of his own Reason ; it may be so far from being a duty, which he owes to God, that it may be reckoned amongst his most criminal presumptions. And the pleading for this authority of his own Reason, may have the guilt of pleading for his greatest vanity. And if, as this Writer observes, *spiritual pride be the worst sort of pride,** a confident reliance upon our own Reason, as having a right to determine all matters between God and man, if it should prove to be a *groundless pretension*, bids fair to be reckoned the highest instance of the *worst* kind of the worst of sins.

Every other instance of vanity, every degree of personal pride, and self-esteem, may be a pardonable weakness in comparison of this. For how small is that pride which only makes us prefer our own personal beauty or merit to that of our fellow creatures, when compared with a self-confiding Reason, which is too haughty to adore anything in the divine counsels, which it cannot fully comprehend ; or to submit to any directions from God, but such as its own wisdom could prescribe? Thus much is certain, that there can be no *medium* in this matter. The claiming this authority to our own Reason, must either be a very great duty, or amongst the greatest of sins.

If it be a *sin* to admit of any *secrets* in divine providence, if it be a *crime* to ascribe wisdom and goodness to God in things we cannot comprehend. If it be a *baseness* and *meanness* of spirit to believe that God can teach us *better*, or *more* than we can teach ourselves. If it be a *shameful apostasy* from the dignity

---

* Page 150.

of our nature, to be humble in the hands of God, to submit to any *mysterious providence* over us, to comply with any other methods of *homage* and *adoration* of him, than such as we could of ourselves contrive and justify; then it is certainly a great duty to assert and maintain this authority of our own Reason.

On the other hand; If the profoundest humility towards *God*, be the highest instance of piety. If everything within us and without us, if everything we know of God, everything we know of ourselves preaches up humility to us, as the foundation of every virtue, as the life and soul of all holiness. If *sin* had its beginning from *pride*, and *hell* be the effect of it, if *devils* are what they are through spiritual pride and self-conceit, then we have great reason to believe, that the claiming this authority to our Reason, in opposition to the revealed wisdom of God, is not a frailty of *flesh* and *blood*, but that same spiritual pride which turned *Angels* into *apostate* Spirits.

Since therefore this appealing to our own Reason, as the absolutely *perfect measure and rule* of all that ought to pass between God and man, has an *appearance* of a pride of the *worst* kind, and such as unites us both in temper and conduct with the fallen spirits of the kingdom of darkness, it highly concerns every pleader on that side, to consider what grounds he proceeds upon, and to ask himself, what there is in the *state* and *condition* of human nature, to oblige him to think that nothing can be *divine* or *holy*, or *necessary*, in religion, but what *human* Reason dictates?

I hope the reader will think this a fair state of the case, and that all the light we can have in this Matter, must arise from a thorough consideration of the *state* and *condition* of man in this world. If without revelation he is free from mysteries as a *moral* and *religious* agent, then he has some plea from his *state* and *condition* to reject *revealed* mysteries.

But if in a state of natural religion, and mere morality, he cannot acknowledge a divine providence, or worship and adore God, without *as much* implicit faith, and humble submission of his Reason, as any revealed mysteries require; then his *state* and *condition* in the world, condemns his refusal of any revelation sufficiently attested to come from God. This enquiry therefore into the state and condition of man, being so plainly the true point of the controversy, I hope to obtain the reader's impartial attention to it.

Had mankind continued in a state of *perfect innocence*, without ever failing in their duty either to God or man, yet even in such a state, they could never have known what God would or would not reveal to them, but by some express revelation from him. And as God might intend to raise them to some higher, and unknown state of perfection; so he might raise them to it by the revelation of such things as their own Reason, though innocent and uncorrupt, yet could not have discovered.

But if man, in a state of *innocence*, could have no pretence to set himself against divine revelation, and make his own Reason the *final judge* of what God could, or could not reveal to him; much less has he any pretence for so doing in his present state of *sin, ignorance*, and *misery*, His *nature* and *condition* is so far from furnishing him with reasons against revelation, against any *supernatural* help from God; that it seems to be inconsolable without it; and every circumstance of his life prepares him to hope for terms of *mercy* and deliverance from his present guilt and misery, not according to *schemes* of his *own* contrivance, not from his *own Knowledge* of the *nature*, and *reason*, and *fitness* of things, but from some *incomprehensible depth* of divine goodness.

For if sin, and misery, and ignorance, cannot convince us of our own weakness, cannot prepare us to accept of any *methods* of *atoning* for our guilt, but such as our own guilty disordered Reason can suggest, we are not far from the hardened state of those miserable spirits that make war against God.

For to insist upon the *prerogative* of our own nature, as qualifying us to make our own peace with God, and to reject the *atonement* which he has provided for us, because we esteem it more fit and reasonable, that our *own repentance* should be sufficient without it, is the same height of *pride* and *impiety*, as to affirm, that we have no need of any repentance at all.

For as mankind, if they had continued in a state of *Innocence*, could not have known how their innocence was to be rewarded, or what changes of state God intended them for, but as revelation had discovered these things unto them: So after they were *fallen* into a state of guilt and sin, they could never know what *effects* it was to have *upon them*, what *misery* it would expose them to, or *when*, or *how*, or whether they were ever to be delivered from it, and made as happy as if they had *never* sinned; these are things that nothing but a revelation from God could teach them.

So that for a Sinner to pretend to appoint the *atonement* for his own Sins, or to think himself able to tell what it *ought* to be, or what *effect* it must have with God, is as foolish and vain a presumption, as if man in *innocence* should have pretended to appoint his own method of being changed into a *Cherubim*.

The Writers against Revelation appeal to the *Reason* and *Nature* of things, as *infallibly* discovering everything that a Revelation from God can teach us.

Thus our Author; *If the relations between things, and the fitness resulting from thence, be not the sole Rule of God's actions, must not God be an arbitrary Being? But if God only commands what the nature of things shew to be fit, it is scarce possible that men should mistake their duty; since a mind that is attentive can as easily distinguish fit from unfit, as the Eye can beauty from deformity.**

It is granted, that there is a fitness and unfitness of actions founded in the nature of things, and resulting from the relations that persons and things bear to one another. It is also granted, that the reasonableness of most of the duties of children to their parents, of parents to their children, and of men to men, is very apparent, from the relations they bear to one another; and that several of the duties which we owe to God, plainly appear to us, as soon as we acknowledge the relation that is between God and us.

But then, all this granted, this *whole argument* proves directly the contrary to that which this author intended to prove by it.

I here therefore join with this Author: I readily grant, that the Nature, Reason and Relations of things and persons, and the fitness of actions resulting from thence, is the *sole rule* of God's actions. And I appeal to this one common and confessed principle, as a sufficient proof that a man cannot thus abide by the *sole Light* of his own Reason, without contradicting the nature and reason of things, and denying this to be the *sole Rule* of God's actions.

For if the *fitness* of actions is founded in the *nature* of things and persons, and this fitness be the *sole Rule* of God's actions, it is certain that the Rule by which he acts, must in many instances be *entirely* inconceivable by us, so as not to be known *at all*, and in no instances *fully* known, or *perfectly* comprehended.

For if God is to act according to a *fitness founded* in the *nature* of things, and nothing can be fit for him to do, but what has its fitness founded in his own *divinely perfect* and *incomprehensible* nature, must he not necessarily act by a Rule *above* all human comprehension? This argument supposes that he cannot do what is *fit* for him to do, unless what he does has its *fitness* founded in his own *Nature;* but if he must govern his actions by his own nature, he must act by a *Rule* that is just as *incom*prehensible to us as his own nature.

And we can be no farther *competent judges* of the *fitness* of the conduct of God, than we are competent judges of the divine nature; and can no more tell what is, or is not *infinitely wise*

---

* Page 30.

in God, than we can raise ourselves to a *state* of infinite wisdom.

So that if the *fitness* of actions is founded in the *particular nature* of things and persons, and the fitness of God's actions must arise from that which is *particular* to his nature, then we have from this argument, the *utmost certainty* that the *Rule* or *Reasons* of God's actions must in many cases be entirely inconceivable by us, and in no cases perfectly and fully apprehended; and for this very reason, because he is not an *arbitrary being*, that acts by *mere will*, but is governed in everything he does, by the reason and nature of things. For if he is not arbitrary, but acts according to the nature of things, then he must act according to his *own nature*. But if his own nature must be the *reason, rule* and *measure* of his actions; if they are only fit and reasonable because they are according to this *Rule and Reason*, then it necessarily follows, that the fitness of many of God's actions must be incomprehensible to us, *merely* for this reason, because they have their *proper fitness;* such a fitness as is founded in the divine nature.

How mistaken therefore is this author, when he argues after this manner. *If God requires things of us, whose fitness our Reason cannot prove from the nature of things, must he not be an arbitrary being?* For how can that prove God to be an arbitrary agent, which is the necessary consequence of his not being arbitrary?

For supposing God to be an arbitrary Being, there would then be a bare possibility of our comprehending the fitness of everything he required of us. For as he might act by *mere will*, so he might choose to act according to our nature, and suitable to our comprehensions, and not according to his own nature, and infinite perfections.

But supposing God not to be an *arbitrary Being*, but to act constantly, as the perfections of his own nature make it *fit* and *reasonable* for him to act, then there is an utter impossibility of our comprehending the reasonableness and fitness of many of his actions.

For instance; look at the *reason* of things, and the *fitness* of actions, and tell me how they moved God to create mankind in the state and condition they are in. Nothing is more above the reason of men, than to explain the reasonableness and infinite wisdom of God's providence in creating man of such a *form* and *condition*, to go through *such* a state of things as human life has shewn itself to be. No revealed mysteries can more exceed the Comprehension of man, than the state of human life itself.

Shew me according to what *fitness*, founded in the *nature* of things, God's infinite wisdom was determined to form you in such a manner, bring you into such a world, and suffer and preserve *such a state* of things, as human life is, and then you may have some pretence to believe no revealed doctrines, but such as your own reason can deduce from the nature of things and the fitness of actions.

But whilst your own *form*, whilst *Creation* and *Providence* are depths which you cannot thus look into, 'tis strangely absurd to pretend, that God cannot reveal anything to you as a matter of religion, except your own reason can shew its foundation in the nature and reason of things.

For does not your own *make*, and *constitution*, the reasonableness of God's providence, and the *fitness* of the State of human life, as much concern you, as any *revealed* doctrines? Is it not as *unfit* for God to create man in such a *state*, subject to such a *course* of providence, as he cannot *prove* to be founded in the *fitness* and *reasonableness* of things; as to reveal to him such truths, or methods of salvation, as he cannot by any arguments of his own prove to be necessary

Revelation, you say, is on your account, and therefore you ought to see the *reasonableness* and *fitness* of it. And don't you also say, that God has made you for your *own sake*, ought you not therefore to know the reasonableness and fitness of God's forming you as you are? Don't you say, that providence is for the *sake* of Man? is it not therefore fit and reasonable, in the nature of things, that there should be no *mysteries*, or *secrets*, in providence, but that man should so see its methods, as to be able to prove all its steps to be constantly fit and reasonable?

Don't you say, that the *world* is for the *sake* of man; is it not therefore fit and reasonable that man should see, that the *past* and *present* state of the world has been such as the reason and fitness of things required it should be?

Now if the *imperfect* state of human nature, the *miseries* and *calamities* of this life, the *diseases* and mortality of human bodies, the *methods* of God's continual providence in governing human affairs, are things that as much concern us, and as nearly relate to us, as any methods of revealed religion; and if these are things that we cannot examine or explain, according to any *fitness* or *unfitness* founded in the *nature* of things, but must believe a great deal more of the infinite wisdom of God, than we can so explain; have we any reason to think, that God cannot, or ought not to raise us out of this unhappy state of things, help us to an higher order of life, and exalt us to a nearer enjoyment of himself, by any means, but such as our own poor Reason can grope out of the nature and fitness of things?

Now what is the reason, that all is thus mysterious and unmeasurable by human Reason, in these matters so nearly concerning human nature? 'Tis because God is not an *arbitrary Being*, but does that which the *incomprehensible perfections* of his own nature, make it *fit* and *reasonable* for him to do. Do but grant that nothing can be *fit* for God to do, but what is *according* to his own *infinite perfections*: Let but this be the *rule* of his actions, and then you have the *fullest* proof, that the fitness of his actions must be above our comprehension, who can only judge of a *fitness* according to our *own perfections*; and then we must be surrounded with mystery for this very reason, because God acts according to a *certain rule*, his own Nature.

Again: What is the nature of a human soul, upon what *terms*, and in what manner it is *united* to the body, how far it is *different* from it, how far it is *subject* to it, what powers and faculties it *derives* from it; are things wherein the *wisdom* and *goodness* of God, and the *happiness* of man are deeply concerned. Is it not necessary that these things should have their foundation in the *reason*, and *fitness* of things, and yet what natural Reason, uninspired from above, can shew that this *state* of soul and body is founded in the reason and fitness of things?

Again: The *origin* of the soul, at what time it enters into the body, whether it be *immediately* created at its entrance into the body, or comes out of a *pre-existent state*, must have its fitness or reasonableness founded in the nature of things.

For who can say, that it is the same thing, whether human souls are created *immediately* for human bodies, or whether they come into them out of some *pre-existent state?* Now one of these ways may be exceeding *fit* and *wise*, and the other as entirely *unjust* and *unreasonable*, and yet when Reason left to its own light examines either of these ways, it finds itself *equally perplexed* with difficulties, and can affirm nothing with certainty about it.

Again: Who can say that it is the same thing to man, as a *moral agent*, or that he is to have the same treatment from God, or that the same *kinds* or *degrees* of piety must be exactly required, whether human souls be *fallen spirits*, that pre-existed before the creation of bodies, or were *immediately* created, as bodies were prepared for them?

Now here comes another act of *implicit faith* in natural religion, in a point of the *greatest moment* to the moral world. For as to God's proceeding in this matter of the greatest *justice* or *injustice* in his conduct over us, mere Reason has no ability to examine into it by any pretended fitness or unfitness founded in the nature of things; but must be forced to *believe* that God deals with us according to infinite wisdom and goodness, or else be amongst those judicious believers, that believe there is no God.

Again: The origin of *sin* and *evil*, or how it entered into the world consistently with the infinite wisdom of God, is a mystery of *natural religion*, which reason cannot unfold. For who can shew from the *reason* and *nature* of things, that it was *fit* and *reasonable*, for the providence of God to suffer sin and evil to enter, and continue in the world as they have? Here therefore the man of natural religion must drop his method of reasoning from the nature and fitness of things, and that in an article of the highest concern to the moral world, and be as mere a believer, as he that believes the most incomprehensible mystery of revealed religion.

Now as there have been in the several ages of the world, some *impatient, restless* and *presuming* spirits, who because they could not in these points explain the justice of God's providence, have taken refuge in horrid *Atheism*, so they made just the same *sober use* of their reason, as our *modern unbelievers*, who because they cannot comprehend, as they would, the *fitness* and *necessity* of certain Christian doctrines, resign themselves up to an hardened *infidelity*. For it is just as wise and reasonable to allow of no mysteries in *Revelation*, as to allow of no mysteries or secrets in *Creation* and *Providence*.

And whenever this writer, or any other, shall think it a proper time, to attack *natural* religion with as much freedom, as he has now fallen upon *revealed*, he need not enter upon any *new* hypothesis, or *different* way of reasoning. For the same turn of thought, the same manner of cavilling may soon find materials in the natural state of man, for as large a bill of complaints against natural religion, and the mysteries of providence, as is here brought against revealed doctrines.

To proceed: If the *fitness of actions is founded in the nature and relations of beings*, then nothing can be fit for God to do, but so far as it is fit for the *Governor of all created beings*, whether on earth, or in any other part of the universe; and he cannot act fitly towards mankind, but by acting as is fit for the Governor of all beings.

Now what is fit for the *Governor* of *all created* nature to do in this or that particular part of his creation, is as much above our reason to *tell*, as it is above our power to *govern* all beings. And how mankind ought to be governed, with relation to the whole creation, of which they are so small a part, is a matter equally above our knowledge, because we know not how they are a part of the whole, or what relation they bear to any other part, or how their state affects the whole, or any other part, than we know what beings the whole consists of.

Now there is nothing that we know with more certainty than that God is Governor of the *whole*, and that mankind are a *part* of the whole; and that the uniformity and harmony of divine providence, must arise from his infinitely wise government of the *whole*; and therefore we have the utmost certainty, that we are *vastly incompetent* judges of the fitness or unfitness of any methods, that God uses in the government of so small a part of the universe, as mankind are.

For if the actions of God cannot have their *proper fitness*, unless they are according to the *incomprehensible greatness of his own nature*, and according to his incomprehensible greatness, as *Lord* and *Governor of all created nature;* have we not the most undeniable certainty, that the fitness of the divine providence over mankind, cannot possibly be seen by those, who are resolved to know nothing of God, but that which their own Reason can teach them?

Again : If the *fitness of actions is founded in the relations of beings to one another*, then the fitness of the actions of God's providence over mankind, must be in many instances altogether mysterious and incomprehensible to us.

For the relation which God bears to mankind, as their *all-perfect Creator* and continual *Preserver*, is a relation that our Reason conceives as imperfectly, and knows as little of, as it does of any of the divine attributes. When it compares it to that of a *Father* and his children, a *Prince* and his subjects a *Proprietor* and his property, it has explained it in the best manner it can, but still has left it as much a *secret*, as we do the divine nature when we only say, it is *infinitely* superior to everything that is *finite*.

By the natural Light of our Reason we may know with certainty, several *effects* of this relation, as that it puts us under the care and protection of a wise, and just, and merciful providence, and demands from us the highest instances of humility, duty, adoration and thanksgiving. But what it is in its own nature, what kind of state, or degree of *dependency* it signifies, what it is to exist in and by God, what it is to see by a *light* that is his, to act by a power from him, to live by a *life* in him; are things as incomprehensible to Reason, *left to itself*, as what it is to be in the *third heavens*, or to hear words that cannot be uttered.

But if this relation consists in these *inconceivable* things, in a communication of *life, light,* and *power,* if these are enjoyed in God, and in ourselves, our own and yet his, in a manner not to be explained by anything that we ever heard, or saw; then we must necessarily be poor judges of what is fit for God to require of us, because of this *relation*. It teaches us nothing but the superficialness of our own knowledge, and the unfathomable depths of the divine perfections.

How little this Writer has considered the nature and manner of this *relation* between God and Man, may be seen by the following paragraphs. *The Holy Ghost*, says he, *cannot deal with men as rational creatures, but by proposing arguments to convince their understandings, and influence their wills, in the same manner as if proposed by other agents.* As absurd, as to say, God cannot *create* us as rational beings, unless he creates us by such means, and in the same *manner*, as if we were created by other agents. For to suppose that other agents can possibly act upon our understanding, and will, in the *same manner* that God does; is as gross an absurdity, as to suppose that other agents can create us in the same manner that God creates us.

And to *confine* the manner of the Holy Ghost's acting upon us, to the manner of our acting upon one another by *arguments* and *syllogisms*, is as great weakness, as to *confine* the manner of God's creating us, to the manner of our making a *Statue* with *tools* and *instruments*.

But he proceeds and says, *For to go beyond this, would be making impressions on men, as a seal does on wax; to the confounding of their reason, and their liberty in choosing; and the man would then be merely passive, and the action would be the action of another being acting upon him, for which he could be no way accountable.**

Here you see the Holy Spirit has but these two possible ways of acting upon men, it must either only propose an argument, just as a man may propose one, or it must act like a *seal upon wax*.

I only ask this writer, Whether God communicates *life*, and *strength*, and *understanding*, and *liberty of will* to us, only as men may communicate anything to one another? or as a seal acts upon wax? If so, it may be granted, that the Holy Ghost cannot act upon us any other way.

But it must be affirmed, that we do, by a continual influx from God, enjoy all these powers, and receive the continuance of all these faculties from him, not as men receive things from one another, nor as *wax* receives the *impression* of the *seal*, but in a way as much above our conception, as creation is above our power; if we have all our *power* of acting, by a *continual communication* from him, and yet are free-agents, have all our *light*

---

* Page 199.

or Natural Religion Stated. 69

from him, and yet are *accountable intelligent* Beings: then it must be great weakness to affirm, that the Holy Ghost cannot act upon us in the same manner: For it would be saying, God cannot act upon us as he does act upon us.

The short of the matter is this. Either this *writer* must affirm, that our *rational nature*, our *understanding faculties*, our *power* of action, our *liberty* of will, must *necessarily* subsist without the *continual action* of God upon them, or else he must grant, that God can *act* upon our *understandings* and *wills* without making us as *merely passive* as the wax under the seal.

This writer says, *Though the relation we stand in to God, is not artificial, as most are amongst men——yet this does not hinder, but that we may know the end he had in being related to us as Creator and Governor, and what he requires of his creatures and subjects.* But how are we to know this? *This*, says he, *the Divine Nature*, which *contains in it all perfection and happiness, plainly points out to us.**

If he had said, since God must act over us as Creator and Governor, according to his own infinite *perfection and happiness*, therefore his conduct over us may be *very mysterious*, he had drawn a *plain* conclusion. But he proves all to be plain, because God is to govern us according to something that is not plain, according to his own *incomprehensible nature*.

His argument therefore proceeds thus. God must govern us according to his own *infinite perfection and happiness*; but we *do not know* what his infinite perfections and happiness are:

Therefore we *plainly know* how he is to govern us.

Now if this Writer is capable of taking such an argument as this to be demonstrative, it is no wonder that all his principles of Religion are founded upon demonstration.

But if he knows no more of what arises from the *Relation* between God and his creatures, than he has here demonstrated, he might be very well content with some farther knowledge from Divine Revelation.

It is because of this incomprehensible Relation between God and his creatures, that we are unavoidably ignorant of what God may justly require of us either in a state of *innocence* or *sin*. For as the fitness of actions between Beings *related*, must result from their respective Natures, so the incomprehensibility of the Divine Nature, on which the Relation between God and man is founded, makes it utterly impossible for mere natural reason to say, what *kind* of *homage*, or *worship*, he may fitly require of man in a state of *innocence*; or what *different* worship and homage he may, or must require of men, as *sinners*.

---
* Page 29.

And to appeal to the infinite Perfections of God, as *plainly pointing this out*, is the same extravagance, as to appeal to the *incomprehensibility* of God, as a plain proof of our comprehending what God is.

As to the obligations of moral or social duties, which have their foundation in the conveniences of this life, and the several relations we bear to one another, these are the same in the state of *Innocence* or *Sin*, and we know that we truly act according to the Divine Will, when we act according to what these relations require of us.

But the question is, What distinct kind of *Homage*, or *Service*, or *Worship*, God may require us to render to Him, either in a state of *Innocence* or *Sin*, on account of that Relation he bears to us as an all-perfect Creator and Governor?

But this is a question that God alone can resolve.

Human Reason cannot enter into it, it has no principle to proceed upon in it. For as the *necessity* of Divine Worship and Homage, so the *particular matter* and *manner* of it, must have its reason in the Divine Nature.

Sacrifice, if considered only as a *human Invention*, could not be proved to be a reasonable service. Yet considered as a *Divine Institution*, it would be the greatest folly not to receive it as a reasonable service. For as we could see no reason for it, if it was of human invention, so we should have the greatest reason to comply with it, because it was of Divine Appointment. Not as if the Divine Appointment altered the *nature* and *fitness* of things; but because nothing has the *nature* and *fitness* of Divine Worship, but because it is of Divine Appointment.

Man therefore, had he continued in a state of Innocence, and without Revelation, might have lived in an awful fear, and pious regard of God, and observed every duty both of moral and civil life, as an act of obedience to him. But he could have no foundation either to invent any particular *matter* or *manner* of Divine Worship himself, or to reject any that was appointed by God, as *unnecessary*. It would have been ridiculous to have pleaded his innocence, as having no need of a Divine Worship? For who can have greater reason, or be fitter to worship God, than innocent Beings? It would have been more absurd, to have objected the sufficiency and perfection of their reason; for why should men reject a *revealed method and manner* of Divine Worship and Service, because God had given them sense and reason of their own, sufficient for the duties of social and civil life?

And as reason in a state of such innocence and perfection, could not have any pretence to state, or appoint the matter or manner of Divine Worship, so when the state of innocence was changed for that of sin, it then became more difficult for bare reason to know what kind of Homage, or Worship could be acceptable to God from sinners.

For what the *Relation* betwixt God and sinners makes it fit and reasonable for God to require or accept of them, cannot be determined by human reason.

This is a *new State*, and the foundation of a *new Relation*, and nothing can be fit for God to do in it, but what has its *fitness resulting* from it. We have nothing to help our conceptions of the forementioned *relative Characters* of God, as our *Governor* and *Preserver*, but what we derive from our idea of human *Fathers* and *Governors*. Which idea only helps us to comprehend these *relations*, just as our idea of human power helps us to comprehend the *Omnipotence* of God. For a father or governor, no more represents the *true state* of God as our *Governor* and *Preserver*, than our living in our Father's *family*, represents the *true manner* of our living in God.

These relations are both very plain and very mysterious; they are very plain and certain, as to the *reality* of their existence; and highly mysterious and inconceivable, as to the *manner* of their existence.

That which is *plain* and *certain*, in these relative characters of God, plainly shews our obligations to every instance of *duty, homage, adoration, love* and *gratitude*.

And that which is *mysterious* and *inconceivable* in them, is a just and solid foundation of that *profound humility, awful reverence, internal piety*, and *tremendous sense* of the divine Majesty, with which devout and pious persons think of God, and assist at the *offices* and *institutions* of religion. Which excites in them a higher zeal for doctrines and institutions of divine revelation, than for all things human; that fills them with regard and reverence for all *things*, places, and offices, that are either by divine or human authority, appointed to assist and help their desired intercourse with God.

And if some people, by a *long* and *strict* attention to *Reason*, clear ideas, the *fitness* and *unfitness* of things, have at last arrived at a demonstrative certainty, that all these sentiments of piety and devotion, are mere *bigotry, superstition*, and *enthusiasm;* I shall only now observe, that *youthful extravagance, passion*, and *debauchery*, by their own *natural tendency*, without the assistance of any other guide, seldom fail of making the same discovery. And though it is not reckoned any reflection upon *great wits*, when they hit upon the same thought, yet it may seem some disparagement of that *reason* and *philosophy*, which teaches *old men* to think and judge the same of religion, that *passion* and *extravagance* teaches the young.

To return: As there is no state in human life, that can give us a true idea of any of the forementioned relative characters of God, so this relative state of God towards sinners is still more remote, and less capable of being truly comprehended by anything observable in the relations, betwixt a *judge* and criminals, a *creditor* and his debtors, a *physician* and his patients, a father or prince, and their disobedient children and subjects.

For none of these states separately, nor all of them jointly considered, give us any just idea, either of the *nature* and *guilt* of sin, or how God is to deal with sinners, on the account of the relation he bears to them.

And to ask, whether God in punishing sinners, acts as a *physician* towards patients, or as a *creditor* towards debtors, or as a *prince* towards rebels, or a *judge* over criminals; is the same weakness, as to ask, whether God as our *continual preserver*, acts as our parents, from whom we have our *maintenance*, or as a prince, that only *protects* us. For as the *maintenance* and *protection* that we receive from our parents and prince, are not proper and true representations of the *nature* and *manner* of our *preservation* in God, but only the properest words that human language affords us, to speak of things not human, but divine and inconceivable in their own proper natures: So a *physician* and his patients, a *creditor* and his debtors, a *prince* and his rebels, or a *judge* over criminals, neither separately nor jointly considered, are proper and strict representations of the *reasons* and *manner* of God's proceedings with sinners, but only help us to a more proper language to speak about them, than any other states of human life.

To ask, whether *sin* hath solely the *nature* of an offence, against a prince or a father, and so is pardonable by mere goodness; whether it is like an *error* in a *road* or *path*, and so is entirely at an end, when the right path is taken; whether its guilt hath the nature of a debt, and so is capable of being discharged, just as a debt is; whether it affects the soul, as a *wound* or *disease* affects the body, and so ought only to move God to act as a good physician? all these questions are as vain, as to ask, whether knowledge in God is really *thinking*, or his nature a real *substance*. For as his knowledge and nature cannot be strictly defined, but are capable of being signified by the terms *thinking* and *substance*, so the nature of sin is not *strictly represented* under any of these characters, but is capable of receiving *some representation* from every one of them.

When sin is said to be an offence against God, it is to teach us, that we have infinitely more reason to dread it on *God's account*, than to dread any offence against our parents, or governors.

When it is compared to a *debt*, it is to signify, that our sins make us accountable to God, not in the *same manner*, but with the same certainty, as a debtor is answerable to his creditor ; and because it has some likeness to a debt, that of ourselves we are not able to pay.

When it is compared to a *wound*, or disease in the body, it is not to teach us, that it may as justly and easily be healed as bodily wounds, but to help us to conceive the greatness of its evil ; that, as diseases bring death to the body, so sin brings a worse kind of death upon the soul.

Since therefore the *nature* and *guilt* of sin can only so far be known, as to make it highly to be *dreaded*, but not so known as to be *fully* understood, by anything we can compare it to.

Since the *relation* which God bears to *sinners*, can only be so known, as to make it highly reasonable to prostrate ourselves before him, in every instance of humility and penitence ; but not so fully known as to teach us how, or in what manner, God must deal with us ; it plainly follows, that if God is not an *arbitrary* Being, but acts according to a *fitness, resulting* from this relation, he must, in this respect, act by a *rule* or *reason* known only to himself, and such as we cannot *possibly* state from the *reason* and *nature* of things.

For if the nature of things, and the fitness of actions resulting from their relations, is to be the rule of our Reason, then *Reason* must be here at a full stop, and can have no more light or knowledge to proceed upon, in stating the *nature*, the *guilt*, or proper *atonement* of sin in men, than of sin in *Angels*.

For *Reason*, by consulting the *nature* and *fitness* of things, can no more tell us, what the *guilt* of sin is, what *hurt* it does us, how far it *enters* into, and *alters* our very nature, what *contrariety to*, and *separation* from God, it necessarily brings upon us, or what *supernatural* means are, or are not, necessary to abolish it ; our *Reason* can no more tell this, than our *senses* can tell us, what is the *inward*, and what is the *outward* light of Angels.

Ask Reason, what *effect* sin has upon the soul, and it can tell you no more, than if you had asked, what effect the *omnipresence* of God has upon the soul.

Ask Reason, and the nature of things, what is, or ought to be, the *true nature* of an atonement for sin, how far it is like *paying* a *debt, reconciling* a *difference*, or *healing* a *wound*, or how far it is different from them ? and it can tell you no more, than if you had asked, what is the *true degree* of power that *preserves* us in existence, how far it is *like* that which at first created us, and how far it is *different* from it.

All these enquiries are, by the nature of things, made impossible to us, so long as we have no light but from our own natural capacities, and we cannot take upon us to be *knowing*, and *philosophers*, in these matters, but by deserting our Reason, and giving ourselves up to *vision* and *imagination*.

And we have as much authority from the reason and nature of things, to appeal to *hunger* and *thirst*, and *sensual pleasure*, to tell us *how* our souls shall live in the beatific presence of God, as to appeal to our *reason* and *logic*, to demonstrate how sin is to be *atoned*, or the soul *altered*, *prepared*, and *purified*, for future happiness.

For God has no more given us our Reason to *settle* the nature of an atonement for sin; or to find out what can, or cannot, take away its guilt, than he has given us *senses* and *appetites* to state the nature, or discover the ingredients, of future happiness.

And he who rejects the *atonement* for sins made by the Son of God, as *needless*, because he cannot prove it to be *necessary*, is as extravagant, as he that should deny that God created him by his *only Son*, because he did not *remember* it. For our memory is as proper a faculty to tell us, whether God at first created us, and all things, by his only Son, as our *Reason* is to tell us, whether we ought to be restored to God, with, or without the mediation of Jesus Christ.

When therefore this writer says, *Can anything be more evident, than that if doing evil be the only cause of God's displeasure, that the ceasing to do evil, must take away that displeasure?**

Just as if he had said, if conversing with a *leper* has been the only cause of a man's getting a *leprosy*, must not departing from him, be the removal of the *leprosy*? For if anyone, guessing at the *guilt* of sin, and its *effects* on the soul, should compare it to a *leprosy* in the body, he can no more say, that he has reached its *real, internal* evil, than he, that comparing the happiness of heaven to a crown of glory, can be said to have described its real happiness.

This *writer* has no occasion to appeal to reason, and the nature of things, if he can be thus certain about things, whose nature is not only obscure, but *impossible* to be known. For it is as impossible for him to know the *guilt* and *effects* of sin, as to know the shape of an Angel. It is as impossible to know by the mere light of reason what God's *displeasure* at sin is, what *contrariety* to, or *separation* from sinners it implies, or how it *obliges*

---

* Page 4.

God to deal with them; as to know what the internal essence of God is. Our author therefore has here found the utmost degree of evidence, where it was *impossible* for him to have the *smallest degree* of knowledge.

For though it is very evident, that in the case of sin, Reason can prescribe nothing but repentance; yet it is equally evident, that Reason cannot say, nothing more is required, to destroy the effects of sin, and to put the sinner in the *same state*, as if it had never been committed.

If a man, having *murdered* twenty of his fellow creatures, should afterward be sorry for it, and wish that he had a power to bring them to life again, or to create others in their stead, would this be an *evident* proof, that he was no *murderer*, and that he had never killed one man in his life? Will his ceasing to kill, and wishing he had a power to create others in their stead, be a *proof*, that he is just in the *same state* with God, as if he had never murdered a man in his life? But, unless this can be said, unless a man's repentance sufficiently proves that he *never* was a sinner, it cannot be evident, that repentance is sufficient to put a man in the *same state*, as if he never had sinned.

He therefore that says, *If sin be the only cause of God's displeasure, must not ceasing from sin take away his displeasure?* has just as much sense and reason on his side, as if he had said, if a man's *murdering* of himself, is the cause of God's displeasure, must not his restoring himself to life again, take away God's displeasure?

For there is as much foundation in reason, and the nature of things, to affirm, that the soul of a *self-murderer* must have a sufficient power to undo the effects of murder, and put him in his former state; as to affirm, that *every sinner* must have a sufficient natural power of undoing all the effects of sin, and putting himself in the same state as if he had never sinned.

This objection therefore, against any *super-natural* means of atoning for sin, taken from the *sufficiency* of our own repentance, is as *clear* and *philosophical*, as that *knowledge* that is without *any ideas;* and as justly to be relied upon, as that *conclusion* which has no *premises*.

This writer has two more objections against the atonement for sin, made by Jesus Christ. *First*, as it is an *human sacrifice, which nature itself abhors;* and which was looked upon as the great abomination of idolatrous *pagan* worship.

The *cruelty, injustice*, and *impiety*, of shedding *human* blood in the sacrifices of the *pagan* religion, is fully granted: but *Reason* cannot thence bring the smallest objection against the sacrifice of Christ, as it was *human*.

For how can Reason be more disregarded, than in such an argument as this? The *pagans* were unjust, cruel, and impious, in offering human blood to their false gods, therefore the true God cannot receive any *human* sacrifice for sin, or allow any persons to die, as a punishment for sin.

For, if no human sacrifice can be fit for God to receive, because human Sacrifices, as parts of *pagan* worship, were unjust and impious; then it would follow, that the *mortality*, to which all mankind are appointed by God, must have the *same cruelty* and *injustice* in it. Now that *death* is a punishment for sin, and that all mankind are by death offered as a *sacrifice* for sin, is not only a doctrine of revealed Religion, but the plain dictate of Reason. For, though it is Revelation alone that can teach us, how God threatened death, as the punishment of a particular sin, yet reason must be obliged to acknowledge, that men die, because they are sinners. But, if men die because they are sinners, and reason itself must receive this, as the most justifiable cause of death; then reason must allow, that the death of all mankind is received by the true God, as a *sacrifice* for sin. But if reason must acknowledge the death of all mankind, as a sacrifice for sin, then it can have no just objection against the sacrifice of Christ, *because* it was *human*.

Revelation therefore teaches nothing more hard to be believed on this point, than reason teaches. For if it be just and fit in God, to *appoint* and *devote* all men to death, as the proper *punishment*, and *means* of their deliverance from their sins; how can it be proved to be unjust and unfit in God, to receive the death of Jesus Christ, for the same ends, and to render thereby the common death and sacrifice of mankind truly effectual?

I need not take upon me to prove the *fitness* and *reasonableness* of God's procedure in the *mortality* of mankind; Revelation is not under any necessity of proving this; because it is no difficulty that arises from revelation, but equally belongs to natural religion; and both of them must acknowledge it to be fit and reasonable; not because it can be proved to be so from the nature of things, but is to be believed to be so, by faith and piety.

But if the necessary faith and piety of natural religion, will not suffer us to think it *inconsistent* with the justice and goodness of God, to appoint all mankind victims to death on the account of sin, then *reason*, or *natural* religion, can have no objection against the sacrifice of Christ, as it is an *human sacrifice*.

And all that *revelation* adds to *natural* religion, on the point of *human* sacrifice, is only this; the knowledge of *one*, that gives *merit*, *effect*, and *sanctification*, to all the rest.

Secondly, It is objected, that the atonement made by Jesus Christ represents God as punishing the *innocent* and acquitting the *guilty ;* or, as punishing the innocent *instead* of the guilty.

But this proceeds all upon mistake : for the atonement made by Jesus Christ, though it procures pardon for the guilty, yet it does not acquit them, or excuse them from any punishment, or suffering for sin, which *reason could impose upon them.* Natural religion calls men to repentance for their sins : the atonement made by Jesus Christ does not acquit them from it, or pardon them without it; but calls them to a *severer* repentance, a *higher* self-punishment and penance, than natural religion, alone, prescribes. So that *reason* cannot accuse this atonement, of *acquitting* the guilty ; since it brings them under a necessity of doing *more*, and performing a *severer* repentance, than reason, alone, can impose upon them.

God therefore does not by this proceeding, (as is unreasonably said) shew his *dislike* of the *innocent* and his *approbation* of the *wicked*.

For how can God be thought to punish our blessed Saviour out of *dislike*, if his sufferings are represented of such infinite merit with him ? Or how can he shew thereby his *approbation* of the guilty, whose repentance is not *acceptable* to him, till recommended by the infinite merits of Jesus Christ ?

Reason therefore has nothing that it can justly object, against the atonement made by our blessed Lord, either as it was an *human sacrifice*, or as *freeing* the *guilty*, and punishing the innocent in their stead ; because this very sacrifice calls people to a *higher state* of suffering and punishment for sin, than reason, alone, could oblige them to undergo.

As to the fitness and reasonableness of our blessed Lord's sufferings, as he was God and man ; and the *nature* and *degree* of their worth ; reason can no more enter into this matter, or *prove* or *disprove* anything about it, than it can enter into the state of the whole creation, and shew, how it could, or could not, be in the whole, better than it is.

For you may as well ask any of your *senses*, as ask your *reason* this principal question, *Whether any supernatural means be necessary for the atonement of the sins of mankind ?* Or, supposing it necessary, whether the *mediation, death,* and *intercession* of Jesus Christ, as God and man, be that true supernatural means ?

For as the fitness or unfitness of any *supernatural* means, for the atonement of sin, must result from the *incomprehensible relation* God bears to sinners, as it must have such *necessity, worth,* and *dignity*, as this relation *requires*, and because it requires it ; it necessarily follows, that if God acts according to *this relation*, the *fitness* of his actions cannot be according to our comprehension.

Again: Supposing some *supernatural means* to be necessary, for destroying the guilt and power of sin; or that that *mediation, sufferings*, and *intercession*, of the Son of God incarnate, is that true supernatural means, it necessarily follows, that a revelation of such, or any other *supernatural* means, cannot possibly be made obvious to our reason and senses, as the things of human life, or the transactions amongst men are; but can only be so revealed, as to become just occasions of our *faith, humility, adoration*, and *pious resignation*, to the divine wisdom and goodness.

For, to say that such a thing is *supernatural*, is only saying, that it is something, which, by the *necessary state* of our own nature, we are as incapable of knowing, as we are incapable of seeing *spirits*.

If therefore supernatural and divine things are by the letter of Scripture ever revealed to us, they cannot be revealed to us, as they are in their *own nature*: for if they could, such things would not be *supernatural*, but such as were suited to our capacities.

If an *angel* could appear to us, as it is in its own nature, then we should be *naturally* capable of seeing angels; but, because our nature is not *capable* of such a sight, and angels are, as to us, *supernatural* objects; therefore, when *angels* appear to men, they must appear, not as they are in themselves, but in some *human*, or *corporeal* form, that their appearance may be suited to our capacities.

It is just thus, when any *supernatural* or *divine* matter is revealed by God, it can no more possibly be revealed to us, as it is in its *own nature*, than an *Angel* can appear to us, or make itself visible by us as it is in its own nature; but such supernatural matter can only be revealed to us, by being represented to us, by its likeness to something, that we already *naturally* know.

Thus revelation teaches us this *supernatural* matter; that Jesus Christ is making a *perpetual intercession for us in heaven*: For Christ's *real state*, or *manner* of existence with God in heaven, in regard to his Church, cannot, as it is in its *own nature*, be described to us; it is in this respect ineffable, and incomprehensible. And therefore, this high and inconceivable manner of Christ's existence with God in heaven, in regard to his church, is revealed to us under an idea, that gives us the truest representation of it, that we are capable of; *viz.*, the idea of a *perpetual intercession* for his church.

But if anyone should thence infer, that the Son of God must therefore either be always upon his knees in acts of *mental* or *vocal* prayer, or *prostrate* in some humble form of a supplicant, he would make a very weak inference.

Because this revealed Idea of Christ, as a perpetual Intercessor in heaven, is only a comparative representation of something, that cannot be *directly* and *plainly* known as it is in its own nature; and only teaches us, how to believe something, though imperfectly, yet *truly* and *usefully*, of an incomprehensible matter.

Just as our own ideas of *wisdom* and *goodness* do not teach us what the divine wisdom and goodness are in their *own natures*, but only help us to believe something *truly* and *usefully* of those perfections of God, which are in themselves inconceivable by us.

But then there is no inferring anything from these ideas, by which divine and supernatural things are represented to us, but only the *truth* and *certainty* of that *likeness* under which they are represented.

Thus from our own idea of goodness in ourselves, we can infer nothing concerning goodness, as it is a perfection inherent in God, but only this, that there certainly is in God some *inconceivable, infinite* perfection, *truly answerable* to that which we call goodness in ourselves, though as *infinitely* different from it, as *Omnipotence* is infinitely different from all that we *naturally* know of *power*.

But then we can proceed no farther than to the *truth* and *certainty* of this *likeness;* we cannot by any farther considerations of the *nature* and *manner* of goodness, as it is in ourselves, infer anything farther, as to the *nature* and *manner* of the *divine goodness*. This is as impossible, as to state the real nature and manner of *Omnipotence*, by considering the *particulars* of *human power*.

In like manner, our revealed idea of Jesus Christ as an *Intercessor* for us in heaven, gives us the utmost certainty that he is in heaven for our benefit, in a manner *truly* and *fully* answerable to that of a *powerful Intercessor*. But if from considering our own ideas of *human Intercessors*, we should thence pretend to infer the *real supernatural* manner of Christ's existence in heaven, we should fall into the same absurdity, as if we undertook to represent the *true* nature of *Omnipotence*, by considering what we knew of the *nature* and *manner* of human power.

Again: When it is by the letter of Scripture revealed to us, that the blessed Jesus is the one *Mediator* between God and man; that he is the *Atonement*, the *Propitiation*, and *Satisfaction* for our sins: These expressions only teach us *as much* outward knowledge of so great a mystery, as *human* language can represent. But they do not teach us the *real* or *perfect* nature of Christ's *state* between God and sinners. For that being a *divine* and *supernatural* matter, cannot by any outward words be revealed to us as it is in its *own Nature*, any more than the *essence* of God can be made *visible* to our eyes of Flesh.

But these expressions teach us thus much with certainty, that there is in the *state* of Christ between God and sinners, something infinitely and inconceivably beneficial to us; and *truly answerable* to all that we mean by *meditation, atonement, propitiation,* and *satisfaction.*

And though the *real, internal manner,* of this meditation and atonement, as it is in its *own nature,* is *incomprehensible* to the natural man, yet this does not lessen our knowledge of the *truth* and *certainty* of it, any more than the *incomprehensibility* of the divine nature, lessens our *certainty* of its real existence.

And as our idea of God, though consisting of incomprehensible perfections, helps us to a real and certain knowledge of the divine nature; and though all mysterious, is yet the solid foundation of all piety; so our idea of Jesus Christ, as our *mediator* and *atonement,* though it be mighty incomprehensible in itself, as to its real nature, yet helps us to a *certain* and *real* knowledge of Christ, as our *mediator* and *atonement;* and, though full of mystery, is yet full of motives to the highest degrees of piety, devotion, love, and gratitude unto God.

All objections therefore, raised from any difficulties about the nature of *atonements, propitiations,* and *satisfactions,* as these words are used to signify in human life, and common language, are vain, and entirely groundless.

For all these objections proceed upon this supposition, that *atonement,* or *satisfaction,* when attributed to Jesus Christ, signify neither *more* nor *less,* nor operate in any other manner, than when they are used as terms in *human laws,* or in *civil* life: Take away this supposition, and all objections are entirely removed with it.

Thus our author thinks this an unanswerable difficulty in the present case, when he asks, How *Sins freely pardoned, could want any expiation?* Or how, after a full *equivalent paid, and adequate satisfaction given, all could be mercy, and pure forgiveness?**

And yet all this difficulty is founded upon this absurd supposition, that atonement and satisfaction, when attributed to Jesus Christ, signify neither more nor less, than atonements and satisfactions, when spoken of in human laws, and human life.

---

* Page 419.

Which is full as absurd, as to suppose, that *power* and *life,* when attributed to God, signify neither more nor less, than when they are spoken of men: For there is no reason why we should think there is anything mysterious and incomprehensible in *power* and *life,* when attributed to God; but what is the same reason for our thinking, that *atonement* and *satisfaction,* when ascribed to the Son of God, must be mysterious and incomprehensible.

To return: I have granted this writer his great principle, *that the relations of things and persons, and the fitness resulting from thence, is the sole rule of God's actions:* and I have granted it upon this supposition, that it must thence follow, that God must act according to his *own nature;* and therefore nothing could be fit for God to do, or worthy of him, but what had the reason of its fitness in his own nature: and if so, then the *rule* of his actions could not fall within our comprehension. And consequently, *reason alone,* could not be a *competent judge* of God's proceedings; or say, what God might, or might not, require of us: and therefore I have, by this means, plainly turned his main argument against himself, and made it fully confute that doctrine, which he intended to found upon it.

But though I have thus far, and for this reason, granted the *nature* and *relations* of things and beings, to be the rule of God's actions, because that plainly supposes, that therefore his *own nature* must be the rule of his actions; yet since our *author,* and other modern opposers of revealed doctrines of religion, hold it in another sense, and mean by it, I know not what *eternal, immutable* reasons and relations of things, *independent* of any being, and which are a *common rule and law of God and man,* I entirely declare against it, as an erroneous and groundless opinion.

Thus, when the writer says, *If the relations between things, and the fitness resulting from thence, be not the sole rule of God's actions, must he not be an arbitrary being?* As he here means some *eternal, immutable relations, independent* of God; so, to suppose, that God cannot be a *wise* and *good* being, unless such eternal, independent relations, be the *sole rule* of his actions, is as erroneous, as to affirm, that God cannot be *omniscient,* unless *mathematical demonstrations* be his *sole manner* of knowing all things. And it is just as reasonable to fix God's knowledge *solely* in mathematical demonstrations, that we may thence be assured of his *infallible knowledge,* as to make I know not what independent relations of things, the *sole rule* of his actions, that we may thence be assured, he is not *arbitrary,* but a wise and good Being.

And we have as strong reasons to believe God to be, in the highest degree, *wise* and *good*, without knowing on *what*, his wisdom and goodness is *founded;* as we have to believe him to be *omniscient*, and *eternal*, without knowing on *what*, his *omniscience* is founded; or to *what*, his *eternity* is owing. And we have the same reason to hold it a vain and fruitless enquiry, to ask what *obliges* God to be *Wise* and *Good*, as to ask what obliges him to be *Omniscient*, or *Eternal.*

And as it would be absurd to ascribe the *Existence* of God to *any cause*, or found it upon any *independent relations* of things, so it is the same absurdity, to ascribe the infinite wisdom and goodness of God to *any cause*, or found them upon any independent relations of things.

Nor do we any more *lose* the notion, or *lessen* the certainty of the Divine Wisdom and Goodness, because we cannot say on *what* they are founded, or to *what* they are to be ascribed, than we *lose* the notion of God, or render his existence *uncertain*, because it cannot be founded on anything, or ascribed to any cause.

And as in our account of the existence of things, we are obliged to have recourse to a Being, whose existence must not be ascribed to *any cause*, because everything cannot have a cause, no more than everything can be created, so in our account of *Wisdom* and *Goodness*, there is the same necessity of having recourse to an infinite Wisdom and Goodness, that never *began* to be, and that is as different as to its *reason* and *manner* of existence, from all other wisdom and goodness, that have a beginning, as the *existence* of God is *different* from the existence of the creatures.

But if it be necessary to hold, that there is an infinite wisdom and goodness that *never began* to be, then it is as necessary to affirm, that such wisdom and goodness can no more be *founded* upon the *relations* of things, than the *unbeginning existence* of God can be *founded* upon the existence of things. And to seek for any *reasons* of a wisdom and goodness that could not begin to be, but was always in the *same infinite* state, is like seeking the cause of that which can have no cause, or asking *what* it is that *contains* infinity.

But to derive the wisdom and goodness of God from the directions he receives from the *Relations* of things, because our wisdom and goodness is directed by them, is as weak and vain, as to found his *knowledge* upon sensation and reflection, because our rational knowledge is *necessarily* founded upon them.

When therefore this writer saith, *Infinite wisdom can have no commands, but what are founded on the unalterable reason of*

or *Natural Religion Stated.* 83

things ;* he might as justly have said, an *infinite Creator* can have no *power* of creating, but what is founded on the *unalterable nature* of creatures.

For the *reason* of things, is just as unalterable, as the *nature* of creatures. And if the reasons and relations of things are nothing else but their *manner* of existence, or the *state* of their nature, certainly the relations of things must have the same *beginning*, and the same *alterable* or unalterable nature, as the things from whence they flow. Unless it can be said, that a thing may exist in *such a manner*, though it does not exist at all.

Nothing is more certain, than that the relations of things is only the *particular state* of their nature, or *manner* of existence ; there can therefore no eternal, and unalterable relations exist, but of things that eternally and unalterably exist. Unless a thing may be said to exist eternally and unalterably in such a particular *state* of nature, or *manner* of existence, and yet have no eternal existence.

When therefore he says again, *The will of God is always determined by the nature and reason of things ;*† It is the same as if he had said, the *omnipotence* of God is always determined by the *nature* of *causes* and *effects.* For as all causes and effects are what they are, and *owe* their *nature* to the omnipotence of God, so the relations of things are what they are, and owe their nature to the wisdom and will of God.

Nor does this dependence of the relations of things on the will of God, destroy the nature of relations, or make them doubtful, any more than the existence of things depending on the *power* of God, destroys the certainty of their existence, or renders it doubtful. For as God cannot make things to exist, and not to exist at the same time, though their existence depends upon his power, so neither can he make things to have such relations, and yet not to have such relations at the same time, though their relations depend upon his will.

So that the ascribing the relations of things to the will of God, from whence alone they can proceed, brings no uncertainty to those duties or rules of life, which flow from such relations, but leaves the state of nature with all its relations, and the duties which flow from them, in the greatest certainty, so long as nature itself is continued ; and when that either *ceases entirely*, or is only *altered*, it is not to be wondered at, if all its relations cease, or are altered with it.

Our author says, *Dare anyone say, that God's laws are not founded on the eternal reason of things ?*‡

---

* Page 247.   † Page 65.   ‡ Page 425.

6—2

I dare say it with the same assurance, as that his *existence* is not founded on the *eternal existence* of things. And that it is the same extravagance to say, that God's laws are founded on the *eternal reasons* of things, as to say, that his *power* is founded on the *eternal capacities* of things. For the *capacities* of things have just the same *solidity* and *eternity*, as the relations of things have, and are just such *independent realities*, as they are: And are just the same *proper materials* to found the omnipotence of God upon, as the relations of things are, to found his infinite wisdom upon.

And as we can say, that the *omnipotence* of God in preserving and supporting the creation, will certainly act *suitably* to itself, and *consistent* with that omnipotence which first made things be what they are, and put nature into such a state of causes and effects as it is in; so we can say, that the *infinite wisdom* of God in giving laws to the world, will act *suitably* to itself, and *consistent* with that wisdom which at first made the *nature* and *relations* of the rational world be what they are.

But then as the *omnipotence* of God, though it acts suitably to the laws and state of the creation, and the nature of causes and effects, which it first ordained, yet cannot be said to be founded upon the nature of causes and effects, because neither causes nor effects have *any nature*, but what they *owe* to omnipotence; so the infinite wisdom of God, though in giving laws to the world, it acts *suitably* to the natures and relations of rational beings, yet cannot be said to be *founded* upon such relations, because such relations are the *effects* of the divine wisdom, and owe their existence to it.

And the *reason* or *relations* of things shew God's *antecedent* wisdom, and are effects of it, just as the nature of *causes* and *effects* shew his *antecedent* power, and are the effects of it. And as he is infinitely powerful, but not from the *nature* of causes and effects; so he is infinitely wise, but not from the *reason* and *nature* of things.

Again; if God is *infinite* wisdom, then his wisdom cannot be founded on the relations of things, unless things *finite*, and relations that began to be, can be the foundation of that wisdom which is infinite, and could not begin to be.

And to ask what thein finite wisdom of God can be founded upon, if it is not founded upon the *natures* and *relations* of things, is the same absurdity, as to ask, How God's wisdom could be *without* a beginning, if we cannot tell *how it began?* For if his wisdom is infinite, it can no more be founded upon anything, or have any reason of its existence, than it can have anything before it.

Therefore to ask, *what* it is founded upon, when it can have no foundation upon *anything*, is asking, what an *independent* being is dependent upon, or *how* that began, which could have *no* beginning?

And to ask the reason or foundation of *anyone* of the divine attributes, is the same as asking the reason or foundation of them all. And to seek for the reason or foundation of *all* the divine attributes, is seeking for the *cause* of God's existence.

And as we do not come to God's existence, till we come to the *end* of *causes*, so nothing that is divine, can be attributed to any cause.

Nor is it any more a contradiction to say, there is something whose nature is without any cause or foundation of its existence, than to say, something exists without ever *beginning* to exist. For as nothing can have a beginning, but as it proceeds from some cause; so that which can have no beginning, can have no cause. If therefore the divine wisdom ever *began* to be *infinite*, and we could know when that beginning was, we should have some pretence to search for *that*, upon which its infinity was *founded;* but if it never could begin to be, then to seek for its reason, or foundation, is seeking for its beginning.

This writer affirms, that God's wisdom and goodness must be founded on the nature and reason of things, otherwise it could not be proved, that God was not an *arbitrary being*.

Now to seek for reasons to prove that God is not an arbitrary being, that is, a being of the *highest freedom* and *independency*, that does everything according to his *own will* and *pleasure*, is as vain, as to seek for reasons to prove, that *all things* and *all natures* are not the effect of his *will*. For if everything besides God, received its existence from him; if everything that exists, is the effect of his will, and he can do nothing, but because he *wills* the doing it, must he not be free and arbitrary in as *high* a *manner*, as he is powerful?

For if God is omnipotent, he must act according to his own will. And to say, that his *will* must be *governed* and *directed* by his wisdom and goodness, is the same, as to say his omnipotence must be governed by something *more powerful*. For if either his *will*, or his *omnipotence* wanted to be governed, there could be nothing to govern them; unless we could suppose, that he had a will *superior* to his will, and a power *superior* to his omnipotence. And though *will* and *power* when considered, as *blind*, or *imperfect* faculties in men, may pass for *humour* and *caprice*, yet as attributes of God, they have the *perfection* of God.

This *writer* says, *It is not in our power to love the Deity, whilst* we consider him to be an arbitrary being, acting out of humour and caprice.*

But if God's *will* is as *essentially* opposite to *humour* and *caprice*, as his *omnipotence* is essentially opposite to *weakness and inability;* then it is as absurd to suppose, that God must act according to humour and caprice, because he acts according to his own will, as to suppose that he must act with inability, because he acts by his omnipotence.

And if the will of God, *as such*, is in the highest state of perfection, then we have the *highest reason* to love and adore God, because he is arbitrary, and acts according to his *own all-perfect will*. And if it be asked, what it is that makes the will of God *all-perfect*, it may as well be asked, what it is that makes him omnipotent, or makes him to exist. For, as has been already observed, we have not found out a God, till we have found a being that has no *cause;* so we have not found the *will* of God, till we have found a *will*, that has no *mover*, or *director*, or *cause* of its perfection. For that *will* which never began to be, can no more be anything, but what it is in itself, than it can begin to be.

And if any of God's attributes *wanted* to be governed and directed by the other, it might as well be said, that his infinite goodness was governed by his *will*, as that his will was governed by his goodness, because he cannot be good against his will.

That which makes people imagine, that *will alone* is not so adorable, is because they consider it as a blind imperfect faculty that wants to be directed. But what has such a will as this to do with the *will* of God?

For if the will of God is as *perfect* a *will*, as his omniscience is a *perfect knowledge*, then we are as sure, that the *will* of God cannot want any direction, or *will* anything amiss, as we are, that his omniscience cannot need any information, or fall into any mistake. And if the *will* of God wanted any direction or government, it is impossible it should have it; for having no superior, it could only be so governed, because it *willed* it, and therefore must be always under its own government.

All the perfection therefore that can be ascribed to God, must be ascribed to his *will*, not as if it was the production of his will (for nothing in God is produced) but as eternally, essentially, and infinitely inherent in it.

And as God's will has thus all the perfection of the divine nature, and has no rule, or reason, or motive to any goodness, that comes from it, but its own *nature* and *state* in God; so this

---

* Page 31.

great will is the only law of all creatures, and they are all to obey and conform to it, for this reason, because it is the will of God.

Nothing has a *sufficient moral* reason, or fitness to be done, but because it is the will of God that it should be done.

It may be asked, Is there then no *reason* or *nature* of things? Yes; as certainly as there are things. But the nature and reason of things, considered *independently* of the divine will, or *without* it, have no more *obligation* in them, than a *divine worship* considered independently of, and without any regard to the *existence* of God. For the *will* of God is as absolutely necessary to found all *moral obligation* upon, as the existence of God is necessary to be the foundation of religious worship. And the fitness of *moral obligations*, without the *will* of God, is only like the fitness of a *religious* worship without the *existence* of God.

And it is as just to say, that he destroys the *reason* of religion and piety, who founds it upon the nature and existence of God, as to say, he saps the foundation of moral obligations, who founds them upon the will of God. And as religion cannot be justly or solidly defended, but by shewing its connection with, and dependence upon God's existence; so neither can moral obligations be asserted with strength and reason, but by shewing them to be the will of God.

It may again be asked, Can God make that fit in *itself*, which is in *itself absolutely* unfit to be done?

This question consists of improper terms. For God's will no more make actions to be fit *in themselves*, than it makes *things* to exist *in, or of themselves*. No things, nor any actions have any *absolute* fitness, of and in *themselves*.

A *gift*, a *blow*, the making a *wound*, or *shedding* of *blood*, considered in themselves, have no *absolute* fitness, but are fit or unfit according to any variety of accidental circumstances.

When therefore God by his will makes anything fit to be done, he does not make the thing fit in *itself*, which is just in the *same state* considered in *itself*, that it was before, but it becomes fit for the person to do it, because he can only be happy, or do that which is fit for him to do, by doing the will of God.

For instance, the *bare eating* a fruit, considered in *itself*, is neither fit nor unfit. If a fruit is appointed by God for our food and nourishment, then it is as fit to eat it, as to preserve our lives. If a fruit is poisonous, then it is as unfit to eat it, as to commit self-murder. If eating of a fruit is prohibited by an express order of God, then it is as unfit to eat it, as to eat our own damnation.

But in none of these instances is the eating or not eating,

considered in *itself, fit* or *unfit;* but has all its fitness, or unfitness, from such circumstances, as are entirely owing to the will of God.

Supposing therefore God to require a person to do something, which according to his present circumstances, *without* that command, he ought not to do, God does not make that which is *absolutely* unfit in *itself,* fit to be done; but only adds *new circumstances* to an action, that is neither fit, nor unfit, moral, nor immoral in *itself,* but *because* of its circumstances.

To instance in the case of *Abraham,* required to sacrifice his son. The killing of a man is neither good nor bad, considered *absolutely* in *itself.* It was lawful for *Abraham* to kill his son, because of the *circumstances* he was in with regard to his son. But when the divine command was given, *Abraham* was in a *new state,* the action had *new circumstances,* and then it was as lawful for *Abraham* to kill his son, as it was lawful for God to require any man's life, either by *sickness,* or any *other means* he should please to appoint.

And it had been as unlawful for *Abraham* to have disobeyed God in this extraordinary command, as to have cursed God at any *ordinary calamity* of providence.

Again, it is objected, *If there is nothing right or wrong, good or bad, antecedently and independently of the will of God, there can then be no reason, why God should will, or command one thing, rather than another.*

It is answered, *first,* That all goodness, and all possible perfection, is as *eternal* as God, and as essential to him as his existence. And to say, that they are either *antecedent* or *consequent, dependent* or *independent* of his will, would be equally absurd. To ask therefore, whether there is not something right and wrong, antecedent to the will of God, to render his will *capable* of being right, is as absurd, as to ask for some antecedent cause of his existence, that he may be proved to exist necessarily. And to ask, how God can be good if there is not something good independently of him, is asking how he can be infinite, if there be not something infinite independently of him. And to seek for any other *source* or *reason* of the divine goodness, besides the divine nature, is like seeking for some external cause and help of the divine omnipotence.

The goodness and wisdom, therefore, by which God is wise and good, and to which all his works of wisdom and goodness are owing, are neither *antecedent,* nor *consequent* to his will.

Secondly, Nothing is more certain, than that all *moral obligations* and *duties* of creatures towards one another, *began* with the existence of moral creatures. This is as certain, as that all *physical relations*, and corporeal qualities and effects, *began* with the existence of bodies.

As therefore nothing has the nature of a cause or effect, nothing has any quality of any kind in bodies, but what is entirely owing to matter so created and constituted by the *will* of God; so it is equally certain, that no actions have any *moral qualities*, but what are wholly owing to that state and nature in which they are created by the will of God.

Moral obligations therefore of creatures have the same *origin*, and the *same reason*, that natural qualities and effects have in the corporeal world, *viz.*, the sole will of God. And as in a different state of matter, bodies would have had different qualities and effects; so in a different state of rational beings, there would be different moral obligations, and nothing could be right or good in their behaviour, but what began then to be right and good, because they then began to exist in such a state and condition of life. And as their state and condition could have no other cause or reason of its existence, but the sole will of God, so the cause and reason of right and wrong in such a state, must be equally owing to the will of God.

The pretended *absolute independent fitnesses*, or *unfitnesses* of actions therefore *in themselves*, are vain *abstractions*, and philosophical *jargon*, serving no ends of morality, but only helping people to wrangle and dispute away that sincere obedience to God, which is their only happiness. But to make these imaginary *absolute fitnesses* the *common law* both of God and man, is still more extravagant. For if the *circumstances* of actions give them their *moral nature*, surely God must first be in our circumstances, before that which is a law to us, can be the same law to him.

And if a father may require that of a son, which his son, because of his *different state*, cannot require of his brother; surely that which God may require of us, may be as different from that, which a father may require of a son, as God is different from a father.

Thus this writer speaking of the law founded on absolute fitnesses, says, *It is a law by which God governs his own actions, and expects that all the rational world should govern theirs.** And lest you should think that God is not in the same state of necessary subjection and obedience to this law, he farther adds, *that God cannot dispense, either with his creatures, or himself, for not observing it.*†

Now to say, that the *reason* of things is the same law to God that it is to us, is saying, that God is in the *same state* with *regard*

---

* Page 59.   † Page 189.

to the nature of things, as we are. For as things are a law to us, because we are in *such* a state; if they are the *same law* to God, it must be because God is in the same state that we are.

Again, if God is as much under a law as we are, then he is as much under authority; for law can no more be without authority, than without a law-giver. And if God and we are under the *same law*, we must be under the *same authority*.

But as God cannot be under any law in common with us his creatures, any more than he can be of the same rank or order with us; so neither can he be under any law at all, any more than he can be under any authority at all.

For that which is the *rule*, or *reason* of God's actions, is no more different from his own will, than his power is different from his will.

And though God is not to be looked upon as an *arbitrary being*, in the sense of this author, who will not distinguish arbitrary from *humour* and *caprice;* yet in a better, and only true sense of the word, when applied to God, he must be affirmed to be an arbitrary being, that acts only from himself, from his *own will*, and according to his *own pleasure*.

And we have no more reason to be afraid to be left to a God without a law, than to a God that had no beginning; or to be left to his will and pleasure, than to be left under the protection and care of a being, that is all love, and mercy, and goodness. For as the existence of God, as such, necessarily implies the existence of all perfection; so the will of God, as such, necessarily implies the *willing* everything, that *all perfection* can will.

And as the existence of God, because it contains all perfection, cannot for that reason have any external cause; so the will of God, because it is *all perfection*, cannot, for that reason, have any external *rule* or *direction*. But his own will is wisdom, and his wisdom is his will. His goodness is arbitrary, and his arbitrariness is goodness.

To bring God therefore into a state of moral obligation and subjection to any external *law* or *rule*, as we are, has all the absurdity of supposing him to be a finite, dependent, temporary, imperfect, improvable, governable being as we are.

But this writer does not only thus bring God into this state of law and obligation with us, but makes farther advances in the same kind of errors.

Hence, says he, *we may contemplate the great dignity of our rational nature, since our reason for* kind, *though not for degree, is of the* same nature *with* that of God's.*

---

* Page 24.

Here you see *our reason*, that is, our *faculty* of reasoning, for reason cannot be called *our's* in any other respect, has no other difference from reason as it is in God, but that of degree. But what greater absurdity can a man fall into, than to suppose, that a being whose existence had a beginning but a few years ago, differs only in degree from that which could not *possibly* have a beginning; or that a *dependent* and *independent* being, should not be different in *kind*, but *only* in degree. For if nothing that had a beginning, can be without a beginning; if nothing that is dependent can be independent, then no faculties or powers of dependent beings that began to be, can be of the *same kind* with the powers of that independent being, that could not begin to be.

For to say, that the faculties of a dependent and independent being, may be of the same kind, is as flat a contradiction, as to say, the same kind of thing may be dependent, and independent, as it is the same kind of thing.

How extravagant would he be, who should affirm, *existence*, *life*, *happiness*, and *power*, to be of the same *kind* and *nature* in us, as they are in God, and only to differ in degree?

And yet it would be more extravagant to suppose, that though God cannot *possibly* have our *kind* of *existence*, *life*, *happiness*, and *power*, yet he must have *our kind* of reason.

Reason belongs to God and man, just as *power, existence, life*, and *happiness*, belong to God and man. And he that can from happiness being common to God and man, prove our happiness to be of the *same kind* and nature with God's, may also prove reason in God and man to be of the same kind.

This writer indeed says, *Our happiness is limited*, because *our reason is so;* and that God has *unlimited happiness*, because *he alone has unlimited reason.**

But if that which is *necessarily limited*, is certainly different from that which is *necessarily unlimited*, then we have proof enough from this very argument, that a reason *necessarily* limited, cannot be of the *same kind* with that reason, which is *necessarily* unlimited. Unless it can be said, that necessary and unnecessary, limited and unlimited, finite and infinite, beginning and unbeginning, have no contrariety in *kind*, but only differ, as a *short* line differs from a *long* one.

The truth of the matter is this; reason is in God and man, as power is in God and man. And as the divine power has some degree of likeness to human power, yet with an *infinite* difference from it; so that perfection which we call *reason* in God, has

---

* Page 24.

some degree of likeness to reason as it is in man, yet is *infinitely* and beyond all conception different from it.

Nor can anyone shew, that we enjoy reason in a *higher degree* in respect of God, than we enjoy power; or that the *manner*, or *light* of our reason, bears any greater likeness to the light and knowledge of God, than the *manner* and *extent* of our power bears to the omnipotence of God.

And as our enjoyment of power is so limited, so imperfect, so superficial, as to be scarce sufficient to tell us, what power is, much less what omnipotence is; so our share of reason is so small, and we enjoy it in so imperfect a manner, that we can scarce think or talk intelligibly of it, or so much as define our own faculties of reasoning.

Chapter II.

Shewing from the state *and* relation *between God and man, that human reason cannot possibly be a competent judge of the* fitness *and* reasonableness *of God's proceedings with mankind, either as to the* time, *or* matter, *or* manner *of any external revelation.*

AS our author has laid it down as an undeniable rule of God's actions, that he must, if he be a wise and good being, act according to the relation he stands in towards his creatures; so I proceed upon this principle, to prove the incapacity of *human reason*, to judge *truly* of God's proceedings in regard to divine revelation.

For if the fitness of actions *results from the nature and relations* of beings, then the *fitness* of God's actions, as he is an *omniscient creator* and *governor*, to whom everything is *eternally foreknown*, over beings endued with *our freedom of will,* must be to us very incomprehensible.

We are not so much as capable of comprehending by our own reason the *possibility* of this relation, or how the foreknowledge of God can consist with the free agency of creatures. We know that God foreknows all things, with the same certainty as we know there is a God. And if *self-consciousness* is an infallible proof of our own existence, it proves with the same certainty the freedom of our will. And hence it is, that we have a full assurance of the consistency of God's foreknowledge with freedom of will.

Now this *incomprehensible* relation between an *eternally foreknowing creator* and *governor*, and his free creatures, is the *relation* from whence arises the *fitness* of God's providence over us. But if the *relation* itself is incomprehensible, then those actions that have their *fitness* from it, must surely be incomprehensible. Nothing can be fit for God to do, either in *Creation* or *Providence*, but what has its fitness founded in his own *fore-knowledge* of everything that would follow, from *every kind* of creation, and *every manner* of providence: But if nothing can be fit, but because it is according to *this fore-knowledge* of *everything* that would follow from *every kind* of creation, and *every manner* of providence; then we have the utmost certainty, that the *fitness* of God's actions as a *fore-knowing Creator*, and *Governor* of free agents, must be founded upon *reasons* that we cannot *possibly* know anything of.

And a *child* that has but just learned to speak, is as well qualified to state the fitness of the laws of *matter* and *motion* by which the whole *vegetable* world is preserved, as the wisest of men is qualified to comprehend, or state the fitness of the methods, or proceedings, which a *fore-knowing providence* observes over free agents. For every reason on which the fitness of such a providence is founded, is not only *unknown* to us, but by a necessity of nature *impossible* to be known by us.

For if the *fitness* of God's acting in this, or that manner, is founded in his *fore-knowledge* of everything that would *happen*, from *every possible way* of acting, *then* it is just as absolutely impossible for us to know the reasons, on which the fitness of his actions are founded, as it is impossible for us to be omniscient.

What human reason can tell, what kind of beings it is *fit* and *reasonable* for God to create, on the account of his own *eternal fore-knowledge?* And yet this is as possible, as for the same reason to tell, how God ought to govern beings already created, on the account of his own eternal fore-knowledge; and yet God can neither *create*, nor *govern* his creatures, as it is *fit* and *reasonable* he should, unless he creates and governs them in *this* or *that* manner, on the *account* of his own fore-knowledge. And therefore, if he acts *like* himself, and *worthy* of his own nature, the fitness of his proceedings must for this very reason, *because* they are fit, be vastly above our comprehension.

Who can tell what *different kinds* of rational creatures, distinguished by variety of natures, and faculties, it is fit and reasonable for God to create, because he *eternally foresaw* what would be the *effect* of such different creations? Who can explain the *fitness* of that vast *variety* there is amongst rational creatures of the *same species*, in their rational faculties, or shew that all their different faculties ought to be as they are? And yet the *fitness* of this providence has its *certain reason* in the divine fore-knowledge, and it could not be fit, but because of it.

Who can tell what *degree* of reason rational creatures ought to enjoy, *because* they are rational; or what degrees of *new* and *revealed* knowledge it is fit and reasonable for God to give, or not give them, because they seem, or seem not to themselves to want it, are disposed, or not disposed to receive it? For as mankind cannot tell why it was *fit* and *reasonable* for God to create them of such a *kind*, and *degree*, as they are of; so neither can they tell how God ought, or ought not to add to their natural knowledge, and make them as *differently accountable* for the use of revealed rules of life, as for the use of their natural faculties.

And as the reason why God created them of *such* a *kind*, and with *such faculties*, was because of his own fore-knowledge of the *effects* of such a creation; so if ever he does reveal to them any *supernatural* knowledge, both the doing it, the *time*, and *matter* and *manner* of it, must have their *fitness* in his own *eternal fore-knowledge* of the effects of such a revelation.

The reasons therefore on which the *fitness* of this or that revelation, *why* or *when*, of *what matter*, in *what manner*, and to *whom* it is to be made, must, from the nature and reason of things, be as unsearchable by us, as the reasons of *this* or *that* creation of rational beings, at such a *time*, of such a *kind*, in such a *manner* and in such a *state*.

This may help us to an easy solution of those unreasonable questions, which this writer puts in this manner.

If the design of God in communicating anything of himself to men was their happiness, would not that design have obliged him, who at all times alike desires their happiness, to have at all times alike communicated it to them? If God always acts for the good of his creatures, what reason can be assigned, why he should not from the beginning have discovered such things as make for their good, but defer the doing it till the time of Tiberius: *since the sooner this was done, the greater would his goodness appear?**

---

* Page 393.

And again, *How is it consistent with the notion of God's being universally benevolent, not to have revealed it to all his children, when all had equal need of it? Was it not as easy for him to have communicated it to all nations, as to any one nation or person? Or in all languages, as in one?**

Now all this is fully answered, by our author's own great and fundamental principle.

For if the relations between things and persons, and the fitness resulting from thence, be the sole rule of God's actions,† as he expressly affirms: then the *sole rule* or reason of God's revealing anything to any man, or men, at any time, must have its *fitness resulting* from the divine fore-knowledge of the effects of *such* a revelation, at *such* a time, and to *such* persons. If God does not act thus, he does not act according to the *relation* betwixt a *fore-knowing Creator*, and his free creatures. But if he does act according to a *fitness resulting* from this *relation*, and makes, or does not make revelations, according to his own fore-knowledge of the fitness of times, and persons for them; then to ask how a God, *always equally* good, can make a revelation at *any* time, and not make the *same* at *all* times, is as absurd as to ask, how a God, always equally good, can reveal that at one time, because it is a *proper* time for it, and not reveal it at every other time, though every other time is *improper* for it.

God's goodness, directed by his own fore-knowledge of the *fitness* of times, and of the *state* and *actions* of free agents, deferred a certain revelation to the time of *Tiberius*, because he *foresaw* it would then be an act of the *greatest* goodness, and have its *best effects* upon the world: To ask therefore, *what reason can be assigned*, why so good and beneficial a revelation was not *sooner*, or even from the *beginning* made to the world, is asking, *What reason can be assigned*, why God is good, and intends the *greatest* good by what he does, or stays for the doing anything, till such time, as makes it a greater good than if he had done it sooner; it is asking, why God should act, according to his *own fore-knowledge* of the *state* and *actions* of *free agents*, and order all things, according to a fitness resulting from such a fore-knowledge.

These questions suppose, that if God shewed his *goodness* to mankind by a revelation at such time, he must be *wanting* in goodness before that time, because he did not make it *sooner;* whereas if his deferring it till *such* a time, was owing to his *fore-knowledge* of the actions and state of free agents, and of the *effects* of his revelation, and because it would then have its *best*

---

* Page 196. † Page 28.

effects, then God is proved to be *equally* good before he made it, for this very reason, because he did not make it before its *proper* time; and he had been wanting in goodness, if he had not *deferred* it till that time.

Now this appealing to God's fore-knowledge of the state and actions of *free agents*, as the cause of all that is particular in the *time* and *manner* of any revelation, and deducing its fitness from thence, cannot be said to be *begging the question* in dispute, but is resolving it directly according to the *rule*, which this writer lays down for God to act by, which is this: That *the relations between things and persons*, and *the fitness resulting from thence, must be the sole rule of God's actions, unless he be an arbitrary being*.

But if this is the *sole rule*, then God in giving any revelation, must act as the *relation* betwixt a *fore-knowing* Creator and his *free* creatures requires; and his actions must have their *fitness resulting* from his fore-knowledge of the *state* and *actions* of free agents. And if this is God's sole rule, made necessary to him from the nature of things, then to ask why *this* or *that* revelation *only* at *such* a time, is to ask why God *only* does that which is *fit* for him to do. And to ask, why not the same revelation at any other time, is asking why God does not do that, which it is *not fit* for him to do.

This writer asks, *How it is consistent with the notion of God's being universally benevolent, not to have revealed it to all his children, who had equal need of it?* But if they had *equal need* of it, yet if they were not *equally fit* for it, but prepared only to have their *guilt* increased by it, and so be exposed to a greater damnation by refusing it; then God's goodness to them is very manifest, by withholding such information from them, and reserving it for those that would be made happier by it.

Judas and *Pontius Pilate*, and the *Jews* that called for our Saviour's crucifixion, had *equal need* of a Saviour with those that believed in him. *Chorazin* and *Bethsaida* wanted the light of the Gospel as much as those that received it; but if the rest of the world had been, at that time, as much indisposed for the light of the Gospel, as they were, God's goodness had been greater to that age, if he had left them as they were, and reserved the light of the Gospel till a better age had succeeded.

So that this argument, founded on the *equal need* of all, or former ages, has no force, unless it could be shewn, that the same revelation made to any of these former ages, would have produced all those good effects, which God foresaw would follow, from its being reserved for such a *particular time* and *state* of things and persons.

He asks again, *Was it not as easy for God to have communicated it to all nations, as to any one nation or person ? Or in all languages, as in any one ?* This argument is built upon the *truth* and *reasonableness* of this supposition, That God does things because they are *easy,* or forbears things because they are *difficult* to be performed. For it can be no argument, that God ought to have revealed such things to *all* nations or persons, because it was as *easy* to him, as to do it to *any one* nation or person ; unless it be supposed, that the *easiness* of a thing is a reason why God does it, and the difficulty of a thing a reason why he does not do it. But if this supposition be very absurd, then the argument founded upon it must be liable to the same charge.

But if God does things, not because they are easy, but because they are infinitely good and fit to be done, and founded in the *relation* of a fore-knowing Creator to his free creatures; then the reason why God has afforded different revelations, to different ages and persons, is this, That his *manner* of revealing everything, might be *worthy* of his own *fore-knowledge* of the effects of it, and that everything that is particular in the *time* or *manner* of any revelation, might have its *fitness resulting* from the *relation* betwixt a good God and his creatures, whose *changing* state, *different* conduct, *tempers* and *actions,* are all eternally fore-known by him.

If it should here be said, that this *writer* only means, that it is as *possible* for God to make the same revelation, have the *same* effects, and produce *as much* good in one age as in another ;

This is only saying, It is as *possible* for God to *destroy* the difference of times and states, to *overrule* the nature of things, and turn all mankind into *mere machines,* as it is to govern and preside over them according to their natures. For if the natures of things are not to be destroyed ; if the *nature,* and *state,* and *tempers* of men, and the *freedom* of their wills, are to be suffered to act according to themselves ; then to say, it is as possible for God to make the same revelation to have the same effect in one age as in another, is as absurd as to say, it is as possible for him to make the *same heat* of the *Sun,* have the same effects upon any one place of the earth, that it has upon another, upon *rocks* and *barren sands,* as it has upon a fertile soil, without altering the nature of *rocks* and *sands.*

Again, it is objected, that a divine revelation must either be the effect of *justice,* or else of *mercy* and *free goodness;* but in either of these cases it ought to be *universal ;* for justice must be done to all. But if it is the effect of *mercy* and *free goodness,* this writer asks, *How a being can be denominated merciful and good, who is so only to a few, but cruel and unmerciful to the rest?**

It is answered, That there is neither justice in God without mercy, nor *mercy* without justice; and to ascribe a *revelation* to either of them separately, in *contradistinction* to the other, has no more truth or reason in it, than to ascribe the *creation* separately either to the *Wisdom*, or *Power* of God, in contradistinction to the other.

Secondly, A divine revelation is not owing to the *justice* or *free goodness* of God, either *separately* or *jointly* considered; but to the goodness, mercy, and justice of God, *governed* and *directed* by his eternal fore-knowledge of all the effects of every revelation, at any, or all times.

God ordains a revelation in this, or that manner, time, and place; not because it is a *justice* that he cannot refuse, not because it is matter of *favour* or *free* goodness, and therefore may be given in any manner at pleasure; but because he has the whole *duration* of human things, the whole *race* of mankind, the whole *order* of human changes and events, the whole *combination* of all causes and effects of human tempers, all the *actions* of free agents, and *all the consequences* of every revelation, plainly in his sight; and according to this eternal fore-knowledge, every revelation receives everything that is *particular* in it, either as to *time, matter, manner*, or *place*.

He shews his goodness in a revelation to *this part* of the world, not because it is a *part* that *alone* wants it, not because he can bestow his *favours* as he pleases, but because by acting *so* with *such* a part, he *best* shews his goodness and regard to the *whole*. He reveals himself at *such* a *time*, not because he at *that time* begins to have a *partial* or *particular* kindness, but because by so *timing* his goodness, he *best shews* his care and goodness throughout the *whole duration* of human things, from the beginning to the end of the world. And it is because he had the *same good* will towards mankind in *every age*, that he does what he does in any *particular* age.

And if by the *particular* time and manner of any revelation, the *whole race* of mankind receive more benefit from it; if more are raised to happiness by it, and fewer are made miserable by a blamable *using* or *refusing* it, than could have happened by *any other* time, or manner of giving it to the World, consistent with the natural freedom of men; then God, by being particular in the time and place of giving it, is not merciful to a *few*, and cruel to *many*, but is *most* merciful to *all*; because he only chose *such*

---

* Page 401.

time, and *place*, and *persons*, because *all* would receive more benefit from it, than they possibly could from the choice of any other time, or place, or persons.

All complaints therefore about that which is *particular*, or *seemingly* partial in the time and manner of any revelation, are very unjustifiable; and shew, that we are discontented at God's proceedings, because he acts like himself, does what is *best* and *fittest* to be done, and governs the world, not according to our weak imaginations, but according to his own infinite perfections.

We will not allow a Providence to be *right*, unless we can comprehend and explain the reasonableness of all its steps; and yet it could not *possibly* be right, unless its proceedings were as much *above* our comprehension, as our wisdom is *below* that which is infinite.

For if the *relations* of *things* and *persons*, and the *fitness* resulting from thence, be the *rule* of God's actions; then all the revelations that come from God, must have their *fitness* resulting from the relation his fore-knowledge bears to the *various states, conditions, tempers*, and *actions* of free agents, and the *various effects* of every manner of revelation.

But if God cannot act worthy of himself in any manner of revelation, unless he acts according to a fitness resulting from this relation; then we have the highest certainty, that he must act by a *rule* that lies out of our sight, and that his Providence in this particular must be incomprehensible to us; for this very reason, because it has that very fitness, wisdom and goodness in it, that it ought to have.

CHAPTER III.

Shewing how far human reason is enabled to judge of the reasonableness, truth and certainty of divine Revelation.

THE former chapter has plainly shewn, from the state and relation between God and man, that we must be strangers to the true reasons on which a divine revelation is founded, both as to its *time, matter*, and *manner*.

But it is here objected, *If God by reason of his own perfections must be thus mysterious and incomprehensible, both in the matter* and manner of divine revelation; How can we know what revelations we are to receive as divine? How can we be blamed for rejecting this, or receiving that, if we cannot comprehend the reasons on which every revelation is founded, both as to its matter and manner?

Just as we may be blamed for some notions of God, and commended for others, though we can have no notions of God, but such as are mysterious and inconceivable. We are not without some natural capacity of judging right of God, of finding out his perfections, and proving what is, or is not worthy to be ascribed to him. Yet what the divine perfections are in themselves, what they imply and contain in their own nature and manner of existence, is altogether mysterious and inconceivable by us at present. If therefore a man may be blamable, or commendable, for his right or wrong belief of a God; then a man may be accountable for a right or wrong belief of such matters, as are in their own nature too mysterious for his comprehension. And though a man knows the reasons of a divine revelation, either as to its *matter* or *manner*, as imperfectly as he knows the divine nature; yet he may be as liable to account for believing *false revelations*, as for *idolatry;* and as full of guilt for rejecting a *true revelation*, as for denying the only *true God*.

Secondly, Though we are insufficient for comprehending the *reasons*, on which the particular *matter* or *manner* of any divine revelation is founded; yet we may be so far sufficient judges, of the *reasons* for *receiving* or not *receiving* a revelation as divine, as to make our conduct therein justly accountable to God.

For if God can shew a revelation to proceed from him, by the *same undeniable* evidence, as he shews the *creation* to be his *work;* if he can make himself as visible in a *particular extraordinary* manner, as he is by his *general* and *ordinary* providence; then, though we are as unqualified to judge of the mysteries of a *revelation*, as we are to judge of the mysteries in *creation* and *providence;* yet we may be as fully obliged to receive a revelation, as to acknowledge the creation to be the work of God; and as highly criminal for disbelieving it, as for denying a general Providence.

Adam, Noah, Abraham, and *Moses,* were very incompetent judges, of the reasons on which the particular revelations made to them were founded; but this did not hinder their sufficient assurance, that such revelations came from God, because they were proved to come from God in the same manner, and for the same reasons, as the creation is proved to be the Work of God.

And as *Adam* and *Noah* must see everything wonderful, mysterious, and above their comprehensions, in those new worlds into which they were introduced by God; so they could no more expect, that he should require nothing of them, but what they would enjoin themselves, than that their own *frame*, the *nature* of the creation, the *providence* of God, or the *state* of human life, should be exactly as they would have it.

And if their posterity will let no *messages* from heaven, no *prophecies* and *miracles* persuade them, that God can call them to any duties, but such they must enjoin themselves; or to the belief of any doctrines, but such as their own minds can suggest; nor to any methods of changing their present state of weakness and disorder for a happy immortality, but such as suit their own *taste, temper*, and way of reasoning; it is because they are grown senseless of the mysteries of creation and providence with which they are surrounded, and forget the awful prerogative of infinite wisdom, over the weakest, lowest rank of intelligent beings.

For the *excellence* of a revelation is to be acknowledged by us, for the same reason that we are to acknowledge the excellence of creation and providence: not because they are wholly according to human conception, and have no mysteries, but because they are proved to be of God.

And a revelation is to be received as coming from God, not because of its internal excellence, or because we judge it to be worthy of God; but because God has declared it to be his, in as *plain* and *undeniable* a manner, as he has declared *creation* and *providence* to be his.

For though no revelation can come from God, but what is truly worthy of him, and full of every internal excellence; yet what is truly *worthy* of God to be *revealed*, cannot possibly be known by us, but by a revelation from himself.

And as we can only know what is worthy of God in creation, by knowing what he has created; so we can no other way possibly know what is worthy of God to be revealed, but by a revelation. And he that pretends, independently of any revelation, to shew *how*, and in what manner God ought to make a revelation worthy of himself, is as great a *Visionary*, as he that should pretend, independently of the creation, or without learning anything from it, to shew how God ought to have proceeded in it, to make it worthy of himself. For as God alone, knows how to create worthy of himself, and nothing can possibly be proved to be worthy to be created by him, but because he has already created it; so God alone knows what is worthy of himself in a revelation, and nothing can possibly be proved worthy to be revealed by him, but because he has already revealed it.

Hence we may see how little this *writer* is governed by the *reason* and *nature* of things, who proceeds upon this as an undeniable principle, that we could not know a revelation to be divine, unless we knew, antecedently to revelation, what God could teach or require of us by it. Thus, says he, *Were we not capable by our reason of knowing what the divine goodness could command, or forbid his creatures, antecedently to any external revelation, we could not distinguish the true instituted religion from the* many *false ones.**

Just as *wild* and *visionary*, as if it was said, Were we not capable by our reason of knowing what kind or order of beings God *ought* to create, *independently* of anything we learn from the creation, we could never prove this or that creation to proceed from him. Did we not, antecedently to facts and experience, know by our own reason what ought to be the method and manner of divine providence, we could never prove that the providence which governs nations and persons is a divine providence.

For if a revelation could have no proof that it was divine, unless we by our reason, *antecedently* to *all* revelation, knew *all* that *any* revelation could contain, or require of us; then it undeniably follows, that no *providence* or *creation* could be proved to be divine, unless we by our reason, *independently* of creation and providence, could tell what *kind* of beings God ought to create, or what *manner* of providence he ought to observe.

For that which cannot be ascribed to God in revelation, because it is unworthy of his wisdom and goodness, cannot be ascribed to God in creation and providence.

Again, He proceeds to shew, that a revelation from God cannot contain anything, but what human reason can prove from the nature of things; for this reason, because if God could require anything more of us, than what our own reason could thus prove, he must then require *without* reason, be an *arbitrary* being, and then there is an end of all religion.

Now this argument proceeds thus; If God does not act according to the *measure* of *human* reason, he cannot act according to *reason itself*. If he requires anything more of us, than what we *think* the nature of things requires of us, then he cannot act according to the nature of things. If he makes anything a rule or law to us, which we would not impose upon ourselves, then he must make laws by *mere will*, without any reason for them. If he requires us to believe anything of his own nature, or our nature, more than we could have known of ourselves, then he must act by *caprice* and *humour*, and be an arbitrary being. If

---

* Page 66.

his *infinite* wisdom is in any matters of revelation *greater* than ours; if it is not in everything he reveals *measurable* by ours, it cannot be wisdom at all, much less can it be infinite wisdom.

That is, if he is *more powerful* than we are, he cannot be *omnipotent;* if he is *more perfect* than we are, he cannot be *all perfection;* if he acts upon *greater*, or *higher*, or *more* reasonable motives than we do, he cannot be a *reasonable* being.

Now if these absurdities are not plain and manifest to every common understanding, it is in vain to dispute about anything; but if they are, then it is as plain, this writer's great argument against Christianity, and first principle of his *rational religion*, is in the same state of undeniable absurdity, as being solely built upon them.

Thus, says he, *Natural religion takes in all those duties which flow from the reason and the nature of things.** That is, natural religion takes in all those things that bare human reason can of itself discover from the nature of things. This is granted; but what follows? Why, says he, *Consequently, was there an instituted religion which differs from that of nature, its precepts must be arbitrary, as not founded on the nature and reason of things, but depending on mere will and pleasure, otherwise it would be the same with natural religion.*†

That is, since natural religion contains all that bare human reason can of itself discover, if God was to reveal anything more than human reason can discover, he must be an arbitrary being, and act by mere will and pleasure; otherwise his revelation would be the same with, and nothing more than human reason.

Here you see all the absurdities just mentioned, are expressly contained in this argument. God is all *humour, caprice,* and *mere arbitrary will*, if his revelation is not strictly, in every respect, the same with human reason. That is, he is *without* wisdom, *without* reason, if his wisdom and reason *exceed* ours. He has *no reason*, nor *wisdom*, if his reason and wisdom are *infinite*.

Secondly, This argument, if it were allowed, leads directly to *atheism*. For if a revelation cannot be divine, if it contains anything mysterious, whose fitness and necessity cannot be explained by human reason, then neither *creation* nor *providence* can be proved to be divine, for they are both of them more mysterious than the Christian revelation. And revelation itself is *therefore* mysterious, because creation and providence cannot be delivered from mystery. And was it possible for man to comprehend

---

* Page 114.   † Page 16.

the reasons, on which the *manner* of the creation and divine providence are founded, then revelation might be without mysteries.

But if the mysteries in revelation are owing to that, which is by the nature of things incomprehensible in creation and providence, then it is very unreasonable to reject revelation, because it has that which it must necessarily have, not from itself, but from the nature and state of things. And much worse is it, to deny revelation to be divine, for such a reason, as makes it equally fit to deny *creation* and *providence* to be of God.

For if everything is *arbitrary*, whose *fitness and expedience* human reason cannot *prove* and *explain*, then surely an *invisible over-ruling providence*, that orders all things in a manner, and for reasons, known only to itself; that subjects human life, and human affairs, to what changes it pleases; that confounds the best laid designs, and makes great effects arise from folly and imprudence; that gives the race not to the swift, nor the battle to the strong; that brings good men into affliction, and makes the wicked prosperous; surely such a providence must be highly arbitrary.

And therefore if this argument is to be admitted, it leads directly to *atheism*, and brings us under a greater necessity of rejecting this notion of divine providence, on the account of its mysteries, than of rejecting a revelation that is mysterious in any of its doctrines. And if, as this writer frequently argues, God cannot be said to deal with us as rational agents, if he requires anything of us, that our reason cannot prove to be necessary; surely he cannot be said to deal with us as rational and moral agents, if he overrules our persons and affairs, and disappoints our counsels, makes weakness prosperous, and wisdom unsuccessful, in a *secret* and *invisible* manner, and for reasons and ends that we have no means of knowing.

And if it may be said, To what purpose has he given us reason, if that is not solely to give laws to us; surely it may better be said, To what purpose has he given us reason to take care of ourselves, to provide for our happiness, to prepare *proper* means for certain ends, if there is an overruling providence that changes the *natural course* of things, that confounds the best laid designs, and disappoints the wisest counsels?

There is nothing therefore half so mysterious in the Christian revelation, considered in itself, as there is in that *invisible* providence, which all must hold that believe a God. And though there is enough plain in providence, to excite the adoration of humble and pious minds, yet it has often been a rock of *atheism* to those, who make their own reason the measure of wisdom.

Again, Though the *creation* plainly declares the glory, and wisdom, and goodness of God; yet it has more mysteries in it, more things, whose fitness, expedience, and reasonableness, human reason cannot comprehend, than are to be found in Scripture.

If therefore he reasons right, who says, *If there may be some things in a true Religion, whose fitness and expedience we cannot see, why not others: Nay, why not the whole; since that would make God's laws all of a piece? And if the having of these things is no proof of its falsehood, how can any things fit and expedient (which no Religion is without) be a proof of the truth of any one Religion?** If, I say, this is right reasoning, then it may be said, *If there are things in the creation whose fitness we cannot see, why not others: Nay, why not the whole; since that would make all God's works of a piece? And if the being of such things as these in the creation, is not a proof of its not being divine, How can the fitness and expedience of any creation prove that it is the work of God?*

Thus does this argument tend wholly to Atheism, and concludes with the same force against *creation* and *providence*, as it does against revelation.

This is farther plain from our author's account of the *works* and *laws* of God. It is a first principle with him, that God's *laws* and *works* must have the same infinite wisdom in them. *That they both alike have the character of infinite wisdom impressed on them, and both alike discover their divine original.*†

But if so, then nothing can prove any *works* to be of divine original, but that which will prove any *laws* to be of divine original. And nothing can shew any *laws* to be unworthy of God, but what would equally shew *any works* to be unworthy of God. But we have already seen, that no laws can come from God, or be fit for him to make, but such as human reason can prove to be fit and expedient; therefore *no works* can proceed from God, or be worthy of him, but such as human reason can prove to be fit and expedient.

Either therefore there is nothing in the works of the creation, whose fitness and expedience cannot be proved; nothing in God's providence over whole nations, and particular persons, whose fitness and expedience cannot be explained and justified by human reason, or else neither creation nor providence can be ascribed to God.

He says, *It is impossible men should have any just idea of the perfections of God, who think that the dictates of infinite Wisdom,*

---

* *First Address to the Inhabitants of* London, page 57.   † Page 124.

do not carry their own evidence with them, or are not by their own innate worth discoverable to all mankind.*

But if so, then we are obliged, out of regard to the divine perfections, to deny every creature, or part of the creation, to proceed from God, which does not *carry its own evidence of infinite wisdom, and discover its own innate worth to all mankind.*

Anyone must easily see, that I put no force upon this writer's arguments, to give them this atheistical tendency, but barely represent them as they are in his book.

For since it is his own avowed and repeated principle, that God's *works* and *laws* are both of a kind, and that they must both *alike discover their divine original;* it necessarily follows, that if any *law* or *command* must be unfit for God to make, because its fitness cannot be proved by human reason ; then every creature, or part of the creation, whose fitness and expedience cannot be proved by human reason, must be rejected as unworthy of God. So that this argument leads to Atheism, not by any remote consequence, but by its first and immediate tendency.

For according to it, a man is obliged, out of regard to the divine perfections, to deal with *creation* and *providence*, as this writer does with *Scripture ;* and to allow no more of either of them, than suits with his own notions of that which God ought to do in creation and providence.

The true grounds and reasons on which we are to believe a revelation to be divine, are such external marks and signs of God's action and operation, as are a sufficient proof of it. And if God has no ways of acting that are peculiar and particular to himself, and such as sufficiently prove his action and operation, then revelation can have no sufficient proof that it comes from God.

And if a revelation had no other proof of its Divinity, but such an internal excellency and fitness of its doctrines, as is fully known and approved of by *human reason;* such an internal excellency would be so far from being a sufficient proof of its Divinity, that it would be a probable objection against it. For it has an appearance of great probability, that God would not make an external revelation of that *only*, which was *sufficiently* and fully known to the natural man, or mere Reason, without it.

Although therefore no revelation can come from God, whose doctrines have not an *internal excellency*, and the *highest fitness ;* yet the non-appearance of such excellency and fitness to *our*

---

* Page 125.

or Natural Religion Stated. 107

reason, cannot be a disproof of its Divinity, because it is our ignorance of such matters without revelation, that is the *true ground and reason* of God's revealing anything to us.

The credibility therefore of any external divine revelation with regard to human reason, rests wholly upon *such external* evidence, as is a sufficient proof of the divine operation, or interposition. If there be no such external evidence possible; if God has no ways of acting so *peculiar* to himself, as to be a *sufficient* proof to human reason of his action; then no revelation can be sufficiently proved to be a divine, external revelation from God.

I appeal therefore to the miracles and prophecies on which Christianity is founded, as a sufficient proof, that it is a divine revelation. And shall here consider, what is objected against the sufficiency of this kind of proof.

1. It is objected, That miracles cannot prove a *false*, or *bad* doctrine, to be *true* and *good;* therefore miracles, *as such*, cannot prove the truth of any revelation.

But though miracles cannot prove false to be true, or bad to be good; yet they may prove, that we ought to receive such doctrines, both as true and good, which we could not know to be true and good without such miracles. Not because the miracles have any influence upon the things revealed, but because they testify the credibility of the revealer, as having God's testimony to the truth of that which he reveals.

If therefore miracles can be a sufficient proof, of God's sending any persons to speak in his name, and under his authority; then they may be a sufficient proof of the truth and divinity of a revelation, though they cannot prove that which is false, to be true.

Our author therefore brings a farther objection against this use of miracles.

If, says he, *evil beings can impress notions in men's minds as strongly as good beings, and cause miracles to be done in confirmation of them; is there any way to know to which of the two notions thus impressed are owing, but from their nature and tendency, or internal marks of wisdom and goodness?——And if so, Can external proofs carry us any farther, than the internal proofs do?*[*]

This objection supposes, that no miracles, *as such*, can be a sufficient proof of the divinity of a revelation, for this reason, because we do not know the extent of that power, which evil spirits have, of doing miracles. But this objection is groundless. For, granting that we do not know the nature and extent of

---
* Page 243.

that power which evil spirits may have; yet if we know *enough* of it to affirm, that the *creation* is not the work of evil spirits; if we can securely appeal to the creation, as a *sufficient proof* of God's action and operation; then we are fully secure in appealing to miracles, as a sufficient proof of a divine revelation.

For, if the creation must of necessity be allowed to be the work of God, notwithstanding any *unknown degree* of power in evil spirits; if we can as certainly ascribe it to God, as if we really knew there were no *such* spirits; then in some cases, miracles may be as full a proof of the operation, or interposition of God, as if we really knew there were no such spirits in being.

I do not ask, Whether the *same divine* perfection is necessary to foretell such things as are foretold in Scripture, and work such miracles as are there related, as is necessary to *create?* I do not ask, Whether any power less than divine can do such things? I only ask, Whether there is any certainty, that the creation is the work of God? Whether we can be sure of the divine operation, from the existence of that creation that we are acquainted with? Or, Whether we are in any *doubt* or *uncertainty* about it, because we do not know the *true nature* or *degree* of power, that may belong to evil spirits?

For if it can be affirmed with certainty, that the creation is the work of God, notwithstanding our uncertainty about the degree of power that may belong to evil spirits; then we have the same certainty, that the *prophecies* and *miracles* recorded in Scripture, are to be ascribed to God, as his doing, notwithstanding our uncertainty of the power of evil spirits.

And this is affirmed, not because *prophecies* and *miracles* require the *same degree* of divine power, as to create (for that would be affirming we know not what,) but it is affirmed, because the creation cannot be a *better*, *farther*, or *different* proof of the action or operation of God, than such miracles and prophecies are.

For every reason for ascribing the creation to God, is the same reason for ascribing such miracles and prophecies to God; and every argument against the certainty of those miracles and prophecies coming from God, is the same argument against the certainty of the creation's being the work of God; for there cannot be more or less certainty in one case than in the other.

For, if evil spirits have so the creation in their hands, that by reason of their power over it, *no miracles* can prove the operation of God, then the operation of God cannot be proved from the creation itself.

For the creation cannot be proved to be the operation of God, unless it can be proved that God *still presides* over it.

And if *all that* which is extraordinary and miraculous may be accounted for, without the interposition of God; then nothing that is ordinary and common, according to the course of nature, can be a proof of the action of God. For there can be no reason assigned, why that which is *ordinary* should be ascribed to God, if all that is, or has been, or can be miraculous, may be ascribed to evil spirits.

Either therefore it must be said, that there are, or may be miracles, which cannot be the effects of evil spirits; or else nothing that is ordinary and common, can be a proof of the operation of God. For if nothing miraculous can be an undeniable proof of God's action, nothing created can be a proof of it.

The matter therefore stands thus: There are, and may be miracles, that cannot be ascribed to evil spirits, without ascribing the creation to them; and which can no more be doubted to come from God, than we can doubt of his being the Creator of the world. There may be miracles therefore, which, *as such*, and considered *in themselves*, are as full a proof of the *truth* of that which they attest, as the creation is of the *fitness* of that which is created.

And though the *matter* of a revelation is to be attended to, that we may fully understand it, and be rightly affected with it; yet the reason of our receiving it as divine, must rest upon that *external authority*, which shews it to be of God.

And the authority of miracles, sufficiently plain and apparent, are of themselves a full and necessary reason for receiving a revelation, which both as to its *matter* and *manner*, would not be approved by us without them.

It seems therefore to be a *needless*, and too *great* a concession, which some *learned divines* make in this matter, when they grant, that we must first examine the doctrines revealed by miracles, and see whether they contain anything in them *absurd*, or *unworthy* of God, before we can receive the miracles as *divine*. For,

1. Where there can be nothing doubted, nor any more required, to make the miracles sufficiently plain and evident, there can be no doubt about the truth and goodness of the doctrine they attest. Miracles in such a state as this are the last resort, they determine for themselves, and cannot be tried by anything farther.

And as the *existence* of things, is the highest and utmost

evidence of God's having created them, and not to be tried by our *judgments* about the reasonableness and ends of their creation; so a course of plain undeniable miracles, attesting the truth of a revelation, is the *highest* and *utmost* evidence of its coming from God, and not to be tried by our judgments about the *reasonableness* or *necessity* of its doctrines.

And this is to be affirmed, not because God is too good to suffer us to be brought into such a snare, but because we can know nothing of God, if such a course of miracles is not a sufficient proof of his action and interposition. For if doctrines revealed by such an *undeniable change* in the natural course of things, have not thence a sufficient proof, that they are divine doctrines; then *no laws* that are according to the natural state of things, can have *thence* any proof, that they are *divine laws*.

For if *no course* of *miracles* can be of *itself* a sufficient proof, that *that* which is attested by them, is attested by God; then no *settled, ordinary* state of things can of *itself* be a proof, that *that* which is required by the natural state of things, is required by God.

2. To try miracles, sufficiently plain and evident, by *our judgments* of the reasonableness of the doctrines revealed by them, seems to be beginning at the wrong end. For the doctrines had not been revealed, but because of our ignorance of the *nature* and *reasonableness* of them; nor had the miracles been wrought, but to prevent our *acquiescing* in our own judgments about the worth and value of them.

3. To say, That no miracles, however plain and evident are to be received as divine, if they attest any doctrine that appears to *human reason* to be absurd, or unworthy of God, is very unreasonable. For what is it that can be called *human reason* in this respect? Is it anything else than human opinion? And is there anything that mankind are in greater uncertainty, or more contrary to one another, than in their opinions about what is absurd, or unworthy of God in religion? And is it not the very end and design of a divine revelation, to help us to a rule that may put an end to the divisions of human reason, and furnish us with an authority for believing such things, as we should not think it reasonable to believe without it?

And how weak and useless must that revelation be, which has not sufficient authority to teach us *new notions* of religion, and persuade us to believe that to be reasonable and worthy of God, which we could not believe to be so upon a less authority?

But if this be the case, as it seems clearly to be, then we are

or Natural Religion Stated. 111

not to try plain and evident miracles of the *highest kind*, by our judgments of the reasonableness of the doctrines revealed by them; but miracles are to be received, as of sufficient authority, to form and govern our opinions about the reasonableness of the doctrines.

It may perhaps be said, though the authority of miracles, is sufficient to govern our opinions in doctrines that are only mysterious, and above the comprehension of our reason, yet that which is plainly and grossly absurd, or unworthy of God, cannot, nor ought to be received upon any authority of the *greatest miracles*.

This objection is vain and absurd; it is vain, because it relates to a case that never was the case of miracles; and it is absurd, because it is providing against a case, that never can happen to miracles. For to suppose anything in its own nature grossly absurd, or unworthy of God, to be attested with the *highest evidence* of miracles, is as impossible, and contradictory a supposition, as to suppose God to create rational beings wicked in their nature, that they might thereby be of service to the devil. These two suppositions have not the smallest difference, either in absurdity, or impossibility.

Again; The history of magical wonders, and extraordinary things done by evil spirits, is no objection against the sufficiency of that proof, that arises from miracles. For the question is not, whether nothing that is extraordinary can be done by evil spirits, in any circumstances, but whether nothing that is miraculous can, *as such*, be a proof of its being done by God. For these two cases are very consistent. It may be very possible for evil spirits, to do things extraordinary in *some circumstances*, as where people enter into contracts with them, and resign themselves up to their power, and yet that miracles may in *other circumstances*, merely as miracles, be a sufficient proof of their being done by God.

Thus the case of the *Egyptian magicians*, is so far from abating the weight of miracles, that it is a great proof of their authority, considered in themselves; for the *Magicians* could proceed but a little way in their contention with *Moses*, they were soon made to feel his superior power in the same manner, as the rest of the *Egyptians* did, and to confess, that his miracles were done by the *finger of God.* This very instance therefore fully shews, that miracles, *as such*, may be a sufficient proof of God's interposition. For if, in the case of a contention, the superior power must be ascribed to God, then miracles, as *such*, or of *such a kind*, as having none equal to them, or able to stand against them, must in such a state be a sufficient proof of their being done by God, and give a sufficient warrant, to receive any doctrine that is attested by them.

For, let it be supposed, that the *Egyptian* Magicians had destroyed the power of *Moses*, and brought all the *miraculous evils* upon the *Israelites*, as enemies of the *Egyptian* Gods, which he brought upon them; what consequence must *reason* have drawn from such an event? Could reason have proved, that the God that made the world was *one* God, and that he alone ought to be worshipped? Or that the *Egyptians* ought to have left their Gods, who had the *whole creation* in their hands in such a manner, as to change the nature of things as they pleased, and destroy every power that opposed them?

Now either the case here supposed is possible, or it is impossible. If it is possible, then all the reasons for worshipping the *one true God*, taken from the *nature* and *state* of the creation, may entirely cease, and be so many reasons for idolatrous worship. For no one can have any reasons for worshipping the one true God, from the nature and state of the creation, if other Gods have the greatest power over it, and can turn everything into a *plague* upon those that do not worship them.

But if this case is impossible, then it necessarily follows, that miracles, *as such*, and considered *in themselves*, may be *certain* and *infallible* proofs of God's interposition. For this case can only be impossible, because the greatest, plainest miracles, cannot possibly be on the side of error. But if this cannot be, then the greatest, plainest miracles, *as such*, and considered *in themselves*, are an infallible mark of truth.

And he that abides by miracles in such circumstances, as proofs of the operation of the *one true* God, has the same certainty of proceeding right, as he that takes the state, and nature of the creation, to be the effect of the one true God.

And as miracles thus considered in themselves, are the highest and most undeniable evidence of the truth and divinity of any external revelation; so Christianity stands fully distinguished from all other religions, by the highest and most undeniable evidence; since it has all the proof that the *highest state* of miracles can give, and every other religion is without any support from them.

And though this writer, with a boldness worthy of himself, often puts all *traditional religions* upon a level: yet he might have shewn himself as much a friend to truth and sobriety, by asserting, that all *arguments* are equally conclusive, all *tempers* equally virtuous, all *designs* equally honest, and all *histories* and *fables* equally supported by evidence of fact.

But his prodigious rashness in asserting, at all adventures, whatever he pleases, is not confined to matters of fact, but is as remarkably visible in that part of his book which pretends to argument; as may be fully seen by the following paragraphs.

'It is the observation, says he, of *naturalists*, that there is no 'species of creatures, but what have some *innate weakness*, which 'makes them an easy prey to other animals that know how to 'make the advantage of it. Now the *peculiar foible* of mankind 'is *superstition*, which at all times has made them liable to be 'practised on, not by creatures of different species, but by those 'of their own; who by a confident pretence of knowing more 'than their neighbours, have first circumvented the *many*, the '*credulous*, and *unwary;* and afterwards forced the *free-thinking* '*few into an outward compliance.*'* Here it is to be observed:

1. That superstition is the *peculiar foible* in man; as natural and intrinsic to him, as an *innate weakness* in animals. He has it therefore from God and nature, in the same manner as animals have their innate weakness. And therefore it must be as unnatural for men to be without superstition, or not act according to it, as for animals to be without their innate weakness.

2. Mankind are, according to this account, in their natural state, entirely incapable of knowing any true religion. For if, as our author saith, *superstition be the opposite to true religion;* if this superstition be the *innate peculiar foible* of human nature; if mankind are not only to begin and end their lives among those that have all the *same foible*, but, what is worse, have at all times had this innate foible increased and practised upon by the crafty pretenders of their own species; are they not inwardly and outwardly fixed in superstition, the *opposite to true religion?*

Judge therefore by this, what our author *really* thinks of the *excellency* and *perfection* of the light of nature; and how much meaning he has in such exclamations as these: *And now let anyone say, how it is possible God could more fully make known his will to all intelligent creatures, than by making everything within and without them*, a declaration of it?†

That is, How can they have a better *inward guide* to true religion, than by having an *innate* peculiar foible contrary to it? How can they have a better *outward call* to the true religion, than by having all the world conspiring to fix them in superstition?

For this, he says, is their state; this innate peculiar foible has been at all times increased and practised upon by the more cunning of their species, and the *free-thinking few forced into an outward compliance*. It is this inward and outward state of Man,

---

* Page 169.   † Page 19.

that throws our author into so much transport at its absolute perfection, as to matters of religion.

Again; Judge from this with what piety and sincerity he speaks of God, when he says, *Infinite wisdom, directed by infinite goodness, will certainly give us equal degrees of evidence for religious truths, which so much concerns us, as it has done for truths of less importance.** For if our Author believed himself in this assertion, how could he believe superstition to be the *peculiar* inborn foible of man? For can religious truths have the *same degrees of evidence* with things of less importance, if man's *peculiar foible* relates to religion?

Again; He cries out, *In what point is it, that men of the meanest abilities may not know their duty to God? Cannot they tell what sentiments inspire them with love and reverence for the deity?*† Now put these things together, and then his argument will proceed thus: If superstition is *contrary* to true religion, and superstition be the *innate peculiar* foible of all men, how can the *weakest* man be in any mistake about what is right or wrong in religion? Let the reader here judge, whether I put any force upon his words.

Judge again, how serious this Author must be in a variety of such arguments as these: *If*, says he, *men have been at all times obliged to avoid superstition, and embrace true religion, there must have been at all times sufficient marks of distinction.* And again: *Nothing*, says he, *can be a greater libel on the true religion, than to suppose it does not contain such internal marks, as will, even to the meanest capacity, distinguish it from all false religions.*‡ But if superstition is the *innate, peculiar* foible of mankind, where must a man of the *meanest capacity* look for the *internal marks* of true religion? And if all the world is, and always was, over-run with superstition, and the *free-thinking* few have always been forced into an *outward compliance*, where must such a man look for the *outward marks* of true religion?

To give you one instance more of this writer's extravagant and inconsistent notions:

He makes *reason*, or *natural religion*, to be God's *internal revelation*, differing *only* from *external revelation in the manner of its being communicated.* He rejects *external revelation* as unworthy of God, because it has not been sufficiently made known at *all times*, and in *all places*; yet he sets up an internal revelation, as worthy of God, which has never been made known to any *one man* of any *time* or *place* in the world. For what one man ever knew that *reason* was God's *internal revelation*, to which nothing could be added by any external revelation?

---

* Page 131.   † Page 280.   ‡ Page 295.

It is a mighty complaint with our author against Christianity, that so much happiness should be deferred till the time of *Tiberius*, and that it should be communicated to no greater a part of the world, than Christianity hath been. But is not this a *judicious* complaint in the mouth of a person, that is setting up a religion, that has been communicated to nobody but himself?

I know nothing that can be said for our author, in excuse of so much confusion and self-contradiction, unless it be the particular hardships of his *sect*. The *free-thinking few*, he says, *are forced into an outward compliance;* and that which *forces* a man into a state of hypocrisy, may force him into a great deal of confusion and self-contradiction.

To return: I have from a consideration of the state and condition of man, and the several relations which God stands in towards his creatures, shewn that it is utterly impossible for human reason to be a competent judge of the fitness, or unfitness, of all that God may, or may not require of us. The two following chapters shall state the nature and perfection of reason, considered in itself, or as it is a faculty, or principle of action in human nature.

Chapter IV.

Of the state and nature of reason, as it is in man; and how its perfection in matters of religion is to be known.

THIS writer and others, who take to themselves the names of *free-thinkers*, make their court to the world, by pretending to vindicate the right that all men have, to judge and act according to their own reason. Though, I think, the world has no more to thank them for on this account, than if they had pretended to assert the right that every man has, to see *only* with his *own eyes*, or to hear *only* with his *own ears*.

For their own reason always did, does, and ever will, govern rational creatures, in everything they determine, either in speculation or practice. It is not a matter of *duty* for men to use their own reason, but of *necessity:* and it is as impossible to do otherwise, as for a being that cannot act but from choice, to act without choice. And if a man were to try, not to act according to his own reason or choice, he would find himself under the same difficulty, as he that tries to think, without thinking upon something.

And if God were to command us, by fresh revelations every day of our lives, not to act from a principle of reason and choice, such revelations could have no more effect upon us, than if they came from the weakest amongst mankind. For, as our principle of acting is not derived from ourselves, so it is no more in our power to alter it, or contradict it, than it is in the power of matter not to *gravitate*, or to exist, without taking up some *place*.

Man is under the same necessity of acting from his own choice, that *matter* is of not acting at all; and a being, whose principle of action is reason and choice, can no more act without it, or contrary to it, than an extended being can be without extension.

All men therefore are equally reasonable in this respect, that they are, and must be, by a *necessity* of nature, equally directed and governed by their own reason and choice.

For, as the principle of action, in human nature, is *reason* and *choice*, and nothing can be done, or believed, but for *some reason*, any more than a thing can be chosen and not be chosen; so the acting according to one's own reason is not the privilege of the *philosopher*, but essential to human nature; and as inseparable from all persons, as self-consciousness, or a sense of their own existence.

The dispute therefore betwixt Christians and *unbelievers*, concerning reason, is not, whether men are to use their *own reason*, any more than whether they are to see with their *own eyes*; but whether every man's reason must needs guide him by its *own light*, or must cease to guide him, as soon as it guides him by a light borrowed from revelation? This is the true state of the question, not whether reason is to be followed, but when it is *best* followed? not whether it is to be our guide, but how it may be made our *safest guide*?

The *free-thinkers*, therefore, rather appeal to the passions, than reason of the people, when they represent the Clergy and Christianity as enemies to reason, and just thinking, and themselves as friends and advocates for the use of reason.

For Christians oppose unbelievers, not because they *reason*, but because they reason *ill*. They receive revelation, not to suppress the natural power, but to give new and heavenly light to their reason; not to take away their right of judging for themselves, but to secure them from false judgments.

If therefore a poor peasant should call upon our free-thinkers, to lay aside their *bigotry* to *ideas, arguments*, and *philosophy*, and govern themselves by reason; it would be no more absurd, than for them to exhort Christians to lay aside their bigotry to *creeds* and *doctrines* of revelation, and to govern themselves by reason.

For it may as well be affirmed, that a man departs from the use of his reason, because he depends upon *ideas, arguments*, and *syllogisms;* as that he departs from the use of his reason, because he proceeds upon *prophecies, miracles*, and *revelations.*

And if he uses his reason weakly, and is subject to delusion in these points, he no more renounces his reason, or goes over to another direction, than *Hobbes, Spinosa, Bayle, Collins,* or *Toland*, renounce their reason, when they take their own *fancies* to be demonstrations.

Christians therefore do not differ from unbelievers in the *constant use* of their reason, but in the *manner* of using it: As *virtuous* men differ from *rakes*, not in their desire of happiness, but in their manner of seeking it.

And though this writer is very free in his charge of *bigotry* upon Christians, yet I may venture to challenge him to shew, that there can possibly be more *bigotry* on the side of religion, than there may be against it. For as *bigotry* is nothing but weak reasoning, so *infidels* are entitled to as large a share of it, as believers; and to suppose that bigotry may be charged upon those who have a zeal *for* Christianity, but cannot be charged on them that are zealous *against* it, is as just a way of proceeding, as to say of two *brothers*, that one is to be charged with *passion*, because he *loves* his father, but the other cannot be charged with passion, because he *hates* his father.

And as men that write against religion, are as much concerned to have it false, as those who write for it, are to have it true; so all that there is to blind and prejudice the latter, has the same power to blind and prejudice the former.

It appears from what has been said, that every man's own reason is his only principle of action, and that he must judge according to it, whether he receives, or rejects revelation.

Now although every man is to judge according to the light of his own reason, yet his reason has very little light that can be called *its own*. For, as we derive our nature from our parents, so that which we generally call *natural knowledge*, or the light of *nature*, is a knowledge and light that is made natural to us, by the *same authority*, which makes a certain *language*, certain *customs*, and *modes* of behaviour, natural to us.

Nothing seems to be our own, but a *bare capacity* to be instructed, a nature *fitted* for any impressions; as capable of vice as virtue; as ready to be made a vicious animal, as a religious rational creature; as liable to be made a *Hottentot*, by being born among Hottentots, as to be a *Christian*, by being born among Christians.

It is not my intention by this, to signify, that there is not a *good* and *evil*, *right* and *wrong*, founded in the nature of things; or that morality has any dependence upon the *opinions* or *customs* of men; but only to shew, that we *find* out this right and wrong, come to a *sense* of this good and evil, not by any inward strength, or light, that our *natural reason* of itself affords, but by such *external means*, as people are taught *articulate* language, *civility*, *politeness*, or any other *rules* of civil life.

Men do not prefer virtue to vice, from a philosophical contemplation of the fitness of the one, and the unfitness of the other, founded in the nature of things; but because it is a judgment as *early* in their minds, as their knowledge of the words, virtue and vice.

And it can no more be reasonably affirmed, that our knowledge of God and divine things, our opinions in morality, of the excellency of this, or that virtue, of the immortality of our souls, of a future life of rewards and punishments, are the effects of our natural light; than it can be reasonably affirmed, that our living in *society*, our *articulate* language, and *erect posture*, are owing to the light of nature.

For, as all mankind find themselves in this state, before any reasoning about it; as *education*, and *human authority* have set our bodies *upright*, taught us *language*, and accustomed us to the *rules* and *manners* of a social life; so *education*, and the *same human* authority, have impressed and planted in our minds, certain notions of God and divine things, and formed us to a sense of good and evil, a belief of our soul's immortality, and the expectation of another life.

And mankind are no more left to find out a God, or the fitness of moral virtue, by their own reason, than they are left by their own reason to find out who are their parents, or to find out the fitness of speaking an articulate language, or the reasonableness of living in society.

On the contrary; we know that our manner of coming into the world, subjects us, without any choice, to the *language*, *sentiments*, *opinions*, and *manners*, of those amongst whom we are born. And although when we come to any strength, or art of reasoning, or have a *genius* for philosophic inquiries, we may thence deduce proofs of the *Being* and *Attributes* of God, the *reasonableness* of religion and morality, the *nature* of our souls, and the *certainty* of a future state, and find that the opinions and tradition of mankind concerning these things are well founded; yet these are an *after-knowledge,* not common to men, but accidental confirmations of that knowledge and belief of a God, religion and morality, which were before fixed in us, more or less, by education, and the authority of those amongst whom we have lived.

And as no *Philosopher* ever proved the *fitness* of human nature for a *social* life, from principles of reason and speculation, who had not *first* been taught the nature and advantage of Society *another way ;* so no one ever pretended to prove the Being and Attributes of God, or the excellency of moral virtue, who had not *first* been taught the knowledge of God, and moral virtue some *other way.*

Now if this is the state of reason, as it is in man; if this is all the light that we have from our *own nature,* a *bare capacity* of receiving good or bad impressions, right or wrong opinions and sentiments, according to the state of the world that we fall into; then we are but poorly furnished, to assert and maintain the *absolute perfection* of our own reason.

If our light is little more than the opinions and customs of those amongst whom we live, and it be so hard for a man to arrive at a greater wisdom, than the common wisdom of the *place* or *country* which gave him birth and education; how unreasonably do we appeal to the perfection and sufficiency of our own reason, against the *necessity* and *advantage* of divine revelation?

If we are *nothing* without the assistance of men; if we are a kind of foolish, helpless animals, till education and experience have *revealed* to us the wisdom and knowledge of our fellow-creatures; shall we think ourselves too wise and full of our own light, to be farther enlightened with a knowledge and wisdom revealed to us by God himself?

This gentleman, speaking of education, saith, *Education is justly esteemed a second nature ; and its force is too strong, that few can wholly shake off its prejudices, even in things unreasonable and unnatural; and must it not have the greatest efficacy in things agreeable to reason, and suitable to nature?**

All that I shall add to this account, is only this, That we are, by the circumstances and condition of human life, *necessarily* subjected to this *second nature,* and cannot avoid coming under its power.

But here let me ask this pleader for the sufficiency of the light of nature, how those that resign themselves up to the light of their *own nature,* shall know, whether it is their *first,* or their *second* nature that directs them?

---

* Page 166.

Here are, it seems, *two natures;* they may be as different as good and evil; yet as they are both *natures,* both *internal light,* how shall a man know which he follows? He does not know which was first, or why he should call one first, and the other second; they are both internal, and without anything to distinguish them. And as he is not to *resist* the motions of nature, or *stifle* its directions; so he must be as *obedient* to the directions of the *second,* as of the first nature, because he does not perceive their difference, nor has any means to distinguish their operations.

He therefore that asserts the light of nature to be a *sufficient unerring* guide in divine matters, ought either to shew, that our *second* nature is as *safe* a guide as the first; or that though it is nature, yet it has no *natural power* over us.

For since every man is *necessitated* to take upon him a *second* nature, which he does not *know* to be a second, or *when* it began, or *how far* it has proceeded, or how *contrary* it is to his first nature; he that would prove the light of nature to be so perfect, that nothing can be added to it, is obliged to prove, that our second nature, which we receive by education, has the *same degree* of perfection. For so far as our second nature is *different* from the first, so far it has *changed* the first; and if we are to follow nature exclusive of revelation, we may take *revenge, self-murder, incontinence, sensuality, pride, haughtiness, self-conceit,* and a *contempt* of all things *sacred,* to be the true dictates and directions of nature.

For as it may be very easy, and I am afraid often happens to people, to be thus educated; so if education is a *second nature,* and nature is to be esteemed a *true* and *perfect* guide; a man thus educated, has all his vices made so many glorious laws of nature; and through the strength of his natural light, he condemns humility, self-denial, and devotion, as foolish bigotry.

This writer says, *Natural religion,* that is, the religion of nature, *is a perpetual standing rule for men of the meanest, as well as the highest capacities, and carries its own evidence with it, those internal, inseparable marks of truth.** But if education is a *second nature,* and, as this writer affirms, *has the force of a second nature even in things unreasonable and unnatural;* then this second nature has not only its natural religion, which is also a *perpetual standing rule for men of the meanest, as well as the highest capacities; which carries its own evidence with it, those internal, inseparable marks of truth;* but it may also have a natural religion, both *unreasonable and unnatural;* since it is

---

* Page 243.

here affirmed, that education has the force of nature even in things of this kind.

Again; If education has this force of nature even in things unreasonable and unnatural, and still greater force in things agreeable to nature; if it is also absolutely necessary for all men to come under the power of *some second* nature; what can be more vain or groundless, than to pretend to *state* the *light*, or *rectitude* of human nature, since it must be for the most part in every man, as the *uncertainty, variety, happiness* or *unhappiness* of education has rendered it?

And our author can no more tell, what man would be, without human education, or what nature would do for those who had no foreign instruction, than he can tell what sort of beings dwell in the *moon*. And yet he that does not know this, how can he know what the light of nature is in itself?

For if most of our judgments, opinions, tempers, and ways of thinking, are owing to education, and the authority of that part of the world where we dwell; if these impressions have the power of a *second nature* upon us, then the light of *nature* can no more be distinguished from the light of *education*, than the strength which we have from *nature*, can be distinguished from the strength which we have from our *food*.

So that to declare the light of nature so absolutely perfect, as to be incapable of all improvement even by divine revelation, is no less an extravagance, than to declare the education of mankind to be absolutely perfect in the *same degree*.

For if nature not only *wants*, but cannot possibly *avoid* education; if this *necessary unavoidable* education becomes *another nature*, undiscernible from the first; then nothing can possibly be affirmed of the perfection of the light of nature, but what must be affirmed in the *same degree* of the perfection of education. And he that affirms that mankind have had, at *all times*, and in *all places* of the world, the *same sufficient, perfect* light of nature, must affirm, that mankind have had, at all times and in all places of the world, the same *perfect, unerring* education.

When therefore it is just, and fitting for all people, to abide by the *absolute perfection* of their *education*, the *infallible* light of their *second nature*, as the unerring standard, measure, and rule of all that is to be esteemed *moral, religious,* and *divine;* then it may be just to appeal to the *natural light* of all men, of all ages, and all places, as a *sufficient teacher* of all that ought, or ought not to be a matter of religion.

For till it can be shewn, that men are not liable to a *second nature* from education, or that there is, or can be any nature without it; the *state* of nature must *differ* all over the world, and in every age of the world, just as the light, and advantages of education, have *differed* in the several parts, and ages of the world.

In a word, the religious and moral light of our *first nature*, is just as great as the *first strength* of infants; and the religious and moral light of our *second nature*, is just as perfect as our *education*, and as much of our own growth, as the first language that we are taught to speak.

May not therefore one justly wonder, what it is that could lead any people into an imagination of the absolute perfection of *human reason?* There seems no more in the state of mankind, to betray a man into this fancy, than to persuade him, that the reason of *infants* is absolutely perfect. For sense and experience, are as full and strong a proof against one, as against the other.

But it must be said for these writers, that they decline all arguments from facts and experience, to give a better account of human nature; but with the same justice, as if a man was to lay aside the authority of *history*, to give you a truer account of the life of *Alexander*.

They argue about the perfection of human reason, not as if it were something *already* in being, that had its *nature* and *condition*, and shewed itself to be what it is; but as if it were something that might take its state and condition, according to their fancies and speculations about it.

Their objection against revelation is founded upon the pretended *sufficiency*, and *absolute perfection*, of the light and strength of human reason, to teach all men all that is wise, and holy, and divine, in religion. But how do they prove this perfection of human reason? Do they appeal to mankind as proofs of this perfection? Do they produce any body of men, in this, or any other age of the world, that without any assistance from revelation, have attained to this perfection of religious knowledge? This is not so much as pretended to: The history of such men is entirely wanting. And yet the want of such a fact as this, has even the force of demonstration against this pretended sufficiency of natural reason.

Because it is a matter not capable of any other kind of proof, but must be admitted as certainly true, or rejected as certainly false, according as fact and experience bear witness for, or against it.

For an inquiry about the light, and strength, and sufficiency of reason, to guide and preserve men in the knowledge and practice of true religion, is a question, as *solely* to be resolved by *fact and experience*, as if the inquiry was about the *shape* of man's body, or the *number* of his senses. And to talk of a light and strength of reason, natural to man, which fact and experience have never yet proved, is as egregious nonsense, as to talk of natural senses, or faculties of his body, which fact and experience have never yet discovered.

For as the *existence* of man cannot be proved, but from fact and experience; so every *quality* of man, whether of body or mind, and every degree of that quality, can only be proved by fact and experience.

The degrees of human *strength*, the nature of human *passions*, the duration of human *life*, the light and strength of human *reason* in matters of religion, are things not possible to be known in any *other degree*, than *so far* as fact and experience prove them.

From the bare consideration of a rational soul in union with a body, and bodily passions, we can neither prove man to be *strong* or *weak, good* or *bad, sickly* or *sound, mortal* or *immortal*: all these qualities must discover themselves, as the *eye* discovers its degree of *sight*, the *hand* its degree of *strength, &c.*

To inquire therefore, whether men have by nature light and strength sufficient to guide, and keep them in the true religion; is the same appeal to fact and experience, as to inquire, whether men are *mortal, sickly*, or *sound;* or how far they can *see* and *hear*. For nothing that relates to human nature, as a quality of it, can possibly have any other proof.

As therefore these Gentlemen are, in this debate, without any proof, or even pretence of proof, from fact and experience, so their cause ought to be looked upon to be as vain and romantic, as if they had asserted, that men have senses naturally fitted to hear sounds, and see objects at all distances, though fact and experience, the only means of knowing it, if it was so, has, from the creation to this time, proved the quite contrary.

For he that asserts the sufficiency of the light and strength of reason, to guide men in matters of religion, is not only without any positive proof from fact or experience on his side, but has the history of all ages, for near six thousand years past, fully demonstrating the quite contrary.

If some other enquirers into human nature, should affirm, that there is in mankind a *natural instinct* of mutual love, *sufficient* to make every man, at all times, love every other man, with the *same degree* of affection, as he loves himself; I suppose such an opinion would be thought too absurd and extravagant, to need any confutation. And yet all the absurdity of it would lie in this, that it affirmed something of the *sufficiency* of a natural quality in man, which could not be supported by a single instance of any one man, and was contrary to the experience and history of every age of the world.

Now this is exactly the case of these gentlemen: their opinion has neither more nor less absurdity in it: they only affirm such a sufficiency of light and reason to be natural to all men, as cannot be supported by a single instance of any one man, that ever lived, and is fully contradicted by the experience and history of every age since the creation of the world.

By what has been here said, I hope the reader will observe, that this inquiry about the perfection or imperfection, the strength or weakness, of reason in man, as to matters of religion, rests *wholly* upon fact and experience; and that therefore all speculative reasonings upon it, are to be looked upon as idle, and visionary, as a sick man's dreams about health; and as wholly to be rejected, as any speculative arguments that should pretend to prove, in spite of all facts and experience, the *immortality*, and *unalterable* state of human bodies.

Our author himself seems very sensible, that the argument drawn from facts and experience pressed hard upon his cause; and therefore has given the best answer to it, he can yet think of.

It cannot, says he, *be imputed to any defect in the light of nature, that the* Pagan *world ran into idolatry; but to their being entirely governed by priests, who pretended Communication with their Gods, and to have thence their revelations, which they imposed on the credulous, as divine oracles.*

The truth and justness of this assertion, will fully appear by the following illustration.

'It cannot be imputed to any defect in the health, and sound-
'ness of man's natural constitution, that the world has, in all
'ages, been over-run with diseases and distempers; but to their
'being entirely governed by physicians, who pretended to I
'know not what secret knowledge of medicines, which they
'imposed on the sickly, as infallible remedies.'

For, as a perfect state of health, conscious to itself of a sufficiency of natural strength to keep clear of all diseases, seems to be out of all danger from physicians: so had mankind been ever conscious to themselves, of a sufficient natural knowledge of what is true or false in religion; or, as this author saith, such *as enabled men of the meanest capacity to distinguish between religion and superstition,** what *room* had there been for frauds and impostures in religion?

If a man whose business it was to provide himself with a quantity of *pure gold*, should be continually buying *lead*, and *brass*, and *iron*, instead of it; would you say, that his falling into

---

* Page 3.

such mistakes, was not to be imputed to any *defect* in his knowledge of *pure gold*, or how to distinguish it from other metals: but to the *lies* and *affirmations* of those who told him, that such lead, and brass, and iron, were pure gold?

Farther; This author saith, the world did not run into idolatry through any defect in the light of nature, but because they were *credulous*.

Now credulity, *so far* as it goes in any matter, supposes an *equal degree* of ignorance in that matter, whatever it is. No man is credulous of false accounts, or fabulous relations, where he knows the truth.

Children are exceeding *credulous*, because they are exceeding *ignorant;* and in the same degree as their knowledge increases, their credulity abates. So that to say, men ran into idolatry, not through want of light, or ignorance of what is true and false in religion, but because they were *credulous ;* is as nice a distinction, as if it should be said, that children believe any fable that you can tell them, not because they are *ignorant* of what is true or false, but because they are *credulous*.

Or as it may be said, in another matter, with the same justness of thought, that such an *army* ran away from the enemy, not through any defect in *natural courage*, but because they were *affrighted*.

For men may as justly be said to have a perfect courage, and yet be governed by their fears, as to have perfect knowledge of that which is true in religion, and yet be credulous of that which is false.

This *Anti-pastor*, in his *second Address* says, *Can the superstition of the* Pagans *be imputed to any defect, or insufficiency in the light of reason, when it was wholly owing to their abandoning that divine light ; and in defiance of it, running into senseless traditions ?**

But how came it, that they ran into senseless traditions? What was it that admitted these traditions, as just and good? Why, it was that faculty which judges of everything, and which this writer recommends as an unerring guide. And to say, a man's superstition is not owing to any defect or weakness of his reason, but to his admitting senseless traditions, is as vain an observation, as to say, a man's false reasoning is not owing to any weakness of his reason, but to his admitting and proceeding upon foolish, and absurd arguments.

For, foolish and absurd arguments do not more shew the state of his reason, who proceeds upon them, than senseless traditions shew the state of his reason, who admits them : For they are as

---
* Page 37.

much the objects of his reason, as arguments; and all that is senseless and absurd in either of them, must either be charged equally upon the reason of him that admits them, or both equally removed from it. So that if senseless traditions, are not a proof of the weakness of their reason that approve of them, neither are foolish and absurd arguments a proof of the weakness of their reason, who proceed upon them.

Again; Supposing, as he saith, that the *Pagans, in defiance of their reason*, received such traditions: Does this do any credit to the light of reason? For how can a man renounce his reason, but by an act of his reason?

But, is it not as great a reproach to reason, to renounce itself, as to credit a false tradition? For a *reason* that can, *knowingly*, lay aside itself, is in a more defective and disordered state, than a reason that is only capable of being deluded. But if reason, in this case, lays aside itself, *without* knowing it, then, I suppose, such an *accident* may be fairly attributed to some weakness and defect of reason.

He proceeds thus: *It is certainly no good argument against the sufficiency of the divine light of nature, that men could not err, except they left it, and followed vain traditions.**

This observation has just the same sense and acuteness in it, as if it had been said, *It is certainly no good argument against* the sufficiency of the divine healthfulness of *human nature, that men could not be* sickly, *except they left it*, and *fell into various distempers: Or, against the* sufficiency of the divine strength of *natural courage, that men could not* be timorous, *till they* left it, and followed *vain fears*. For, to prove that reason is sufficient, because everything that is absurd, is contrary to reason, is like proving our healthfulness to be sufficient, because all distempers are contrary to it; or our courage to be sufficient, because fears and cowardice are contrary to it.

Besides, how is it that men *leave* their reason? Why, just as *ignorant* men leave their *knowledge;* as *dull* people leave their *wit*, or *cowards* leave their *courage*. The first part of this paragraph tells you of a *sufficiency of the divine light of nature:* Well; what has this divine light of nature done? what sufficient effects has it had? Why, it has covered all the world with darkness. For, as a proof of the sufficiency of this divine light, he adds, in the very next words, *Whoever considers how all mankind, even the wisest nations, have been imposed on by senseless tales, and idle stories, consecrated by length of time;* well, what then? what should he conclude from this consideration? Ought

---

* *Second* Address, page 39.

he not to conclude, that the *reason* of the wisest men of all nations, runs very low in matters of religion? This is the only conclusion that common sense can draw from such an observation: But, our author says, *Whoever considers this, will not be very fond of relying upon tradition in matters of religion.*

As if he had said, Whoever considers how all mankind, even the wisest of men, have been imposed upon by absurd arguments, will not be very fond of relying upon arguments. For idle tales, and senseless traditions in matters of religion, impose upon men, in no other manner, than false arguments, and absurd conclusions, impose upon them. And as it is their own reason, that gives the strength and appearance of truth to a senseless argument; so it is their own reason, that gives the credibility, and appearance of truth to senseless traditions.

And to lay the fault upon tradition, and not upon reason that approves it, is as just, as to lay the fault upon an abominable argument, and not upon reason, that proceeds upon it.

Again; Supposing that *all mankind, even the wisest nations*, have for this six thousand years been thus imposed upon, not knowing how to distinguish idle tales and senseless traditions from true religion; is not this a noble foundation for this writer to build the *sufficiency of the divine light of nature upon?* For supposing it had been in the greatest degree *insufficient*, what other effect could have followed from it, but only this, that *all mankind*, even the *wisest nations*, should have been over-run with error? And is it not strange, that effects should bear no proportion to their causes; that the same things should follow from the *sufficiency* of the divine light of nature, which must have followed from its *greatest imperfection* and *insufficiency?*

And must not the enemies of *reason* and *free-thinking* be forced to confess, that this writer has chosen an excellent guide for himself; since he so fully acknowledges, that no one yet has been rightly guided by it? Must not his present undertaking be granted to be the effect of cool and sober deliberation, since it only calls people of *all*, even the *meanest, capacities*, to such an use of their reason, as the wisest of men and nations have always been strangers to?

Again; It is pretended, that the absurdities of the Pagan world are not owing to any defect of reason, but to their *undue use* of reason. The Bishop of *London* very justly observes, that such a pretence is *begging the question*. Our author thinks not. I will therefore grant, that it was through an *undue use* of their reason. For granting that mankind fell into all those absurdities, by an undue use of their reason, the charge against reason is rather increased than abated. For an undue use of it, is as great an accusation of reason, as any *weakness* or *blindness* that can be attributed to it. For to distinguish betwixt the defect of reason, and the undue use of reason, is as solid, as to distinguish betwixt the perfection of reason, and a due use of reason. For is not a due use of reason, so far as it proceeds, a certain sign of its perfection? Must not therefore the *undue* use of reason, so far as it proceeds, be an equally certain sign of its imperfection?

For what can make an undue use of reason, but itself? And if reason is so universally liable to an *undue use* of itself, that the universal ignorance and corruption of mankind is to be ascribed to it, then this undue use of reason, is as great a sign of its universal weakness and imperfection, as anything else can be.

This *undue use* of reason, is either voluntary and known, or involuntary and unknown. If it is the latter, then it resolves itself into that natural weakness and infirmity, which his Lordship has so fully proved to belong to human reason. If it is the former, then it may justly be reckoned a *greater disorder*, and such as makes reason more unfit to be a guide, than all the weakness, blindness, and corruption, which his Lordship hath accused it of.

Chapter V.

Shewing, that all the mutability *of our tempers, the* disorders *of our passions, the* corruption *of our hearts, all the* reveries *of the imagination, all the* contradictions *and* absurdities *that are to be found in human life, and human opinions, are strictly and precisely the mutability, disorders, corruption, and absurdities of* human reason.

IT is the intent of this chapter to shew, that although common language ascribes a variety of faculties and principles to the soul, imputing this action to the blindness of our *passions*, that to the inconstancy of our *tempers;* one thing to the heat of our *imagination*, another to the coolness of our *reason;* yet, in strictness of truth, everything that is done by us, is the action and operation of our reason, and is to be ascribed to it, as the sole faculty or principle from whence it proceeded, and by which it is governed and effected.

This writer takes a great deal of pains to prove, by *long quotations*, what nobody denies, that there is a *law* or *light* of reason common to men. All this is as freely granted, as that *love* and *hatred*, *feeling* and *sensation*, are common to men; and is granting no more, than that men are by nature intelligent and rational beings: For the faculties of man, as he is an intelligent being, as necessarily perceive some difference in actions, as to *good* and *bad*, as they perceive some things they like, and some things they dislike. In this sense there is a law or light of reason common to all men: And the law of reason is in men, as the law of *thinking*, of *liking*, and *disliking*, is in men.

And the different degrees of reason are in men, as the different degrees of love and aversion; as the different degrees of wit, parts, good nature, or ill nature, are in men.

And as all men have naturally more or less of these qualities, so all men have naturally more or less of reason: And the bulk of mankind are as different in reason, as they are in these qualities.

As love is the same passion in all men, yet is infinitely different; as hatred is the same passion in all men, yet with infinite differences; so reason is the same faculty in all men, yet with infinite differences.

And as our passions not only make us different from other men, but frequently and almost daily different from ourselves, loving and hating under great inconstancy; so our reason is not only different from the reason of other men, but is often different from itself; by a strange inconstancy, setting up first one opinion, and then another.

So that when we talk of *human reason*, or a reason *common* to mankind, we talk of as *various*, *uncertain*, and *unmeasurable* a thing, as when we talk of a *love*, a *liking*, an *aversion*, a *good nature*, or *ill nature*, common to mankind; for these qualities admit of no variation, uncertainty, or mutability, but such as they directly receive from the *reason* of mankind.

For it is as much the reason of man that acts in all these tempers, and makes them to be just what they are, as it is the reason of man that demonstrates a mathematical proposition.

Was our reason steady, and of one kind, there would be just the same steadiness and regularity in our tempers; did not reason fall into mistakes, follies and absurdities, we should have nothing foolish or absurd in our love or aversion. For every humour, every kind of love or aversion, is as strictly the *action* or *operation* of our reason, as judgment is the act of our reason.

And the tempers and passions of a child, differ only from the tempers and passions of a man, exactly in the same degree, as the reason of a child differs from the reason of man.

So that our passions and tempers, are the natural actions and real effects of our reason, and have no qualities, either good or bad, but such as are to be imputed to it.

A laudable good nature, or a laudable aversion, is only reason acting in a *certain manner;* a criminal good nature, or a criminal aversion, is nothing else but an ill-judging reason; that is, reason acting in another certain manner.

But still it is reason, or our understanding that is the *only agent* in our bad passions, as well as good passions; and as much the *sole agent* in all our passions and tempers, as in things of mere speculation.

So that the state of reason in human life, is nothing else but the state of human tempers and passions: And right reason in morality, is nothing else but right love, and right aversion.

And all our tempers and ways of liking and disliking, are as much the acts and operations of our reason, as the wisest actions of our life; and they only differ from reason, as reason differs from itself, when it judges rightly, and when it judges erroneously.

All *that* therefore which we commonly call the weakness, blindness, and disorder of our *passions*, is in reality the weakness, blindness, and disorder of our *reason*. For a right love, or wrong love, denotes only reason acting in a *certain, particular* manner.

So that if anything can be said precisely, or with exactness, of love, aversion, good nature, or ill nature, as common to mankind; the same may be said of reason, as common to mankind.

And if it would be very foolish and absurd, to ascribe an absolute perfection to human love, making it alone a sufficient guide to all good, or an absolute perfection to human hatred, as a sufficient preservative from all vice; it is equally absurd to ascribe the same perfection to human reason, because neither love nor hatred have anything perfect or imperfect, good or bad in them, but what is solely the action and operation of reason.

For the distinction of our reason from our passions, is only a distinction in language, made at pleasure; and is no more real in the things themselves, than the *desire* and *inclination* are really different from the *will*. All therefore that is weak and foolish in our passions, is the weakness and folly of our reason; all the inconstancy and caprice of our humours and tempers, is the caprice and inconstancy of our reason.

It is not *flattery* that compliments vice in authority; it is not *corruption* that makes men prostitute their honour; it is not *sensuality* that plunges men into *debauchery;* it is not *avarice* that makes men sordid; it is not *ambition* that makes them restless; it is not *bribery* that makes men sell their consciences; it is not *interest* that makes them lie, and cheat, and perjure themselves. What is it therefore? Why, it is that *absolutely perfect* faculty, which our author sets up as the *unerring* standard of all that is *wise, holy* and *good;* it is in his strong language, *reason,* the *use of reason, human reason,* that does all this.

For whether anything be fit to be done, it is, as he says, *reason alone which must judge; as the eye is the sole judge of what is visible, the ear of what is audible, so reason of what is reasonable.*

Everything therefore that is done, everything that is chosen or preferred in human life before anything else, is as strictly done, or chosen by reason, as everything that is seen, is seen by the eye; and everything that is heard, is heard by the ear.

To suppose that reason permits itself to be governed by passions or tempers, but is not the *immediate, full agent* of all that is done by them, is as absurd, as to suppose that reason permits itself to be governed by the *hand* when it is writing falsely, or the *tongue* when it is talking profanely, but is not the immediate, direct agent of all that is written and spoken by them.

Brutes are incapable of imprudence and immorality, because none of their actions are the actions of *reason:* Everything therefore that is imprudence, immorality, baseness, or villainy in us, must be the act of our reason; otherwise it could no more be imprudent or immoral, than the actions of brutes.

If therefore, as this author often saith, reason be the only faculty that distinguisheth us from brutes; it necessarily follows, that those irregularities, whether of humour, passions, or tempers, which cannot be imputed to brutes, must be solely attributed to that faculty by which we are distinguished from brutes; and consequently everything that is foolish, vain, shameful, false, treacherous, and base, must be the sole express acts of our reason; since if they were the acts of anything else, they could have no more vanity, falseness, or baseness, than hunger and thirst.

As therefore all that is faithful, just, and wise, can only be attributed to that which is done by our reason; so by plain consequence, all that is vain, false, or shameful, can only be imputed to any acts, as they are the acts of reason.

It is not my intent in the least to censure, or condemn our common language, which considers and talks of reason and the passions, as if they were as different as a *governor* and his *subjects*.

These forms of speech are very intelligible and useful, and give great life and ornament to all discourses upon morality ; and are even necessary for the Historian, the Poet, and the Orator.

But when certain persons ascribe to human reason, as a *distinct faculty* of human nature, I know not what *absolute perfection*, making it as immutable, and incapable of any addition or improvement, as God himself ; it is necessary to consider human reason, and human nature, not as it is represented in common language, but as it is in reality in itself.

Notwithstanding therefore in common language, our passions and the effects of them, are very usefully distinguished from our reason, I have here ventured to shew, that all the disorders of human nature, are precisely the disorders of human reason, and that all the perfection or imperfection of our passions, is nothing else but the perfection or imperfection of our reason.

And we may as well think, that judgment, prudence, discretion, are things different from our reason, as that humour, temper, approbation, or aversion, are really different from our reason.

For, as it is a right exercise of reason, that denominates its actions to be *prudence, judgment*, and *discretion ;* so it is a wrong exercise of reason, that denominates its actions to be *humour, temper*, and *caprice*.

And it would be as absurd to condemn humour and caprice, if they were not the actions and operations of reason, as to commend a prudence and discretion that were the effects of an irrational principle.

Our follies therefore and absurdities of every kind, are as necessarily to be ascribed to our reason, as the *first, immediate*, and *sole* cause of them, as our wisdom and discretion are to be ascribed to it in that degree.

The difference between reason assenting to the properties of a *square*, and reason acting in motions of desire or aversion, is only this, that in the latter case, it is reason acting under a sense of its own *good* or *evil*, in the former case, it is reason acting under a sense of *magnitude*.

And as the relations of magnitude, as they are the objects of our reason, are only the objects of its *assent* or *dissent ;* so good and evil, as they are objects of our reason, are only the objects of its *desire* or *aversion :* And as the assent or dissent, in matters of speculation, whether right or wrong, is solely the act of our reason; so desire or aversion, in human life, whether right or wrong, is equally the act of our reason.

All the good therefore, that there is in any of the desires or aversions of the mere natural man, is the good of our reason; and all the evil or blindness that there is in any of our passions, is solely the evil and blindness of our reason.

Because love, desire, aversion, considered as operations proceeding from mere nature alone, denote nothing else but our reason acting in a certain manner; just as prudence, discretion, and judgment, when considered as our own abilities, or strength, denote nothing else but our reason acting in a certain manner.

We often say, that our passions deceive us, or persuade us; but this is no more strictly so, than when we say, our *interest* deceived, or a *bribe* blinded us. For bribes and interest are not active principles, nor have any power of deception; it is only our reason that gives them a false value, and prefers them to a greater good.

It is just so in what we call the deceit of our passions: They meddle with us no more than bribes meddle with us; but that pleasurable perception, which is to be found in certain enjoyments, is by our reason preferred to that better good, which we might expect from a self-denial.

We say again, that our passions paint things in false colours, and present to our minds vain appearances of happiness.

But this is no more strictly true, than when we say, our *imagination* forms castles in the air. For the imagination signifies no distinct faculty from our reason, but only reason acting upon our *own ideas*.

So when our passions are said to give false colours to things, or present vain appearances of happiness, it is only our reason acting upon its own ideas of *good* and *evil*, just as it acts upon its own ideas of *architecture*, in forming castles in the air.

So that all *that* which we call different faculties of the soul, tempers and passions of the heart, strictly speaking, means nothing else, but the various acts and operations of one and the same rational principle, which has different names, according to the objects that it acts upon, and the manner of its acting.

In some things it is called speculative, in others it is called practical reason. And we may as justly think our speculative reason, is a different faculty from our practical reason, as that our tempers, aversions, or likings, are not as fully and solely to be ascribed to our reason, as syllogisms and demonstrations.

It was as truly reason that made *Medea* kill her children, that made *Cato* kill himself, that made Pagans offer human sacrifices to idols; that made *Epicurus* deny a providence, *Mahomet* pretend a revelation; that made some men sceptics, others bigots, some enthusiasts, others profane; that made *Hobbes* assert all religion to be human invention, and *Spinosa* to declare trees, and stones, and animals, to be parts of God; that makes free-thinkers deny freedom of will, and fatalists exhort to a reformation of manners; that made *Vaux* a conspirator, and *Ludlow* a regicide; that made *Muggleton* a fanatic, and *Rochester* a libertine: It was as truly human reason that did all these things, as it is human reason that demonstrates mathematical propositions.

Medea and *Cato* acted as truly according to the judgment of their reason at that time, as the *confessor* that chooses rather to suffer, than deny his faith.

And the difference between them does not consist in this, that one power or faculty of the mind acted in one of them, and another faculty or power of the mind acted in another; that is, that reason acted in one of them, and passion in another; but purely in the different state of their reason. For had not *Medea* and *Cato* thought it best to do what they did, at the time they did it, they would no more have done it, than the *confessor* would choose to suffer rather than deny his faith, unless he had judged it best so to do.

It may indeed be well enough said in common language, that passion made *Medea* and *Cato* to do as they did, just as it may be said of a man that affirms a *plenum*, or holds any speculative absurdity, that it is blindness, or prejudice, that keeps him in it. Not as if blindness and prejudice were powers or faculties of his mind, but as they signify the *ill state* of his reason. Just so the passions may be said to govern men in their actions; not as if they were powers of the mind, but as they denote the disordered state of reason. And whenever anything is imputed to the strength and violence of our passions, strictly speaking, it only means the weakness and low condition of our reason at that time.

For reason governs as fully, when our actions and tempers are ever so bad, as it does when our actions and tempers are sound and good. And the only difference is, that reason acting well governs in the one case, and reason acting ill governs in the other.

Just as it is the same reason that sometimes judges strictly right, which at other times judges exceeding wrong, in matters of speculation.

When therefore we say, that reason governs the passions, it means no more, in strict truth, than that reason governs itself;

that it acts with deliberation and attention, does not yield to its first judgments or opinions, but uses second, and third thoughts.

So that guarding against the passions, is only guarding against its own first judgments and opinions; that is, guarding against itself.

To all this it may, perhaps, be objected, that our passions and tempers arise from bodily motions, and depend very much upon the state of our blood and animal spirits, and that therefore what we do under their commotions, cannot be attributed to our reason.

It is readily granted, that the body has this share in our passions and tempers: But then the same thing must be granted of the body, in all the acts and operations of the mind. So that if our desires and aversions cannot be imputed to our reason, as its acts, because of the joint operation of the animal spirits in them; no more can syllogisms and demonstrations be attributed to our reason, as its operations, because the operation of bodily spirits concurreth in the forming of them.

For the most abstract thought, and calm speculation of the mind, has as truly the *concurrence*, and *conjunct* operation of bodily spirits, as our strongest desires or aversions. And it is as much owing to the state of the body, that such speculations are what they are, as it is owing to the state of the body, that such passions are what they are.

For the motions of the bodily spirits are inseparable from, and according to, the state and action of the mind: When reason is in speculation of a trifle, they concur but *weakly;* when reason speculates intensely, their operation is *increased.* And sometimes the attention of the mind is so great, and has so engaged and called in all the animal spirits to its assistance, that the operations of our senses are suspended, and we neither see, nor feel, till the attention of the mind has let the spirits return to all the parts of the body.

Now will anyone say, that these intense thoughts are less the acts of the mind, because they have a greater concurrence of bodily spirits, than when it is acting with indifference, and so has a lesser quantity of bodily spirits?

Yet this might as well be said, as to say, that the assent or dissent, in speculation, is the act of our reason; but liking or disliking, loving or hating, are not so the acts of our reason, because they have a greater concurrence, and different motions of bodily spirits.

For, as the mind is in a different state when it desires good, or fears evil, from what it is when it only compares two triangles; so the motions or concurrence of the bodily spirits, have only *such* a difference, as is strictly *correspondent* to these two states of the mind. They act and join as much in comparing the triangles, as in the desire of good, or fear of evil. And the mind is just so much governed by the body, in its passions, as it is governed by it in its calmest contemplations.

For as the gentle, quiet operation of the animal spirits is then strictly correspondent, and entirely owing to the state and action of the mind; so in all our passions, the strong and increased motion of the animal spirits, is then strictly correspondent, and entirely owing to the state and action of the mind.

So that reason is neither more nor less the agent, in all our tempers and passions, than it is in our most dry and sedate speculations.

It may, and often does happen, that a man may have as great an eagerness and impatience, in the solving a mathematical problem, as another hath to obtain any great good, or avoid any great evil.

But may it therefore be said, that it is not reason that solves, or desires to solve, the problem, because the bodily spirits are so active in it?

In a word; if our passions and tempers might not be imputed to our reason, as its own genuine acts and operations, because they have such a concurrence of bodily spirits, neither could arguing, or reasoning, be attributed to our *reason*, as its proper act and operation, because in all argumentation, the bodily spirits are necessarily employed; and the better and closer the reasoning is, the more they are excited and employed.

If it should farther be objected, that reason is only *right reason*, and therefore cannot be said to act or operate, but where, and so far as, right reason acts.

This is as absurd as to say, that *love* signifies only *pure love*, and *hatred* just hatred; and that therefore a man cannot be said to love, or hate, but when, and so far as, his love is pure, and his hatred just.

To draw now some plain consequences from the foregoing account.

First, If reason be, as above represented, the *universal agent* in the natural man; if all the difference among *such* men, either in speculation, or practice, is only such a difference as reason makes, then nothing can be more extravagant, than to affirm anything concerning the degree of perfection, or imperfection of reason, as *common* to man. It is as wild and romantic, as to pretend to state the measure of folly and wisdom, of fear and courage, of pride and humility, of good humour and ill humour, *common* to mankind: For as these states of the mind, are only so many different states of reason; so no uncertainty belongs to them, but what, in the *same degree*, belongs to *reason*.

Secondly, Granting that all matters of religion, must be agreeable to *right, unprejudiced* reason; yet this could be no ground for receiving nothing in religion, but what *human* reason could prove to be necessary; for *human* reason, is no more *right unprejudiced* reason, than a sinner is *sinless*, or a man an *angel*.

Granting again, that a man may go a great way towards rectifying his reason, and laying aside its prejudices; yet no particular man can be a *better judge* of the rectitude of his *own reason*, than he is of the rectitude of his own *self-love*, the sagacity of his own *understanding*, the brightness of his own *parts*, the justness of his own *eloquence*, and the depth of his own *judgment*.

For there is nothing to deceive him in *self-love*, in the opinion of his *own merit, wit, judgment*, and *eloquence*, but what has the same power to deceive him, in the opinion of his own reason. And if, as our author says, *it be the fate of most sects to be fondest of their ugliest brats*,* none seem so inevitably exposed to this *fatality*, as those whose religion is to have no *form*, but such as it receives from their own hearts.

Thirdly, A man that has his religion to choose, and with this previous privilege, that he need not allow anything to be matter of religion, but what his own right reason can prove to be so, is in as fair a way to be governed by his *passions*, as he that has his *condition* of life to choose, with the liberty of taking that which his own right reason directs him to.

Does anyone suppose now, that nothing but *right reason* would direct him in the choice of his condition? Or that he would make the better choice, because he proceeded upon this maxim, that nothing could be right, but that which was agreeable to his *own reason?* Or that his tempers, his prejudices, his self-love, his passions, his partiality, would have no influence upon his choice, because he had resigned himself to his *own right reason?*

For as our choice of a condition of life is not a matter of speculation, but of good and evil; so however it is recommended to our reason, it chiefly excites our passions. And our choice will be just as reasonable, as our tempers and passions are. And he that is made the most positive, of the sufficiency of his own right reason, will be the most likely to be governed by the blindness of his own passions.

Now it is just the same in the choice of a religion, as in the choice of a condition of life: As it is not a matter of speculation, but of *good* and *evil;* so if it is left to be stated and deter-

---

* Page 184.

mined by our *own reason*, it rather appeals to our *tempers*, than employs our reason ; and to resign ourselves up to our own reason, to tell us what ought, or ought not to be a matter of religion, is only resigning ourselves up to our tempers, to take what we *like*, and refuse what we *dislike* in religion.

For it is not only natural and easy for him, who believes that nothing can be a part of religion, but what his reason can prove necessary to be so, to take that to be *fully proved*, which is only *mightily liked;* and all that to be entirely contrary to *reason*, which is only vastly contrary to his *tempers;* this, I say, is not only natural and easy to happen, but scarce possible to be avoided.

In a word: When *self-love* is a proper arbitrator betwixt a man and his adversary ; when *revenge* is a just judge of meekness; when *pride* is a true lover of humility; when *falsehood* is a teacher of truth ; when *lust* is a fast friend of charity; when the *flesh* leads to the spirit ; when *sensuality* delights in self-denial ; when *partiality* is a promoter of equity ; when the *palate* can taste the difference between sin and holiness ; when the *hand* can feel the truth of a proposition ; then may *human reason* be a proper arbitrator between God and man, the sole, final, just judge of all that ought, or ought not to be matter of a *holy*, *divine* and *heavenly* religion.

Lastly, If this be the state of reason, as has been fully proved, then to pretend, that our reason is too perfect to be governed by anything but its own light, is the same extravagance, as to pretend, that our love is *too pure* to be governed by anything but its own inclinations, our hatred *too just* to be governed by anything but its own motions. For if all that is base and criminal in love, all that is unjust and wicked in hatred, is strictly and solely to be imputed to our reason ; then no perfection can be ascribed to our reason, but such as is to be ascribed to our love and hatred.

Finis.

THE ABSOLUTE UNLAWFULNESS

OF THE

STAGE-ENTERTAINMENT

FULLY DEMONSTRATED.

By *WILLIAM LAW*, M. A.

LONDON:
Printed for M. Richardson, in *Pater-noster-Row*. 1726.

The Absolute Unlawfulness of the Stage-Entertainment.

I AM sensible that the Title of this little Book will, to the Generality of People, seem too high a Flight; that it will be looked upon as the Effect of a fanatical Spirit, carrying Matters higher than the Sobriety of Religion requires. I have only one Thing to ask of such People, that they will suspend their Judgment for awhile, and be content to read so small a Treatise as this is, before they pass any Judgment, either upon the Merits of the Subject, or the Temper of the Writer.

Had a Person some Years ago, in the Time of *Popery*, wrote against the *Worship* of *Images*, as a Worship absolutely unlawful, our Ancestors would have looked upon him as a Man of a very *irregular* Spirit. Now it is possible for the present Age to be as much mistaken in their *Pleasures*, as the former were in their *Devotions*, and that the allowed Diversions of these Times may be as great a Contradiction to the most essential Doctrines of Christianity, as the *Superstitions* and *Corruptions* of the former Ages. All therefore that I desire, is only a little *Free-thinking* upon this Subject; and that People will not as blindly reject all Reason, when it examines their Pleasures, as some blindly reject all Reason, when it examines the Nature of their Devotions.

It is possible that *something* that is called a *Diversion*, may be as contrary to the whole Nature of Religion, as any invented Superstition, and perhaps more dangerous to those that comply with it. As the Worship of *Images* was a great Sin, though under a Pretence of Piety, so the Entertainment of the *Stage* may be very sinful, though it is only intended as a Diversion.

For if the Worship of Images did not cease to be sinful, though it was intended for pious Purposes, it must be great Weakness to imagine, that the Entertainment of the *Stage* cannot be any great Sin, because it is only used as a Diversion.

Yet this is a Way of reasoning that a great many People fall into: They say, Diversions are lawful; that the *Stage* is only a

Diversion; that People go to it without meaning any Harm, and therefore there can be no Sin in it.

But if these People were to hear a Man say, that Religion is lawful; that the Worship of Images was an Act of Religion; that he used Images as a Means of religious Devotion, and therefore there could be no Sin in it; they would mightily lament the Bigotry and Blindness of his Mind. Yet surely this is as wise and reasonable, as for a Person to say, I go to a Play only as to a Diversion: I mean no Harm, and therefore there can be no Sin in it. For if Practices may be exceeding sinful, though they are intended for pious Ends, certainly Practices may be very abominable, though they are only used as Diversions.

When therefore we condemn the *Blindness* of some Christian Countries, for conforming to such gross Corruptions of Religion, we should do well to remember, that they have thus much to be pleaded in their Excuse, that what they do is under a Notion of Piety; that it is in Obedience to the Authority both of Church and State, and that they are at the same time kept entire Strangers to the Scriptures. But how justly may the same Blindness be charged upon us, if it should appear, that without having any of their Excuses, our Public Stated Diversions are as contrary to Scripture, and the fundamental Doctrines of Religion, as any of the grossest Instances of Superstition? If we hold it lawful to go to wicked sinful Diversions, we are as great Strangers to True Religion, as they who are pleased with buying *Indulgences*, and worshipping Pieces of holy Wood.

For a *Sinful Diversion* is the same Absurdity in Religion, as a *Corrupt Worship*, and it shews the same Blindness of Mind, and Corruption of Heart, whether we sin against God in the *Church*, or in our *Closets*, or in the *Play-House*. If there is anything contrary to Religion in any of these Places, it brings us under the same Guilt. There may perhaps be this difference, that God may be less displeased with such Corruptions as we comply with through a blind Devotion, than with such as we indulge ourselves in through a Wantonness of Mind, and a Fondness for Diversions.

The Matter therefore stands thus: If it should appear that the Stage-Entertainment is entirely sinful; that it is contrary to more Doctrines of Scripture than the Worship of *Images;* then it follows, that all who defend it, and take their Share of it, are in the same State as they who worship *Images*, and defend Drunkenness and Intemperance. For to defend or support any sinful Diversion, is the same Thing as supporting or defending any other sinful Practice. It therefore as much concerns us to know whether our Diversions are reasonable, and conformable to Religion, as to know whether our Religion be reasonable and conformable to Truth. For if we allow ourselves in Diversions that are contrary to Religion, we are in no better a State than those whose Religion is contrary to Truth.

I have mentioned the Worship of *Images*, because it is so great a Corruption in Religion, so contrary to Scripture, and so justly abhorred by all the Reformed Churches; that the Reader may hence learn what he is to think of himself, if the Stage is ever his Diversion: For I am fully persuaded, that he will here find Arguments against the *Stage*, as strong and plain as any that can be urged against the Worship of *Images*, or any other Corruption of the most corrupt Religion.

Let it therefore be observed, that the Stage is not here condemned, as some other Diversions, because they are dangerous, and likely to be Occasions of Sin; but that it is condemned, as Drunkenness and Lewdness, as Lying and Profaneness are to be condemned, not as Things that may only be the Occasion of Sin, but such as are in their own Nature grossly sinful.

You go to hear a *Play*: I tell you, that you go to hear *Ribaldry* and *Profaneness;* that you entertain your Mind with extravagant *Thoughts*, wild *Rants*, *blasphemous Speeches, wanton Amours, profane Jests,* and *impure Passions*. If you ask me, Where is the Sin of all this? You may as well ask me, Where is the Sin of *Swearing* and *Lying?* For it is not only a Sin against this or that particular Text of Scripture, but it is a Sin against the *whole Nature* and Spirit of our Religion.

It is a Contradiction to all Christian Holiness, and to all the Methods of arriving at it. For can anyone think that he has a true Christian Spirit, that his Heart is changed as it ought to be, that he is born again of God, whilst he is diverting himself with the Lewdness, Impudence, Profaneness, and impure Discourses of the Stage? Can he think that he is endeavouring to be holy as Christ is holy, to live by his Wisdom, and be full of his Spirit, so long as he allows himself in such an Entertainment? For there is nothing in the Nature of Christian Holiness, but what is all contrary to the whole Spirit and Temper of this Entertainment. That Disposition of Heart which is to take Pleasure in the various Representations of the *Stage*, is as directly contrary to that Disposition of Heart which Christianity requires, as Revenge is contrary to Meekness, or Malice to Good-will. Now that which is thus contrary to the whole Nature and Spirit of Religion, is certainly much more condemned, than that which is only contrary to some particular Part of it.

But this is plainly the Case of the *Stage:* It is an Entertainment that consists of lewd, impudent, profane Discourses, and as such is contrary to the *whole Nature* of our Religion. For all the Parts of Religion, or its whole Nature has only this one Design, to give us Purity of Heart, to change the Temper and Taste of our Souls, and fill us with such holy Tempers, as may make us fit to live with God in the Society of pure and glorious Spirits.

An Entertainment therefore which applies to the Corruption of our Nature, which awakens our disordered Passions, and teaches to relish Lewdness, immoral Rant, and Profaneness, is exceeding sinful, not only as it is a Breach of some particular Duty, but as it contradicts the *whole Nature*, and opposes *every Part* of our Religion.

For, this Diversion, which consists of such Discourses as these, injures us in a very different manner from other Sins. For as Discourses are an Application to our whole Soul, as they entertain the Heart, and awaken and employ all our Passions, so they more fatally undo all that Religion has done, than several other Sins. For as Religion consists in a right Turn of Mind; as it is a State of the Heart; so whatever supports a quite contrary Turn of Mind and State of the Heart, has all the Contrariety to Religion that it can possibly have.

St. *John* says, *Hereby we know that he abideth in us by the Spirit which he hath given us.* There is no other certain Sign of our belonging to Christ; every other Sign may deceive us: All the external Parts of Religion may be in vain; it is only the State of our Mind and Spirit, that is a certain Proof that we are in a true State of Christianity. And the Reason is plain, because Religion has no other End, than to alter our Spirit, and give us new Dispositions of Heart, suitable to its Purity and Holiness. That therefore which immediately applies to our Spirit, which supports a wrong Turn of Mind, which betrays, our Hearts into impure Delights, destroys all our Religion, because it destroys that turn of Mind and Spirit, which is the sole End and Design of all our Religion.

When therefore you are asked, Why is it unlawful to swear? You can answer, Because it is contrary to the Third Commandment. But if you are asked, Why is it unlawful to use the Entertainment of the Stage? You can carry your answer farther, Because it is an Entertainment that is contrary to all the Parts, the whole Nature of Religion, and contradicts every holy Temper which the Spirit of Christianity requires. So that if you live in the use of this Diversion, you have no Grounds to hope that you have the Spirit and Heart of a Christian.

Thus stands the first Argument against the *Stage*: It has all the Weight in it, that the whole Weight of Religion can give to any Argument.

of the Stage-Entertainment.

If you are only for the *Form* of Religion, you may take the Diversion of the Stage along with it. But if you desire the *Spirit* of Religion, if you desire to be truly religious in Heart and Mind, it is as necessary to renounce and abhor the Stage, as to seek to God, and pray for the Guidance of his Holy Spirit.

Secondly. Let the next Argument against the Stage be taken from its manifest Contrariety to this important Passage of Scripture: *Let no corrupt communication proceed out of your mouth, but that which is good, to the use of edifying, that it may minister grace to the hearers. And grieve not the Holy Spirit of God, whereby ye are sealed to the day of redemption.*

Here we see, that all corrupt and unedifying Communication is absolutely sinful, and forbidden in Scripture, for this Reason, because it *grieves the Holy Spirit*, and separates *Him* from us. But if it be thus unlawful to have any corrupt Communication of our own, can we think it lawful to go to Places set apart for that Purpose; to give our Money, and hire Persons to corrupt our Hearts with ill Discourses, and inflame all the disorderly Passions of our Nature? We have the Authority of Scripture to affirm, that *evil Communication corrupts good Manners*, and that *unedifying Discourses grieve the Holy Spirit*.

Now the *Third* Commandment is not more plain and express against *Swearing*, than this Doctrine is plain and positive against going to the *Play-House*. If you should see a Person that acknowledges the *Third* Commandment to be a divine Prohibition against Swearing, yet going to a *House*, and giving his *Money* to Persons who were there met to *Curse* and *Swear* in fine Language, and invent *Musical Oaths and Imprecations*, would you not think him mad in the highest Degree? Now consider whether there be a less Degree of Madness in going to the Play-House. You own that God has called you to great Purity of Conversation; that you are forbid all *foolish Discourse*, and *filthy Jestings*, as expressly as you are forbid *Swearing;* and that you are told to *let no corrupt Communication proceed out of your mouth, but such as is good, for the use of edifying:* And yet you go to a *House set apart* for corrupt Communication: You hire Persons to entertain you with all manner of *Ribaldry, Profaneness, Rant,* and *Impurity* of Discourse, who are to present you with *vile* Thoughts, lewd Imaginations, in *fine Language*, and to make *wicked, vain, and impure Discourse* more lively and affecting, than you could possibly have it in any ill Company. Now is not this Sinning with as high a Hand, and as grossly offending against plain Doctrines of Scripture, as if you were to give your *Money* to be entertained with *Musical Oaths* and *Curses?*

You might reasonably think that *Woman* very ridiculous in her *Piety*, that durst not swear herself, but should nevertheless frequent *Places* to hear *Oaths*. But you may as justly think her very ridiculous in her *Modesty*, who though she dares not to say, or look, or do an immodest Thing herself, should yet give her *Money* to see *Women* forget the *Modesty* of their Sex, and *talk impudently* in a Public *Play-House*. If the *Play-House* was filled with *Rakes* and *ill Women*, there would be nothing to be wondered at in such an Assembly: For *such Persons* to be delighted with such Entertainments, is as natural, as for any *Animal* to delight in its proper *Element*. But for Persons who profess Purity and Holiness, who would not be suspected of *immodest* or *corrupt Communications*, for them to come under the Roof of a *House devoted* to such ill Purposes, and to be pleased Spectators of such Actions and Discourses, as are the Pleasures of the most abandoned Persons; for them to give their Money to be thus entertained, is such a Contradiction to all Piety and common Sense, as cannot be sufficiently exposed.

Consider now, if you please, the Worship of *Images*. You wonder that any People can be so blind, so regardless of Scripture, as to comply with such a Devotion. It is indeed wonderful, But is it not as wonderful, that you should seek and delight in an Entertainment made up of Lewdness, Profaneness, and all the extravagant Rant of disordered Passions, when the Scripture positively charges you to forbear all *corrupt Communication*, as that which *grieves the Holy Spirit*, and separates him from us? Is not this being *blind* and *regardless* of Scripture in as high a degree? For how can the Scripture speak higher, or plainer, or enforce its doctrines with a more dreadful Penalty, than that which is here declared? For without the Holy Spirit of God, we are but Figures of Christians, and must die in our Sins.

If it was said in Scripture, Forbear from all Image-Worship, because it *grieves and removes the Holy Spirit* from you, perhaps you would think the Worshippers of *Images* under greater Blindness, and Corruption of Heart, than they now are. But observe, that if you go to the *Stage*, you offend against Scripture in as high a degree as they, who should worship Images, though the Scriptures forbid it as *grievous to the Holy Spirit*.

If therefore I was to rest here, I might fairly say, that I had proved the Stage to be as contrary to Scripture, as the Worship of *Images* is contrary to the Second Commandment. You think it a strange Contrariety, to see People on their Knees before an *Image* at a Time that the Heart and Mind should raise itself to God. But then, is it not as strange a Contrariety, that a Person should indulge himself in the lewd profane Discourses of the

Stage, who should have his Heart and Mind preserved in the Wisdom, the Purity, and Spirit of Religion? For an Image is not so contrary to God, as Plays are contrary to the Wisdom, the Purity, and the Spirit of Scripture. An Image is only contrary to God, as it has no Power or Perfection: But *Plays* are contrary to Scripture, as the Devil is contrary to God, as they are full of another Spirit and Temper. He therefore that indulges himself in the wicked Temper of the *Stage*, sins against as plain Scripture, and offends against more doctrines of it, than he that uses *Images* in his Devotions.

I proceed now to a Third Argument against the Stage.

When you see the *Players* acting with Life and Spirit, Men and Women *equally bold* in all Instances of *Profaneness*, *Passion*, and *Immodesty*, I daresay you never suspect any of them to be Persons of *Christian Piety*. You cannot, even in your Imagination, join Piety to such Manners, and such a Way of Life. Your Mind will no more allow you to join Piety with the Behaviour of the *Stage*, than it will allow you to think *two* and *two* to be *ten*. And perhaps you had rather see your Son chained to a *Galley*, or your daughter driving *Plough*, than getting their Bread on the *Stage*, by administering in so scandalous a manner to the Vices and corrupt Pleasures of the World. Let this therefore be another Argument, to prove the *Absolute Unlawfulness* of going to a *Play*. For consider with yourself, Is the Business of *Players* so contrary to Piety, so inconsistent with the Spirit and Temper of a true Christian, that it is next to a Contradiction to suppose them united, how then can you take yourself to be *innocent*, who *delight* in their Sins, and *hire* them to commit them?

You may make yourself a Partaker of other Men's Sins, by Negligence, and for want of reproving them: But certainly, if you stand by, and assist Men in their evil Actions, if you make their Vices your Pleasures and Entertainment, and pay your Money to be so entertained, you make yourself a Partaker of their Sins in a very high degree; and consequently, it must be as unlawful to go to a *Play*, as it is unlawful to approve, encourage, assist, and reward a Man for *Renouncing* a Christian Life.

Let therefore all *Men* and *Women* that go to a *Play*, ask themselves this Question; Whether it suits with their Religion, to act the *Parts* that are there acted? Perhaps they would think this as inconsistent with that degree of Piety that they profess, as to do the vilest Things. But let them consider, that it must be a wicked and unlawful Pleasure to delight in anything, that they dare not to do themselves. Let them also consider, that they are really *acting* those *Indecencies* and *Impieties* themselves, which they think is the particular Guilt of the *Players*. For a Person may very justly be said to do that *himself*, which he *pays* for the doing, and which is done for his Pleasure.

You must therefore, if you would be consistent with yourself, as much abhor the Thoughts of being at a *Play*, as of being a *Player* yourself. For to think that you must abhor the one, and not the other, is as absurd as to suppose, that you must be temperate yourself, but may assist, encourage, and reward other People for their Intemperance. The Business of a *Player* is profane, wicked, lewd, and immodest: To be anyway therefore approving, assisting, or encouraging him in such a Way of Life, is as evidently sinful, as it is sinful to assist and encourage a Man in *Stealing*, or any other Wickedness.

This Argument is not far-fetched, or founded in any Subtilties of Reasoning, but is so plain and obvious, that the meanest capacity must needs understand it. I may venture to challenge anyone to shew me, that the Business of the *Player* is a more Christian Employment than that of *Robbers*. For he must know very little of the Nature of Religion, that can look upon Lust, Profaneness, and disorderly Passions, to be less contrary to Religion, than the taking Money from the right Owner. And a Person who devotes himself to this Employment, to get his Bread by gratifying the corrupt Taste of the World with wanton, wild, profane Discourses, may be justly supposed to have a more corrupt Heart himself, than many a Man who has taken unlawful Ways of relieving his Wants.

I speak to this Matter with thus much Plainness, because there is so plain Reason for it; and because I think, there is as much Justice and Tenderness in telling every Player that his Employment is abominably sinful, and inconsistent with the Christian, as in telling the same Thing to a *Thief*. As it ought to be reckoned no Sign of Enmity or Ill-will, if I should attempt to prove to *Malefactors* the horrid Nature of their Sins, and the Necessity of a sincere Repentance, so I hope it will not be looked upon as a Sign of ill Temper, or Anger at any particular Persons, that I set the Business of Players among the most abominable Crimes. For it is with no other Intent, but that they themselves may avoid the dreadful Guilt of so wicked a Profession, and that other People may not dare any longer to support them in it. For it certainly concerns all People, who are not so void of Religion as to be Players themselves, to be strictly careful that they have no Share in the Guilt of so unchristian a Profession.

This we reckon very good Reasoning in all other Cases. A Person that dares not *steal*, thinks it equally sinful to encourage Theft. Anyone that abhors *Perjury*, or *Murder*, knows that he commits those Sins, if he encourages other People in them. What therefore must we think of ourselves, if the Blasphemy, Profaneness, Lewdness, Immodesty, and wicked Rant of Plays, are Parts that we dare not act ourselves, yet make it our Diversion to be delighted with those that do? Shall we think ourselves more enlightened, or more reasonable, than those that worship *Images?* The Second Commandment cannot fright them from the use of Images, but it is because they have had a superstitious Education, are taught to be blindly obedient, and have the Pretence of Piety for what they do. But all the grossest Sins of the *Stage* cannot fright us from it, though we see the Sins, and have nothing to pretend for Compliance, but mere idleness and Diversion.

If anyone was to collect all the foolish vain *Devotions*, which poor mistaken Creatures have paid to *Images*, it would sufficiently justify our Abhorrence of them, and shew the Wisdom of the *Reformation* in abolishing the Use of them. But if a Person was to make a Collection of all the wicked, profane, blaphemous, lewd, impudent, detestable Things, that are said in the Play-House only in *one Season*, it would appear to be such a Mass of Sin, as would sufficiently justify anyone in saying, that the Business of Players is the most wicked and detestable Profession in the World.

All People therefore who ever enter into their House, or contribute the smallest Mite towards it, must look upon themselves, as having been so far Friends to the most powerful Instruments of Debauchery, and to be guilty of contributing to a bold, open, and public Exercise of Impudence, Impurity, and Profaneness. When we encourage any good Design, either with our Consent, our Money, or Presence, we are apt to take a great deal of Merit to ourselves; we presently conclude that we are Partakers of all that is *good and praise-worthy in it*, of all the Benefit that arises from it, because we are Contributors towards it. A Man does not think that he has no Share in some public Charity, because he is but one in ten thousand that contributes towards it; but if it be a religious Charity, and attended with great and happy Effects, his Conscience tells him that he is a Sharer of *all* that great Good to which he contributes. Now let this teach us, how we ought to judge of the Guilt of encouraging anything that is bad, either with our *Consent*, our *Money*, or our *Presence*. We must not consider how much our single Part contributes towards it, nor how much less we contribute than several thousands of other People, but we must look at the *whole thing* in itself, and whatever there is of Evil in it, or whatever Evil arises from it, we must charge ourselves with a Share of the whole

Guilt of so great an Evil. Thus it is that we hope and desire to partake of the Merit of all good Designs, which we any way countenance and encourage; and thus it is that the Guilt of all wicked things, which we countenance and assist, will certainly be laid to our Charge.

To proceed now to a fourth Argument. When I consider *Churches*, and the Matter of *Divine Service*, that it consists of holy Readings, Prayers, and Exhortations to Piety, there is Reason to think that the House of God is a natural Means of promoting Piety and Religion, and rendering Men devout, and sensible of their Duty to God. The very Nature of Divine Assemblies, thus carried on, has this direct Tendency: I ask you whether this is not very plain, that *Churches* thus employed should have this Effect? Consider therefore the *Play-House*, and the Matter of the Entertainment there, as it consists of *Love-Intrigues, blasphemous Passions, profane Discourses, lewd Descriptions, filthy Jests*, and all the most extravagant Rant of wanton profligate Persons of both Sexes, heating and inflaming one another with all the *Wantonness* of Address, the *Immodesty* of Motion, and *Lewdness* of Thought, that Wit can invent; consider, I say, whether it be not plain, that a House so employed is as certainly serving the Cause of *Immorality* and *Vice*, as the House of God is serving the Cause of *Piety?* For what is there in our *Church Service* that shews it to be *useful* to Piety and Holiness, what is there in Divine Worship to correct and amend the Heart, but what is directly contrary to all that is doing in the *Play-House?* So that one may with the same Assurance affirm, that the *Play-House*, not only when some very profane Play is on the *Stage*, but in its *daily common* Entertainments, is as certainly the *House of the Devil*, as the Church is the *House of God*. For though the Devil be not professedly worshipped by Hymns directed to him, yet most that is there sung is to his Service; he is there *obeyed* and *pleased* in as certain a manner, as God is worshipped and honoured in the Church.

You must easily see, that the Charge against the *Play-House* is not the Effect of any *particular Temper*, or Weakness of Mind; that it is not an *uncertain Conjecture*, or *religious Whimsy;* but it is a Judgment founded as plainly in the *Nature* and *Reason* of Things, as when it is affirmed, that the House of God is of Service to Religion: And he that absolutely condemns the *Play-House*, as wicked and of a corrupting Nature, proceeds upon as much Truth and Certainty, as he that absolutely commends the *House of God*, as holy and tending to promote Piety.

When therefore anyone pretends to vindicate the *Stage* to you, as a proper Entertainment for holy and religious Persons,

of the Stage-Entertainment. 151

you ought to reject the Attempt with as much Abhorrence, as if he should offer to shew you, that our *Church Service* was rightly formed for those Persons to join in, who are *devoted to the Devil*. For to talk of the *Lawfulness* and *Usefulness* of the *Stage* is full as absurd, and contrary to the plain Nature of Things, as to talk of the Unlawfulness and Mischief of the Service of the Church. He therefore that tells you, that you may safely go to the *Play-House*, as an innocent useful Entertainment of your Mind, commits the same Offence against common Sense, as if he should tell you, that it was dangerous to attend at Divine Service, and that its Prayers and Hymns were great *Pollutions* of the Mind.

For the Matter and Manner of *Stage-Entertainments* are as undeniable Proofs, and as obvious to common Sense, that the House belongs to the Devil, and is the Place of his Honour, as the Matter and Manner of *Church Service* prove that the Place is appropriated to God.

Observe therefore, that as you do not want the Assistance of anyone to shew you the *Usefulness* and *Advantage* of Divine Service, because the thing is plain, and speaks for itself, so neither, on the other hand, need you anyone to shew the *Unlawfulness* and *Mischief* of the Stage, because there the thing is equally plain, and speaks for itself. So that you are to consider yourself as having the same Assurance, that the *Stage* is wicked, and to be abhorred and avoided by all Christians, as you have, that the Service of the Church is holy, and to be sought after by all Lovers of Holiness. Consider therefore, that your Conduct, with relation to the *Stage*, is not a Matter of *Nicety*, or *scrupulous Exactness*, but that you are as certain that you do wrong in as notorious a manner, when you go to the *Play-House*, as you are certain that you do right, when you go to *Church*.

Now it is of mighty Use to conceive Things in a right manner, and to see them as they are in their own Nature. Whilst you consider the Play-House only as a *Place of Diversion*, it may perhaps give no Offence to your Mind, there is nothing *shocking* in the Thought of it; but if you would lay aside this Name of it for awhile, and consider it in its *own Nature*, as it really is, you would find that you are as much deceived, if you consider the *Play-House* as only a *Place of Diversion*, as you would be, if you considered the House of God only as a Place of *Labour*.

When therefore you are tempted to go to a *Play*, either from your own Inclination, or from the Desire of a Friend, fancy that you was asked in plain Terms to go to the Place of the *Devil's Abode*, where he holds his *filthy Court* of evil Spirits; that you was asked to join in an Entertainment, where he was at the Head of it; where the whole of it was in order to his Glory, that Men's Hearts and Minds might be separated from God, and plunged into all the Pollutions of Sin and Brutality. Fancy that you are going to a Place that as certainly belongs to the Devil, as the *heathen Temples* of old, where *Brutes* were worshipped, where *wanton Hymns* were sung to *Venus*, and drunken Songs to the God of Wine. Fancy that you are as certainly going to the Devil's *Triumph*, as if you were going to those *old Sports*, where People committed Murder, and offered Christians to be devoured by wild Beasts, for the Diversion of the Spectators. Now whilst you consider the *Play-House* in this View, I suppose you can no more go to a *Play*, than you can renounce your Christianity.

Consider now therefore, that you have not been frighting yourself with *groundless Imaginations*, but that which you have here fancied of the *Play-House* is as strictly true, as if you had been fancying, that when you go to Church you go to the House of God, where the heavenly Hosts attend upon his Service; and that when you read the Scriptures, and sing holy Hymns, you join with the Choirs above, and do God's Will on Earth as it is done in Heaven. For observe, I pray you, how justly that Opinion of the *Play-House* is founded. For was it a Joy to God to see *Idols* worshipped, to see Hymns and Adorations offered up to impure and filthy Deities? Were Places and Festivals appointed for such Ends justly esteemed Places and Festivals devoted to the Devil? Now give the Reason why all this was justly reckoned a Service to the Devil, and you will give as good a Reason why the *Play-House* is to be esteemed his *Temple*.

For what though Hymns and Adorations are not offered to impure and filthy Deities, yet if *Impurity* and *Filthiness* is the *Entertainment*, if immodest Songs, profane Rant, if Lust and Passion entertain the Audience, the Business is the same, and the Assembly does the *same Honour* to the Devil, though they be not gathered together in the Name of some *Heathen God*.

For Impurity and Profaneness in the Worshippers of the True God is as acceptable a Service to the Devil, as Impurity and Profaneness in Idolators; and perhaps a *lewd Song*, in an Assembly of Christians, gives him a greater Delight than in a Congregation of *Heathens*.

If therefore we may say, that a *House* or *Festival* was the Devil's, because he was *delighted* with it, because what was there done, was an *acceptable Service* to him, we may be assured that the *Play-House* is as really the House of the Devil, as any other House ever was. Nay, it is reasonable to think, that the *Play-Houses* in this Kingdom are a greater Pleasure to him, than any

Temple he ever had in the Heathen World. For as it is a greater Conquest to make the Disciples of Christ delight in *Lewdness* and *Profaneness*, than ignorant Heathens, so a *House* that, in the Midst of *Christian Churches*, trains up Christians to *Lewdness* and *Profaneness*, that makes the Worshippers of Christ flock together in Crowds, to rejoice in an Entertainment that is as contrary to the Spirit of Christ, as *Hell* is contrary to *Heaven;* a House so employed may justly be reckoned a more delightful Habitation of the Devil, than any Temple in the Heathen World.

When therefore you go to the *Play-House*, you have as much Assurance that you go to the Devil's peculiar Habitation, that you submit to his Designs, and rejoice in his Diversions, which are his best Devices against Christianity, you have as much Assurance of this, as that they who worshipped filthy Deities were in reality Worshippers of the Devil.

Hence it appears, that if instead of considering the Play-House, as only a Place of Diversion, you will but examine what Materials it is made of; if you will but consider the Nature of the Entertainment, and what is there doing; you will find it as wicked a Place, as sinful a Diversion, and as truly the peculiar Pleasure of the Devil, as any wicked Place, or sinful Diversion in the Heathen World. When therefore you are asked to go to a Play, do not think that you are only asked to go to a Diversion, but be assured that you are asked to *yield* to the Devil, to go over to his Party, and to make one of his Congregation. That if you do go, you have not only the Guilt of *buying* so much vain Communication, and paying People for being wicked, but are also as certainly guilty of going to the Devil's House, and doing him the same Honour, as if you were to partake of some *Heathen Festival*. You must consider, that all the Laughter there is not only vain and foolish, but that it is a Laughter among Devils, that you are upon profane Ground, and hearing Music in the very Porch of Hell.

Thus it is in the Reason of the thing. And if we should now consider the State of our *Play-House*, as it is in Fact, we should find it answering all these Characters, and producing Effects suitable to its Nature. But I shall forbear this Consideration, it being as unnecessary to tell the Reader, that our *Play-House* is in Fact the *Sink of Corruption and Debauchery;* that it is the general Rendezvous of the most profligate Persons of both Sexes; that it corrupts the Air, and turns the adjacent Places into public Nuisances; this is as unnecessary, as to tell him that the *Exchange* is a Place of *Merchandise*.

Now it is to be observed, that this is not the State of the *Play-*

House through any accidental Abuse, as any innocent or good thing may be abused; but that Corruption and Debauchery are the truly natural and genuine Effects of the *Stage-Entertainment.* Let not therefore anyone say, that he is not answerable for those Vices and Debaucheries which are occasioned by the *Play-House,* for so far as he partakes of the Pleasure of the *Stage,* and is an Encourager of it, so far he is chargeable with those Disorders which necessarily are occasioned by it. If Evil arises from our doing our Duty, or our Attendance at any *good Design,* we are not to be frighted at it; but if Evil arises from anything as its *natural* and *genuine* Effect, in all such Cases, so far as we contribute to the Cause, so far we make ourselves guilty of the Effects. So that all who any way assist the *Play-House,* or ever encourage it by their Presence, make themselves chargeable, in some degree, with all the Evils and Vices which follow from it. Since therefore it cannot be doubted by anyone, whether the *Play-House* be a Nursery of Vice and Debauchery, since the evil Effects it has upon People's Manners is as visible as the Sun at Noon, one would imagine, that all People of *Virtue* and *Modesty* should not only avoid it, but avoid it with the utmost Abhorrence; that they should be so far from entering into it, that they should detest the very Sight of it. For what a Contradiction is it to common Sense, to hear a Woman lamenting the miserable Lewdness and Debauchery of the Age, the vicious Taste and irregular Pleasures of the World, and at the same time dressing herself to meet the lewdest Part of the World at the Fountain-head of all Lewdness, and making herself one of that Crowd, where every abandoned Wretch is glad to be present? She may fancy that she hates and abominates their Vices, but she may depend upon it, that till she hates and abominates the Place of vicious Pleasures; till she dares not come near an Entertainment, which is the Cause of so great Debauchery, and the Pleasure of the most debauched People; till she is thus disposed, she wants the truest Sign of a real and religious Abhorrence of the Vices of the Age.

For to wave all other Considerations, I would only ask her a Question or two on the single Article of *Modesty.* What is Modesty? Is it a little *mechanical outside* Behaviour, that goes no farther than a few *Forms* and *Modes* at particular Times and Places? Or is it a *real Temper,* a natural Disposition of the Heart, that is founded in *Religion?* Now if Modesty is only a mechanical Observance of a little outside Behaviour, then I can easily perceive how a modest Woman may frequent *Plays;* there is no Inconsistency for such a one to be one thing in one Place, and another in another Place; to disdain an immodest Conversation, and yet at the same Time relish and delight in immodest and impudent Speeches in a public *Play-House*. But if Modesty is a *real Temper* and Disposition of the Heart, that is founded on the Principles of Religion, then I confess I cannot comprehend, how a Person of such Modesty should ever come twice into the Play-house. For if it is Reason and Religion that have inspired her with a modest Heart, that make her careful of her Behaviour, that make her hate and abhor every Word, or Look, or Hint in Conversation that has the Appearance of Lewdness, that make her shun the Company of such as talk with too much Freedom; if she is thus modest in *common Life*, from a Principle of Religion, a Temper of Heart, is it possible for such a one (I do not say to seek) but to bear with the Immodesty and Impudence of the *Stage?* For must not Immodesty and Impudence, must not loose and wanton Discourse be the same *hateful things*, and give the same Offence to the modest Mind, in one Place as in another? And must not that Place, which is the Seat of Immodesty, where Men and Women are trained up in Lewdness, where almost every Day in the Year is a Day devoted to the foolish Representations of *Rant, Lust*, and *Passion;* must not such a Place of all others be the most odious to the Mind, that is *truly modest* upon Principles of *Reason* and *Religion?* One would suppose, that such a Person should as much abominate the Place, as any other filthy Sight, and be as much offended with an Invitation to it, as if she was invited to see an immodest Picture. For the Representations of the *Stage*, the inflamed Passions of Lovers there described, are as gross an Offence to the Ear, as any Representation that can offend the Eye.

It ought not to be concluded, that because I affirm the *Play-House* to be an Entertainment *contrary* to Modesty, that therefore I accuse all People as void of Modesty whoever go to it. I might affirm, that *Transubstantiation* is contrary to all *Sense* and *Reason;* but then it would be a wrong Conclusion, to say that I affirmed that all who believe it are void of all *Sense* and *Reason*.

Now as *Prejudices*, the Force of *Education*, the Authority of *Numbers*, the Way of the World, the Example of *great Names*, may make People *believe*, so the same Causes may make People act against *all Sense and Reason*, and be guilty of Practices which no more suit with the *Purity* of their Religion, than *Transubstantiation* agrees with *common Sense*.

To proceed. *Trebonia* thus excuses herself for going to the *Play-House*. I go but seldom; and then either with my *Mother* or my *Aunt:* We always know the Play beforehand, and never go on the *Sacrament*-Week: And what harm pray, says she, can there be in this? It breaks in upon no Rules of my Life. I neglect no Part of my Duty: I go to *Church,* and perform the same Devotions at home, as on other Days.

It ought to be observed, that this Excuse can only be allowed, where the Diversion itself is innocent: It must therefore first be considered, what the Entertainment is in itself; whether it be suitable to the Spirit and Temper of Religion: For if it is right and proper in itself, it needs no Excuse; but if it be *wrong* and *contrary* to Religion, we are not to use it *cautiously*, but to avoid it *constantly.*

Trebonia must be told, that it is no Proof of the Innocence of a Thing, that it does not interfere with her *Hours of Duty,* nor break the Regularity of her Life; for very wicked Ways of spending Time may yet be consistent with a regular Distribution of our Hours. She must therefore consider, not only whether such a Diversion hinders the Regularity of her Life, or breaks in upon her Hours of Devotion, public or private, but whether it hinders, or any way affects the *Spirit* and *Temper* which all her Devotions aspire after. Is it conformable to that heavenly Affection, that Love of God, that Purity of Heart, that Wisdom of Mind, that Perfection of Holiness, that Contempt of the World, that Watchfulness and Self-denial, that Humility and Fear of Sin, which Religion requires? Is it conformable to those Graces, which are to be the *daily Subject* of all her Prayers? This is the only way for her to know the *Innocence* of going to a Play. If what she there hears and sees, has no *Contrariety* to any *Grace* or *Virtue* that she prays for; if all that there passes, be fit for the *Purity* and *Piety* of one that is led by the Spirit of Christ, and is *working out* her *Salvation with fear and trembling;* if the Stage be an Entertainment that may be thought to be according to the Will of God; then she disposes of an Hour very innocently, though her *Mother* or her *Aunt* were not with her.

But if the *contrary* to all this be true; if most of what she there *hears* and *sees* be as contrary to the *Piety* and *Purity* of Christianity, as *Feasting* is contrary to *Fasting;* if the *House* which she supports with her *Money,* and encourages with her *Presence,* be a notorious Means of Corruption, visibly carrying on the Cause of *Vice* and *Debauchery;* she must not think herself excused for being with her *Mother.*

Trebonia would perhaps think it strange, to hear one of her virtuous Acquaintance giving the like Reason for going now and then to a *Masquerade.*

Now this Diversion is new in our Country; and therefore most People *yet* judge of it in the manner that they ought, because they are not blinded by *Use and Custom.* But let anyone give but the true Reasons, why a Person of Virtue and Piety should not go to *Masquerades*, and the same Reasons will as plainly shew, that Persons of Virtue and Piety should keep at as great a distance from the *Play-House*. For the Entertainment of the *Stage* is more directly opposite to the Purity of Religion, than *Masquerades*, and is besides as certain a Means of Corruption, and serves all bad Ends in as great a degree as they do. They only differ, as bad Things of the same Kind may differ from one another. So that if the evil Use, and ill Consequences of *Masquerades*, be a sufficient Reason to deter People of Piety from partaking of them, the same evil Use, and ill Consequences of the *Stage*, ought to keep all People of Virtue from it. If People will consult their *Tempers* only, they may take the Entertainment of one, and condemn the other; as following the same Guide, they may abhor *Intemperance*, and indulge *Malice:* But if they will consult Religion, and make that the Ground of their Opinions, they will find more and stronger Reasons for a *constant Abhorrence* of the *Stage*, than of *Masquerades*.

Again : If *Trebonia* should hear a Person excusing her Use of *Paint* in this manner; That truly she painted but *very seldom;* that she always said her Prayers first; that she never used it on *Sundays*, or the Week before the *Communion: Trebonia*, would pity such a *Mixture* of Religion and Weakness. She would desire her to use her Reason, and either to allow *Painting* to be innocent, suitable to the *Sobriety* and *Humility* of a Christian, or else to think it is as unlawful at one Time, as at another. But, *Trebonia*, would you not think it still stranger, that she should condemn *Painting* as *odious* and *sinful*, and yet think that the *Regularity* of her Life, and the *Exactness* of her Devotions, might make it lawful for her to paint *now* and *then?*

I doubt not but you plainly see the Weakness and Folly of such a Pretence for *Painting*, under such Rules, at certain Times. And if you would but as impartially consider your Pretences for going sometimes to the Play-House, under the same Rules, you would certainly find them more weak and unreasonable. For *Painting* may with more Reason be reckoned an *innocent Ornament*, than the Play-House an *innocent Diversion*. And it supposes a greater *Vanity* of Mind, a more *perverted* Judgment, and a deeper Corruption of Heart, to seek the Diversion of the *Stage*, than to take the Pleasure of a *borrowed Colour*. Painting, when considered in itself, is undoubtedly a great Sin; but when it is compared to the Use of the Stage, it is but as the *Mote* compared to the *Beam*.

I know you are offended at this *Comparison*, because you judge by your *Temper*, and *Prejudices*, and do not consider the things as they are in themselves, by the pure Light of *Reason* and *Religion*. *Painting* has not been the way of your Family; it is supposed to be the Practice but of *very few;* and those who use it endeavour to *conceal* it: This makes you readily condemn it. On the contrary, your *Mother* and your *Aunt* carry you to the *Play;* you see *virtuous* People there, and the same Persons that fill our *Churches;* so that your *Temper* is as much engaged to think it lawful to go sometimes to a *Play*, as it is engaged to think the Use of *Paint* always odious and sinful.

Lay aside therefore these Prejudices for a while, and fancy that you had been trained up in some Corner of the World in the Principles of Christianity, and had never heard either of the *Play-House* or *Painting*. Imagine now that you was to examine the Lawfulness of them by the Doctrines of Scripture; you would first desire to be told the Nature of these Things, and what they meant. You would be told, that *Painting* was the borrowing of *Colours* from Art, to make the Face look more beautiful. Now though you found no express Text of Scripture against *Painting*, you would find that it was expressly against Tempers required in Scripture; you would therefore condemn it, as proceeding from a Vanity of Mind, and Fondness of Beauty. You would see that the Harm of Painting consisted in this, that it proceeded from a Temper of Mind contrary to the Sobriety and Humility of a Christian, which indeed is harm enough; because this Humility and Sobriety of Mind is as essential to Religion, as Charity and Devotion. So that in judging according to Scripture, you would hold it as unreasonable to *paint sometimes*, as to be sometimes *malicious, indevout, proud,* or *false*.

You are now to consider the *Stage;* you are to keep close to Scripture, and fancy that you yet know nothing of *Plays*. You ask therefore first, what the *Stage* or *Play-House* is? You are told that it is a *Place* where all sorts of People meet to be entertained with *Discourses, Actions,* and *Representations,* which are recommended to the Heart by beautiful Scenes, the Splendour of Lights, and the Harmony of Music. You are told that these Discourses are the Invention of Men of Wit and Imagination, which describe imaginary *Intrigues* and *Scenes* of *Love*, and introduce *Men* and *Women* discoursing, raving, and acting in all the wild indecent Transports of *Lust* and *Passion*. You are told, that the Diversion partly consists of *lewd* and *profane* Songs sung to fine Music, and partly of extravagant Dialogues between *immodest Persons* talking in a Style of *Love* and *Madness*, that is nowhere else to be found, and entertaining the *Christian Audience* with all the Violence of Passion, Corruption of Heart, Wantonness of Mind, Immodesty of Thought, and Profane Jests, that the Wit of the *Poet* is able to invent. You are told, that the *Players*, Men and Women, are trained up to act and represent all the Descriptions of Lust and Passion in the *liveliest manner*, to add a Lewdness of Action to lewd Speeches; that they get their Livelihood by *Cursing, Swearing,* and *Ranting* for three Hours together to an Assembly of *Christians.*

Now though you find no particular Text of Scripture condemning the *Stage*, or *Tragedy* or *Comedy*, in express Words; yet what is much more, you find that such Entertainments are a gross Contradiction to the *whole Nature* of Religion; they are not contrary to this or that particular Temper, but are contrary to that *whole Turn of Heart* and *Mind* which Religion requires. Painting is contrary to Humility, and therefore is to be avoided as sinful; but the Entertainment of the *Stage*, as it consists of *blasphemous* Expressions, *wicked* Speeches, *swearing, cursing*, and *profaning* the Name of God, as it abounds with *impious* Rant, *filthy* Jests, *distracted* Passions, gross Descriptions of *Lust*, and *wanton Songs*, is a *Contradiction to every Doctrine* that our Saviour and his Apostles have taught us. So that to abhor *Painting* at all times, because it supposes a Vanity of Mind, and is contrary to Humility, and yet think there is a lawful Time to go to the *Play-House*, is as contrary to common-Sense, as if a Man should hold that it was lawful sometimes to offend against *all the Doctrines* of Religion, and yet always unlawful to offend against *any one* Doctrine of Religion.

If therefore you were to come (as I supposed) from some Corner of the World, where you had been used to live and judge by the Rules of Religion, and upon your Arrival here had been told what Painting and the *Stage* was; as you would not expect to see Persons of *religious Humility* carrying their Daughters to *Paint-Shops*, or inviting their pious Friends to go along with them, so much less would you expect to hear, that *devout, pious,* and *modest* Women carried their Daughters, and invited their virtuous Friends to meet them at the Play. Least of all could you imagine, that there were any People too *pious* and *devout* to indulge the Vanity of *Painting*, and yet not devout and pious enough to abhor the Immodesty, Profaneness, Ribaldry, Immorality, and Blasphemy of the *Stage.*

To proceed. A *polite Writer** of a late Paper thought he had sufficiently ridiculed a certain Lady's Pretensions to *Piety*, when, speaking of her *Closet*, he says,

Together lie her Prayer-Book and Paint,
At once to improve the Sinner and the Saint.

---

* *Spectator*, No. 79.

Now, whence comes it that this Writer judges so rightly, and speaks the Truth so plainly, in the Matter of Painting? Whence comes it that the generality of his Readers think his Observation just, and join with him in it? It is because Painting is not yet an *acknowledged Practice*, but is for the most part reckoned a *Shameful Instance* of Vanity. Now as we are not prejudiced in favour of this Practice, and have no Excuses to make for our *own Share* in it, so we judge of it impartially, and immediately perceive its Contrariety to a Religious *Temper* and *State* of Mind. This *Writer* saw this in so strong a Light, that he does not scruple to suppose, that *Paint* is as natural and proper a Means to improve the *Sinner*, as the Prayer-Book is to improve the Saint.

I should therefore hope, that it need not be imputed to any *Sourness* of Temper, Religious *Weakness*, or *Dulness* of Spirits, if a *Clergyman* should imagine, that the *Profaneness, Debauchery, Lewdness*, and *Blasphemy* of the *Stage*, is as natural Means to improve the *Sinner*, as the *Bottle of Paint:* Or if he should venture to shew, that the *Church* and the *Play-House* are as ridiculous a Contradiction, and do no more suit with the *same* Person, than the *Prayer-Book and Paint*.

I shall now make a Reflection or two upon the present celebrated Entertainment of the *Stage*, which is so much to the Taste of the People, that it has been acted almost every Night one whole Season.

The first Scene is said to be a *magnificent Palace discovered: Venus attended with Graces and Pleasures.*

Now how is it possible, that such a Scene as this should be fit for the Entertainment of Christians? Can *Venus* and her *Graces* and *Pleasures* talk any Language that is *like* themselves, but what must be *unlike* to the Spirit of Christianity? The very proposing such a Scene as this, supposes the Audience to be fit for the Entertainment of *Lust* and *Wantonness*. For what else can *Venus* and her *Pleasures* offer to them? Had we any Thing of the Spirit of Christianity in us, or were earnestly desirous of those holy Tempers, which are to render us pure in the Eyes of God, we should abominate the very Proposal of such a Scene as this, as knowing that it must be an Entertainment fitter for *public Stews*, than for People who make any Pretences to the Holiness and Purity of the Spirit of Christ. The Scripture says, *Mortify therefore your members which are upon earth, fornication, uncleanness, inordinate affection, evil concupiscence*. This is the Religion by which we are to be saved. But can the Wit of Man invent anything more contrary to this, than an Entertainment from *Venus* attended with her *Pleasures?*

That People should have such a Religion as this, and at the same time such an Entertainment, is an astonishing Instance of the Degeneracy of the present State of Christianity among us. For if the first Scene had been the *Devil attended with Fiends, cursing and blaspheming*, no one could shew that such a Scene was more contrary to the Religion of *Christians*, than a Scene with *Venus* and her *Pleasures*. And if the Devil himself had been consulted by our *Stage Wits*, which of these Scenes he had rather have, he would certainly have chosen *Venus* and her *Pleasures*, as much fitter to debauch and corrupt a Christian Audience, than a Scene of *cursing* and *blaspheming*.

The Scripture thus describes the Infatuation of the old Idolaters. *And none considereth in his heart, neither is there knowledge nor understanding to say, I have burnt part of it in the fire; yea, I have also baked bread upon the coals thereof, and shall I make the residue thereof an abomination? Shall I fall down to the Stock of a Tree?** It is here reckoned a strange Instance of their Blindness, that they did not make so easy a Reflection upon the nature of Things. But how near are we to this Blindness, if we do not make as easy a Reflection upon this Entertainment; for the very mentioning of such a *Scene* as this, is as plain a Demonstration that the Entertainment is contrary to our Religion, as the *burning* of Wood, and its falling into *Ashes*, is a Demonstration that Wood is of a Nature contrary to God. How are we therefore more enlightened, if none of us considers in his Heart, neither is there Knowledge nor Understanding in us to say, *These are the filthy Deities of the Devil's Invention, with which he polluted and defiled the Heathen World. And shall we still preserve their Power among us? Shall we make such Abominations our Diversion?*

For if we worship the God of *Purity*, if we cannot worship him but with hearts devoted to Purity, what have we to do with these Images of Lewdness? If we dress a *Venus*, and celebrate her Power, and make her *Graces* and *Pleasures* meet us in wanton *Forms*, and wanton *Language*, is it not as absurd, as contrary to our Religion, as to set up a *Baal* in the Temple of God? What greater Contradiction is there, either to Reason or Religion, in one Case than in the other? *Baal* is as fit for our Devotions, as *Venus* is for our Rejoicings and Praises.

So that the very naming of such a Scene as this is *unlawful Language*, and carries as great a Contrariety to our Religion, as the Worship of *Baal*.

Two Women (whom I suppose to be baptized Christians)

---

* *Isaiah* xliv. 19.

represent *Venus* and *Diana*, singing, and celebrating their Lusts and Wantonness, *as the Sweets that Life improve.*

Now, if a common *Prostitute* was to come drunk out of a *Brandy-Shop* singing their Words, she would act like herself. No one could say that she had forgot her Character, or was *singing* one way, and *living* another. And I dare say, there is no *Rake* in the Audience so debauched, as not to think this a sufficient Celebration of the Praises and Happiness of his Pleasures.

But what do other People do here? Is there any Entertainment in this Place for *pious, sober,* and *devout* Minds? Does it become them to sing the Praises of Debauchery, or sit among those that do?

When we hear of a *Witches' Feast*, we do not hear of any but *Witches* that go to it: The Mirth and Joy of such Meetings is left wholly to themselves. Now if these impudent Celebrations of *Venus* and her *Pleasures* were left wholly to *Rakes* and *Prostitutes;* if we reckoned it an Entertainment as contrary to Religion, as a *Witches' Feast;* it would only shew, that we judged as rightly in the one Case as in the other. And indeed, one would think, that no Christian need to be told, that *Venus* and her *Graces* are as much the Devil's *Machinery* as *Witches* and *Imps.*

To proceed. If a Person in Conversation was to address himself to a *Modest* Lady in the words of this Entertainment, she would think herself very ill-used, and that she ought to resent such Treatment. She would think, that her *Modesty* might well be questioned, if she bore such Language.

But how it is consistent with such Modesty, to hire People to entertain her with the same Language in Public, is a Difficulty not easily to be explained. Can *Fathers* and *Mothers*, who sit here with their Children, recommend Purity to them at home, when they have carried them to hear the Praises of Lewdness, as the *Sweets which Life improve?*

If a Person was to make a public Harangue in favour of *Image-Worship,* telling us, that it was the finest Means of raising the Heart to a Delight in God, we should think him a *very wicked Man,* and that the Ears and Hearts of Christians ought to detest such Discourses. Yet Christian People can meet in Crowds, and give their Money to have repeated in their Ears, what are here said to be *the Sweets which Life improve.* This, it seems, is no *Idolatry.*

We are told in Scripture, that *Covetousness is Idolatry;* and the Reason is, because it alienates the Heart from God, and makes it rest in something else. The covetous Man is an *Idolater*, because his Heart says, that *Gain* and *Bags* of Gold are the *Sweets which Life improve.* And can we think that that corrupt Heart, that celebrates *Lust* and *Wantonness*, as the *Sweets which Life improve*, is guilty of *less Idolatry*, than he that says the same thing of Riches? As sure as there is such a Sin as *Idolatry*, as sure as the sordid *Miser* is guilty of it, so sure is it that these words are chargeable, not only with excessive *Immodesty*, but plain *Idolatry*. For how do we think that the *Pagans* worshipped *Venus*? We cannot suppose that it was with *Fasting* and *Prayer*, or any *serious* Devotion. No; they paid her such a Devotion, as the *Stage* now does; they called upon her in *lewd* Songs, and praised her, in praising the Pleasures of Lust and Impurity, in rejoicing in her mighty Power, and celebrating her Pleasures, as the *Sweets which Life improve*.

These Women go on, and with Music and Voices, as wanton as their Words, are employed to make a deeper Impression on the Hearts of the Audience. Then enter *Bacchus, Pan*, and *Silenus*, attended with *Satyrs, Fawns*, and *Sylvans*.

And indeed, they enter very properly; for the Discourse is very agreeable to their Nature. But what have Christians to do with this Company? Do they come here to *renounce* their Religion? Or can they think that this Society, with the most beastly *Images* that the Heathen World could invent, is a Society that they may partake of without *Renouncing* Christ?

Our Religion charges us, not to *keep company, if anyone that is called a Brother be a fornicator*,* &c. But where have we left our Religion, if we not only accompany with People devoted to Impurity, but make their Company our Delight, and *hire* them to entertain us with all the lewd Imaginations that can be invented? If we are not content with this, but *conjure* up all the impure *Fictions* of the Heathen World, and make their *imaginary Deities* more vile and wanton than ever they made them, to render them agreeable to our Christian Minds, shall we reckon this among our *small Sins?* Shall we think it a pardonable Infirmity, or partake of such an Entertainment as this?

The Apostle says, *Ye cannot drink the Cup of the Lord, and the Cup of Devils: Ye cannot be partakers of the Lord's Table, and the Table of Devils.*† And can we think that we are not drinking the Cup of Devils, or that we are not at the Devil's Table, when his most favourite Instruments of Impiety, *Venus, Bacchus, Silenus, Satyrs* and *Fawns*, are the Company that we meet to be entertained with? If this is not being at the Devil's Table, he had no Table in the Heathen World. For surely they who call up Devils to their Entertainment, who cannot be enough delighted unless the Impious Demons of the Heathen

---

* 1 Cor. v. 11.   † 1 Cor. x. 21.

World converse with them, are in a stricter Communication with the Devil, than they who only eat of that Meat which had been offered in Sacrifice.

Our blessed Saviour says, *He that looketh upon a Woman to lust after her, hath already committed Adultery with her in his Heart.* Can we reckon ourselves his Disciples, who hire our Fellow-Christians, and Christian Women, whose chief Ornament is a sincere Modesty, to sing in merry Assemblies such Words as are used in this Entertainment.

Who can say that I carry Matters too high, when I call this *renouncing* Christianity? For, can any Words be more expressly contrary to the Doctrine of our Saviour, and that in so important a Point? And does he not sufficiently renounce Christianity, who renounces so great a Doctrine, that has Christ for its Author?

If we were to make a Jest of the *Sacraments* in our merry Assemblies, we should shew as much Regard to Christianity, as by such Discourses as these. For all *lewd Discourses* are as plainly contrary to essential Doctrines of Scripture, as any Ridicule upon the Sacraments that can be invented. It may be you could not sit in the *Play-House*, if you saw *Baptism* made a Jest of, and its Use reproached. But pray, why do not you think that there is as much *Profaneness* and *Irreligion* in impudent Speeches and Songs? Has not Christ said as much about *Purity* of Heart, as about either of the *Sacraments?* Has not he made Chastity of Heart as necessary to Salvation as the Sacraments? How comes it then, that an impudent Praise of Lust and Wantonness is not as *profane,* as a ridicule upon the Sacraments? What Rule of Reason or Religion do you go by, when you think it highly sinful to sit and hear the *Sacraments* jested upon, and yet are cheerful and delighted with such Songs and Discourses, as ridicule *Chastity* of Heart, and religious *Modesty?* Can you suppose, that in the Eyes of God you appear as a better Christian, than those who make merry with profaning the Sacraments? If you can think this, you must hold that the Sacraments are more essential to Religion than *Purity* of Heart; and that it is more acceptable to God to *wash,* than to be *clean;* more pleasing to him to treat the *Altar* as holy, than to live in *Holiness* of Heart.

The Sacraments have nothing valuable in their own Nature; they are only useful to Christians, and to be treated with Reverence, because Christ has appointed them as Means of Holiness. But Purity and Chastity of Heart is an essential and internal Excellence, that by its own Nature perfects the Soul, and renders it more acceptable to God. To abhor therefore a Jest upon the

Sacraments, and yet divert ourselves with *impure* Rant, and *lewd* Songs, is being like those who *abhor Idols*, and yet *commit Sacrilege*.

All therefore who partake of this sinful Entertainment, who take their Share of Mirth in such Scenes of Impurity and Lewdness, must look upon themselves, not only as Offenders against the Laws of *Purity*, but also as chargeable with such *Irreligion* and *Profaneness*, as they are who are merry in such Meetings as ridicule and deride the Use of the Holy Sacraments.

It is a great Aggravation of the Guilt of these Assemblies, that Women are employed to lay aside the peculiar Ornament of their Sex, and to add an Immodesty of Action and Address to immodest Speeches. If we knew of an Assembly, where Clergymen met to ridicule the *sacred Rites* of Religion for the sake of entertaining the Audience with *Eloquence ;* if we should find that great Part of the Audience were *Clergymen*, who could not forbear an Entertainment so contrary to their Profession ; it would easily be seen, that such a sinful Entertainment was more unreasonable, because Clergymen acted in it, and Clergymen came to be entertained with it.

Now this is the Case with the Stage-Entertainment. Women are as particularly called to a *singular Modesty*, as Clergymen are to the Duties of their Profession. If therefore Women act Parts in lewd and impudent Entertainments, they have as much forgot themselves, and appear as *detestable*, as Clergymen that talk *profanely*. And if other Women come to delight themselves with seeing their *Sisters* acting so contrary to themselves, and the peculiar Duties of their Condition, they as much forget themselves as those *Clergy* who should meet to see their *Brethren* raise Diversion out of *Profaneness*. When therefore virtuous and prudent Women think they may go to the *Stage*, where Women so openly depart from the Decencies which are necessary to their Sex, let them consider what they would think of such virtuous and prudent Divines, as should meet to see Clergymen openly contradict the Duties of their sacred Office. For it is the same Absurdity, for modest Women to take Pleasure in a Diversion where Women are *immodest*, as for a good Clergyman to be pleased with a Meeting where Clergymen are *profane*. This must be owned to be strictly true, unless it can be shewn, that *Impudence* and *Immodesty* are not so contrary to the Duties of *Women*, as *Profaneness* is contrary to the Duty of a *Clergyman*. For if there is the same Contrariety, then it must be equally monstrous for Women to encourage a Number of Women in an immodest way of Life, as for *Bishops* and *Priests* to encourage a Number of Clergymen in a State of *Profaneness*.

Let us now take one Step farther in this Entertainment. The *Stage* has now upon it, *Venus, Bacchus, Silenus, Pan, Satyrs, Fawns, Sylvans, Bacchanals,* and *Bacchantes.* Now if there were really such Beings as these, one would not wonder to see them got together. As they have all one common Nature of *Vileness,* they are sufficiently recommended to one another. But is it not astonishing, that these *fictitious Beings,* which are only imaginary Representations of such *Lust, Sensuality,* and *Madness,* as never had any real Existence, but were invented by the Devil for the Delusion of the Heathen World, should be preserved to talk their filthy Language to Congregations of *Christians?* And perhaps *Silenus* never so publicly recommended *Lust* and *Impudence* in any Heathen Assembly, as he does here among Christians. For our *Stage* has made him a fine Singer, that his Lewdness may have all the Recommendation which can be had from it.

Surely no one will now think that I carried the Charge too high, when I called the *Play-House* the House of the *Devil;* for if his *fictitious Beings,* talking his Language, and acting such Parts as they do, be not a sufficient Proof that it is his Work that is here carrying on, it is in vain to pretend to prove anything: There is no Certainty that two and two are four.

If our Eyes could shew us the *holy Angels* in our Church-Assemblies, it would not be a stronger Proof of the Divine Presence, than the seeing such Images as these and hearing their Language is a Proof that the *Stage* is the Devil's Ground. For how can he more certainly assure us of his Presence in any Place, than by *Satyrs, Bacchanals, Bacchantes,* and such like Images of Lewdness? He cannot appear to us as a Spirit; he must therefore get such *Beings* as *these* to appear for him; or, what seems to be more to his Purpose, make deluded Christians supply their Places. If therefore there be any certain Marks of the Devil's Power or Presence in any Assemblies, Places, or Temples of the Heathen World, the same are as certain Marks of his Power and Presence in our *Play-House.*

Again: Is it any Argument that the *Church* is God's House, because we there meet the *Ministers* of God, who act in his Name; because we there sing divine Hymns, hear holy Instructions, and raise our Hearts unto God and heavenly Matters; is this any Proof that we are then drawn near to God? If therefore there be a Place set apart for *lewd* and *profane* Discourses, where the same Beings are introduced as filled Heathen Temples, where we celebrate their Power, and praise their Being with wanton Songs and impure Rant, and where we open our Hearts to the Impressions of wild and disordered Passions, is not this as certain a Proof, that such a *Place* must belong to some Being that is *contrary* to God, and that we are then as certainly drawn near to him? He that does not see this with a sufficient Clearness, could never have seen that the Devil had any Power or Worship in the Heathen World. You must therefore observe, the *Play-House* is not called the House of the Devil, only by way of Terror, and to fright you from a bad Place; but it is called so, because it really is so in the strictest fullest Sense of the Words.

Let us now suppose, that the Disorders of the Stage cannot drive you from it; and that you are no more offended at the Meeting of these filthy Dæmons of the Heathen World, than if you were to meet your Friends.

If this be your Case, how will you prove that your Religion has had any Effect upon you, or that it has done you the least good? For if the same Lewdness and Immorality please you, which pleased the Worshippers of *Venus;* if you delight in such *Rant* and *Madness,* as was the Delight of *Bacchanals,* and *Bacchantes,* is not this a Proof that you have the same *Heart* and *Temper* that they had? And if you are like Idolaters in that which constituted their Idolatry, have you any Reason to think that Christianity has had any Effect upon you? It would even be *Profaneness* in anyone to pretend to the true Spirit of Christianity, so long as he can take pleasure in such an Entertainment as this. For what is there that is unlike to the Spirit of Christ, if this is not? Who that can rejoice in the Lewdness and Beastiality of *Silenus,* and the impure Rant of vile Dæmons, can make any Pretences to a reasonable Piety? Does this Company look as if we had anything holy and divine in our Tempers? Is this living in the Spirit of Christ? Is this the way to be as the Angels of God when we die? Shall we go from the Pleasures of *Bacchus, Silenus, Bacchanals,* and *Bacchantes,* to the Choir of blessed Spirits that are Above? Is there any Reasonableness or Fitness in these Things? Why should we think, that such a Life as this will have an End so contrary to it?

We reckon it strange Grossness of Mind in the *Turks,* to expect a *Paradise* of carnal Delights. But what a Degree of Grossness it is in us, to know the God of Purity, and hope for a Heaven which only the *pure in Heart* shall enjoy, and yet call up all the vile *Fictions* of Lust and Sensuality that corrupted the Heathen World to entertain our Hearts, that from their Mouths we may hear the Praises of Debauchery and Wantonness? Let any one but consider this, as everything ought to be considered, by the pure Light of Reason and Religion, and he will find that the Use of the Stage may be reckoned amongst our worst Sins, and that it is as great a Contradiction to our Religion, as any Corruption or vile Practice of the Heathen World.

I have made these few Reflections upon this Entertainment, not because it exceeds the ordinary Wickedness of the Stage, but for the contrary Reason, because it is far short of it, and is much less offensive than most of our *Plays*. That by shewing the *Stage* to be so impious and detestable, so contradictory to all Christian Piety, in an Entertainment that is moderate, if compared with almost all our Plays, there might be no room left for sober Christians to be at any Peace with it. They who would see how much the Impieties of the Stage exceed what I have here observed of this Entertainment, may consult Mr. *Collier's* short View of the Stage, Sir *Richard Blackmore's* Essays, and *A Serious Remonstrance, &c.*, by Mr. *Bedford*.

To return : *Levis* hears all these Arguments against the *Stage;* he owns they are very plain, and strictly prove all that they pretend to ; he does not offer one word against them; but still *Levis* has an Answer for them *all*, without answering any *one* of them. 'I have, says he, my own Experience, that these Diver-'sions never did me any hurt, and therefore I shall use them.'

But *Levis* does not consider, that this very Answer shews, that he is very much hurt by them; that they have so much disordered his Understanding, that he will defend his Use of them in the most absurd manner imaginable, rather than be driven from them by any Arguments from Religion. For how can a Man shew that he is more hurt by any Practice, or that it has more blinded and perverted his Mind, than by appealing to his own inward Experience in Defence of it, against the plain Nature and Reason of things? Let *Levis* look at this way of reasoning in other Matters. If a Person that prays in an *unknown Tongue*, should disregard all the Arguments that are brought to shew the Absurdity of it, and rest contented with saying, that it never hurt his Devotion, but that he was as much affected in that way, as he could possibly be in any other, *Levis* would certainly tell such a one, that he had lost his Understanding, and that his long Use of such absurd Devotions made him talk so absurdly about them.

Again : If a Worshipper of *Images* was, in Answer to the Second Commandment, only to say, that he had his own Experience that he found no hurt by them ; and that he had the same Devotion of Heart to God, as if he did not worship *Images ;* Or, suppose another Person to keep very ill Company ; and when he is told that *Evil communications corrupt good manners*, should content himself with saying, that he would still use the same ill Company, because he was sure it did him no hurt, nor made any

Impression upon him: Now as *Levis* would be sure that a Man was notoriously hurt by the Worship of *Images*, that should thus blindly defend them, and that the other is sufficiently hurt by ill Company, who should so obstinately stick to it, so he ought to be as sure, that he himself is sufficiently hurt either by Plays, or something else, when with an equal Blindness he defends his Use of them.

Farther: When *Levis* says, that he is sure that the Use of Plays does him no harm, let him consider what he means by that Speech. Does he mean, that though he uses the Diversion of the Stage, yet he finds himself in the true State of Religion; that he has all those holy Tempers in that degree of Perfection which Christianity requires? Now if he cannot say this; how can he say, he is sure that Plays do him no harm? If a Person was to affirm, that Intemperance did him no hurt, it would be expected that he should own that he was in a perfect State of Health; For if he had any Disorder or ill Habit of Body, he could not say, that his Intemperance did not contribute towards it. In like manner, if *Levis* will maintain that Plays do no ways disorder him, or corrupt his Heart; he must affirm, that he has no Disorder or Corruption of Heart belonging to him; for if he has, he cannot say that the Use of Plays does not contribute towards it.

When therefore *Levis* says, Plays do me no harm at all; it is the same thing as if he had said, I have no Disorder at all upon me; my Heart and all my Tempers are in that exact State of Purity and Perfection that they should be.

Again: Let *Levis* consider, that his Taste and Relish of the Stage is a Demonstration that he is already hurt by something or other; and that his Heart is not in a right State of Religion. *Levis* thinks this is a very censorious Accusation, because he is known to be a very good Churchman, to live a regular Life for the most part, to be charitable, and a Well-wisher to all good Designs. All this is true of *Levis*: But then it is as strictly true, that his Taste for Plays is a Demonstration, that his Heart is not in a right State of Religion. For does *Levis* think, that his frequenting the Church is any Sign of the State of his Heart? Am I to believe, that he has inward Dispositions that suit with the holy Strains of Divine Service, because he likes to be at Church? I grant, I am to believe this; there is good Reason for it. But then, if *Levis* uses the *Play-House*, if the disordered Passions, the lewd Images, the profane Rant, and immodest Parts that are there acted, are a Pleasure to him, is not this as strong a Demonstration, that he has some Dispositions and Tempers that suit with these Disorders? If I am to conclude anything from a Man's liking and frequenting Divine Service, is there not as certain a Conclusion to be drawn from a Man's liking and using the Stage? For the Stage can no more be liked, without having some inward Corruptions that are suitable to the Disorders that are there represented, than the Divine Service can be a Pleasure to anyone, that has no Holiness or Devotion in his Heart.

It is infallibly certain, that all Pleasures shew the *State* and *Condition* of our Minds; and that nothing can please us, but what suits with some Dispositions and Tempers that are within us; so that when we see a Man's Pleasures, we are sure that we see a great deal of his Nature. All *Forms* of Life, all *outward* Actions, may deceive us. We cannot absolutely say, that People have such Tempers because they do such Actions; but wherever People place any *Delight*, or receive any *Pleasures*, there we have an infallible Token of something in their Nature, and of what Tempers they have within them.

Diversions therefore and Pleasures, which are reckoned such uncertain Means of judging of the *State* of Men's Minds, are of all Means the most certain; because nothing can please us, or affect us, but what is according to our Nature, which finds something within us that is suitable to it. Had we not inward Dispositions of *Tenderness* and *Compassion*, we should not find ourselves softened and moved with *miserable* Objects. Had we not something *harmonious* in our Nature, we should not find ourselves pleased with Strains of *Music*. In like manner, had we not in our Nature lively Seeds of all those Disorders which are acted upon the Stage, were there not some *inward Corruption* that finds itself gratified by all the irregular Passions that are there represented, we should find no more Pleasure in the Stage, than blind Men find in *Pictures*, or deaf Men in *Music*.

And, on the other Hand, if we were full of the contrary Tempers, were our Hearts full of Affections contrary to those on the *Stage*, were we deeply affected with Desires of Purity and Holiness, we should find ourselves as much offended with all that passes upon the Stage, as *mild* and *gentle* Natures are offended at the Sight of *Cruelty* and *Barbarity*. These Things are of the utmost Certainty.

All People therefore, who use the *Stage*, have as much Assurance that their Heart is not in a right State of Religion, as they possibly can have of anything that relates to themselves.

I hope, none of my Readers will think this too general, or too rash an Assertion; but that they will rather observe, that it is founded on such Evidence of Reason as cannot be rejected, without rejecting everything that is plain and certain in Human

Nature. They must not think it a sufficient Answer to this, to consider either how good they are themselves, or how many excellent Persons they know who do not abstain from the Stage. For this is a way of Reasoning, that is not allowed in any other Case.

Now when it is affirmed, that all Persons who are pleased with the *Stage* must have some Corruptions of Heart, that are gratified with the corrupt Passions which are there acted, is not this as plain and evident, as if it was said, that all who are pleased with seeing barbarous Actions, must have some Seeds of Barbarity in their Nature? If you are delighted with the Stroke of the *Whip*, and love to see the *Blood* fly, is it not past all doubt, that you have a Barbarity within you? And if *impure* Speeches, if *wanton* Amours, if *wild* Passions, and *immoral* Rant, can give you any Delight, is it not equally past all doubt, that you have something of all these Disorders in your Nature? Is it any more uncharitable to affirm this, than to affirm, that all who love to see the *Blood* fly have something barbarous in their Nature? Is there any more Rashness or Severity in it, than in saying, that all who love such or such Strains of *Music* have some Disposition in their Nature that is gratified by them?

It signifies nothing therefore to say, that you know such or such excellent Persons who are pleased with the *Stage*, whom no one ought to suspect to be defective in Piety; it is as absurd as to say, that you know excellent Persons who are pleased with seeing barbarous Actions, whom no one ought to suspect to be defective in *Tenderness*. If you delight in barbarous Sights, and are pleased with the Groans and Pains of the Afflicted, I do not *suspect* you to be defective in *Tenderness*, you have put your Case out of all Suspicion, you have proved that you have a Barbarity in your Nature. So if you delight in the *Stage*, if you taste and relish its *Entertainment*, I do not *suspect* you to be *defective* in Piety; you have put your Case beyond Suspicion; you have proved that you have Dispositions in your Nature, that are gratified by the disorderly Passions of the *Stage*.

Again, consider it in another View: How is it possible that anyone should delight in the *Stage*, but through a Defect in Piety? For is not the Stage guilty of Impurity, Profaneness, Blasphemy, and Immorality? Now though People may differ about the Degree in which they will make this Charge, yet all must own it in some degree. Now if the Charge be but true in *any degree*, must there not be a Want of Piety in those that can partake of an Entertainment chargeable with *Impurity, Profaneness*, and *Immorality*? If People were so pious that they could not bear such an Entertainment as this, if nothing could persuade them to be present at it, this would be no Proof that they were Saints; for to abhor an Entertainment loaded with so much Guilt, is but a small Instance of an advanced Piety. But surely, if they cannot only bear it, but be pleased with it, it is Proof enough, that their Hearts want several Degrees of Piety which become Christians. Besides, can pious Persons, who use the *Stage*, tell you of any *one Play* for this forty or fifty Years, that has been free from *wild* Rant, *immodest* Passions, and *profane* Language? Must they not therefore be defective in Piety, who partake of a Diversion that is at *no time* free from this Guilt in some degree or other? But supposing there was such a thing as an *innocent Play* once or twice in an Age (which is like supposing *innocent* Lust, *sober* Rant, or *harmless* Profaneness) could this make it at all allowable for pious Persons to use the *Stage?* Could this be any Proof that Persons of real Piety might take Pleasure in it? For could it be consistent with an enlivened Piety to use a Diversion, which in its *common ordinary* State is full of monstrous Impiety and Profaneness, because it sometimes happened in a Number of Years, that it might be innocent for a Day or two? But even this does not happen. The Stage never has *one* innocent Play; not one can be produced that ever you saw acted in *either House*, but what abounds with *Thoughts, Passions,* and *Language*, contrary to Religion. Is there therefore any Rashness or Severity in saying, That Persons who use a Diversion, which in its *ordinary* State is full of monstrous Wickedness and Impiety, and in its *best* State is never free from Variety of Sin, must be defective in Piety? How can we know anything with Clearness and Evidence, if we know not this to be clear and evident? For surely it is a necessary Part of Piety to abhor Lewdness, Immorality, or Profaneness, wherever they are; but they who are so pious, as not to be able to be pleased where any of those are, have a Piety that will not permit them ever to see a Play.

There is no Doctrine of our Blessed Saviour, that more concerns all Christians, or is more essential to their Salvation, than this: *Blessed are the pure in heart, for they shall see God.* Now take the *Stage* in its best State, when some admired *Tragedy* is upon it, are the *extravagant Passions* of distracted Lovers, the *impure Ravings* of inflamed Heroes, the *Joys* and *Torments* of Love, and *gross Descriptions* of Lust; are the *indecent* Actions, the *amorous* Transports, the *wanton* Address of the Actors, which make so great a Part of the *most sober* and *modest* Tragedies; are these things consistent with this Christian Doctrine of *Purity of Heart?* You may as well imagine, that *Murder* and *Rapine* are consistent with *Charity* and *Meekness.*

It is therefore as necessary, as reasonable and as consistent with Christian Charity, to tell *Levis* that his Use and Delight in the *Stage* is as certain a Proof of his want of Piety, as to tell the same thing to a malicious, intemperate, or revengeful Person. Some People who are guilty of Personal Vices may have some Violence of Temptation, some natural Disorder to plead in their Excuse; they perhaps may be so tender as to desire to conceal them, and be afraid to encourage others in the like Practices; but the Use and Encouragement of the *Stage* has no Excuses of this kind; it has no *Infirmity*, *Surprise*, or *Violence* of Temptation, to appeal to; it shews no *Tenderness* of Mind, or *Concern* for others, but is a deliberate, continued, open and public Declaration in favour of *Lewdness*, *Immorality*, and *Profaneness*. Let anyone but collect, not all the Wickedness that has appeared on the Stage since he first used it, but only so much as passes there in *anyone* Season, and then he will see what a dreadful Load of Guilt he has brought upon himself. For surely no one can be so weak as to imagine, that he can use and encourage a wicked Entertainment, without making himself a *full Sharer* of all its Wickedness.

Archbishop *Tillotson* treats the Stage in this manner. 'I shall 'now speak a few Words concerning *Plays*, which, as they are 'now ordered among us, are a *mighty Reproach* to the Age and 'Nation.——As now the Stage is, they are *intolerable*, and not 'fit to be permitted in a *civilized*, much less a *Christian* Nation. 'They do most *notoriously* minister to Infidelity and Vice.—— 'And therefore I do not see how any Person *pretending* to 'Sobriety and Virtue, and especially to the *pure* and *holy* 'Religion of our Blessed Saviour, can without *great Guilt*, and 'open *Contradiction* to his holy Profession, be present at such 'lewd and immodest Plays, as too many are; who yet would 'take it very ill to be shut out of the Community of Christians, 'as they would most certainly have been in the first and purest 'Ages of Christianity.'*

Here let it be observed, that this Archbishop, who has generally been reckoned eminent for his *Moderation*, and *gentle* manner of treating everything, says of Plays, that they are a *mighty Reproach* to the Nation; that they are *intolerable*, and not fit to be permitted in a *Civilized*, much less a *Christian Nation;* that they *notoriously* minister to *Infidelity* and *Vice*.

Now this, I suppose, is as high a Charge, as he would have brought against the worst Articles of *Popery*. If I have said, that People cannot use the *Stage* without being defective in

---

* *Sermon upon Corrupt Communication.*

Piety, I have not said it in a declaiming way, but have asserted it from Variety of plain Arguments: But this great Man, so much admired for his *tender* Remarks upon *Persons* and *Things*, goes much farther. He does not say. that People of real and advanced Piety cannot use the *Stage*, but he makes it inconsistent with so much as *pretending to Sobriety and Virtue*, much less the *Purity* of the *holy Religion* of our Blessed Saviour. He does not say, that such People cannot be Excellent and Exemplary Christians, or that they must be defective in Piety, but he charges them with *great Guilt*, and *open Contradiction* to their holy Religion, and assures them, that if they had lived in the *first* and *purest* Ages of Christianity, they would have been excommunicated.

I have appealed to this *great Name*, for no other End, but to prevent the charge of Uncharitableness. For surely, if such an eminent Instance of a *charitable* and *gentle* Spirit can roundly affirm, that the Use of such a *Stage* as ours is an *open Contradiction* to Christianity, and such a scandalous Offence, as would certainly have been punished in the first and purest Ages of the Church with the dreadful Punishment of Excommunication; surely it can be no Proof of an *uncharitable Spirit* in me, that I shew by Variety of Arguments, that the Use of such a *Stage* cannot consist with the true Spirit of Christianity, but that there must be *some Defect* in their Piety, who are able to use it.

Jucunda resolves in great Cheerfulness to hear no Arguments against the *Stage:* She says it can be but a *small Sin;* and considering the Wickedness of the Age, that Person is in a very good State, that is only guilty of going to Plays. Desire her ever so often only to consider the plainest Arguments in the World, she puts all off with only this Reply, *God send I may have no greater Sin to answer for, than seeing a Play!*

Jucunda thinks a Clergyman would do better, to insist only upon the material Parts of Religion, and not lay so much Stress upon Things that are only *Diversions*, lest by making Religion to contradict People in everything, Religion itself should be brought into Dislike. *Jucunda* desires, that she may be instructed in some greater Things, than the Sinfulness of going to a *Play;* for she is resolved to hear no more of that.

But pray, *Jucunda*, consider all that you have here said. You say it can be but a *small Sin*. How is it that you know it is but a *small Sin?* What care have you taken to understand its true Magnitude? You shut your Eyes, and stop your Ears, and resolve against all Information about it, and then call it a *small Sin*. But suppose it was but a *small Sin;* is that a Reason why you should be guilty of it? Does the Smallness of Sins recom-

of the Stage-Entertainment. 175

mend them to your Choice? Our blessed Saviour says,* *If thy foot offend thee, cut it off; it is better for thee to enter halt into life, than having two feet to be cast into hell. And if thine eye offend thee, pluck it out; it is better for thee to enter into the kingdom of God with one eye, than having two eyes to be cast into hell-fire.* Now this passage, I suppose, does not mean, If thou art guilty of some great Sin, either of *Murder, Perjury*, or the like, thou must cut them off. For the Comparison of a *Foot* and an *Eye*, must signify something that is not directly sinful in itself, but only dangerous in its Use; as it sets us too near to some Sins, or is become too full of Temptation. Yet such Ways of Life as these, which are only dangerous, and expose our Virtue to too great a Hazard, however pleasant and useful, though like an Eye, or Foot, are yet to be entirely cut off, that we may not fall into Hell-fire. Can it be supposed that *Jucunda* is of this Religion, who pleases herself with a Diversion, because it is but a *small Sin*? Will she ever think of saving herself by cutting off a *Foot*, or plucking out an *Eye*?

Indeed, to talk of a *small Sin*, is like talking of a *small Law* of God: For as there is no Law of God but is a *great* one, because it comes from God, so every Sin, as it is a Transgression of some Law of God, must needs be a great one. There may be Sins that have a smaller degree of Guilt, because they are committed through *Infirmity, Ignorance*, or *Surprise;* but no Sin is small, that is either carelessly or wilfully continued in. If it be a Sin therefore to use the *Stage*, it cannot be a *small one*, because it has none of those Circumstances which render a Sin a small one. It becomes a very great one to *Jucunda*, because she carelessly and wilfully resolves to continue in it, merely for the sake of a little Diversion.

Let *Jucunda* consider again, what she means by wishing that she may have no greater Sin to answer for than going to a Play. It is a Wish that is silly in itself, because she is not to wish to die in small Sins, but in a perfect Repentance and Abhorrence of all kind of Sin; but it is much sillier still, when it is given as a Reason for going to a *Play*. For it is saying, *I expect to die guilty of greater Sins than of going to a Play, and therefore there is no Occasion to forbear from that.* Now, if she understands herself, she must know, that this is the plain Meaning of her Words. Yet who that understands anything of Religion, or that has any Desire of Holiness, can talk at this rate? It is a Language that is fitter for an *Atheist*, than for a Person that is but *half* a Christian. If a Tradesman that allows himself only

---

* Mark ix. 45, 47.

to lie in the Prices of his Goods, should content himself with saying, *God send I may have no greater Sin to answer for,* no one would suppose him to be much concerned about Religion. Yet as many Christian Reasons might be produced, to shew these Lies to be but small Sins, as to shew that the Use of the Stage is but a *small Sin.*

Jucunda would have a *Clergyman* insist upon the most material Parts of Religion, and not lay so much stress upon Things that are only Diversions. I am of your mind, *Jucunda*, that a Clergyman ought to insist upon the most material Parts of Religion; but then it does not follow, that he must not lay much Stress upon things that are *Diversions.* For as something that is called a Diversion may be entirely sinful, so if this should happen, it is as necessary for a Clergyman to call all Christians from it, as it is necessary to exhort them to keep the Commandments. Religion seems to have as little to do with *Trades,* as with *Diversions;* yet if a Trade be set up, that is in its own Nature wicked, there is nothing more material in Religion, than to declare the Necessity of forsaking such an Employment. But after all, *Jucunda,* the most essential, and most *material* Parts of Religion, are such as relate to *common Life,* such as alter our Ways of living, such as give Rules to all our Actions, and are the Measure of all our Conduct, whether in Business or Diversion. Nothing is so important in Religion to you, as that which makes you sober and wise, holy and heavenly-minded, in the whole Course of your Life. But you are for such *material Parts* of Religion, as should only distinguish you from a *Jew* or an *Infidel,* but make no Difference in common Life betwixt you and *Fops* and *Coquettes.* You are for a Religion that consists in Modes and Forms of Worship, that is tied to *Times* and *Places,* that only takes up a little of your time on *Sundays,* and leaves you all the Week to do as you please. But all this, *Jucunda,* is nothing. The Scripture has not said in vain, *He that is in Christ is a new Creature.* All the Law and the Gospel are in vain to you ; all Sacraments, Devotions, Doctrines, and Ordinances, are to no purpose, unless they make you this *new Creature* in all the Actions of your Life. He teaches you the most material Parts of Religion, who teaches you to be of a *religious Spirit* in everything that you do ; who teaches you to eat and drink, to labour and rest, to converse and divert yourself in such degrees, and to such ends, as best promote a pious Life.

If *Sots* and *Gluttons* should desire a *Clergyman* to insist upon the most material Parts of Religion, and not lay so great a stress upon *Gluttony* and *Intemperance,* which are things which only relate to *eating* and *drinking,* they would shew that they understood Religion as well as *Jucunda.* For everyone must see, that *some Diversions* may as much disorder the Heart, and be as contrary to Religion, as *Gluttony* and *Intemperance.* And perhaps as many People have lived and died unaffected with Religion, through a Course of *Diversions* and *Pleasures*, as through Gluttony and Intemperance.

If it displeases People to be told, that Religion is to prescribe Rules to their Diversions, they are as unreasonable as those are, who are displeased that Religion should prescribe Rules to their Tempers, and Passions, and Inclinations. For as Diversions are only the Gratifications of our Tempers, so if Religion is to forbear us in our Diversions, it is to forbear our Tempers, Passions, and Inclinations. But the Truth is, we ought to be more religiously cautious and watchful about our Diversions, than any other Part of common Life, not only because they take such deep hold of us, but because they have no necessary Foundation in Nature, but are our own Inventions. *Trade* and Business, though they are necessary for great Ends of Life, are yet to be subject to the strictest Rules of Religion; surely therefore *Diversions*, which are but like so many *Blanks* in Life, that are only invented to get rid of Time, surely such things ought of all others to have no *mixture* of anything that is sinful in them. For if the thing itself be hardly pardonable, surely it must be a high Crime to add to it the Sin of doing it in a sinful manner. For as Diversions are at best only Methods of losing Time, the most innocent have something in them that seems to want a Pardon; but if we cannot be content with such as only pass away our Hours, unless they gratify our disordered Passions, we are like those who are not content to sleep away their time, unless they can add the Pleasure of sinful Dreams.

Jucunda therefore is much mistaken, if she thinks that Religion has nothing to do with her Diversions, for there is nothing that requires a more religious Exactness than they do. If we are wrong in them, it is the same thing as if we are wrong in our Religion, or sinful in our Business. Nay, Sin in our Diversions is less excusable, and perhaps does us more harm than in anything else. For such as our Diversions are, such are we ourselves. If Religion therefore is to have any Power over us, if it is to enter into our Hearts, and alter and reform the State of our Souls, the greatest Work that it has to do, is to remove us from such Pleasures and Ways of Life as nourish and support a wrong State of our Souls.

If dying Sinners that go out of the World under a Load of Guilt could see what brought them into that State, it would often be found, that all their Sins, and Impieties, and Neglect of Duty, were solely owing to their Diversions; and perhaps were they to live their Lives over again, there would be no other possible way of living better than they had done, but by renouncing such ways of Life as were only looked upon as Diversions and Amusements.

People of Fashion and Quality have great Advantage above the Vulgar; their Condition and Education gives them a Liveliness and Brightness of Parts, from whence one might justly expect a more exalted Virtue. How comes it then, that we see as ill *Morals*, as open *Impiety*, as little *religious Wisdom*, and as great *Disorders* among them, as among the most rude uneducated Part of the World? It is because the *Politeness* of their Lives, their Course of Diversions and Amusements, and their Ways of spending their Time, as much extinguishes the *Wisdom* and *Light* of Religion, as the Grossness and Ignorance of the dullest Part of the World. A poor Creature that is doomed to a stupid Conversation, that sees nothing but *Drudgery*, and *Eating*, *Drinking*, and *Sleeping*, is as likely to have his Soul aspire to God, and aim at an exalted Virtue, as another that is always in the Brightness and Gaiety, of polite Pleasures. It is the same thing, whether the *good Seed* be burnt up with the Heat and Brightness of the *Sun*, or be lost in *Mud*. Many Persons that live and die in a *Mine*, that are confined to Drudgery and Darkness, are just so fatally destroyed by their way of Life, as others that live in a Circle of Pleasures and polite Engagements are destroyed by their way of Life. Everyone sees and owns the Effects of such a gross way of Life; it is not usual to expect anything wise, or holy, or truly great, from Persons that live and die digging *Coals*. But then it is not enough considered, that there are other ways of Life, of a contrary Appearance, that as certainly and unavoidably produce the same Effects. For a Heart that is devoted to *polite* Pleasures, that is taken up with a Succession of vain and corrupt *Diversions*, that is employed in *Assemblies, Gaming, Plays, Balls*, and such like Business of a *genteel* Life, is as much disposed of, and taken as far out of the way of true Religion, and a divine and holy Life, as if it had been shut up in a *Mine*. These are plain and certain Truths, if there is anything plain and certain, either in the Nature of Religion, or the Nature of Man. Who expects Piety from a *Tapster*, that lives among the Rudeness, Noise, and Intemperance of an *Ale-House?* Who expects Christian Holiness from a *Juggler*, that goes about with his *Cups* and *Balls*? Yet why is not this as reasonable, as to expect Piety and Christian Holiness from a *fine Gentleman* that lives at a *Gaming-Table?* Is there any more reason to look for Christian Fortitude, divine Tempers, or religious Greatness of Mind, in this State of Life?

Had such a one been born in low Life with the same turn of Mind, it had in all probability fixed him in an *Ale-House*, or furnished him with *Cups* and *Balls*.

The sober honest Employments of Life, and the reasonable Cares of every Condition in the World, make it sufficiently difficult for People to live enough to God, and to act with such holy and wise Tempers as Religion requires. But if we make our Wealth and Fortunes the Gratifications of idle and disordered Passions, we may make it as difficult to be saved in a State of *Politeness* and *Gentility*, as in the *basest* Occupations of Life.

Religion requires a steady resolute Use of our best Understanding, and an earnest Application to God for the Light and Assistance of his Holy Spirit.

It is only this watchful Temper, that is full of Attention to everything that is right and good, that watches over our Minds, and guards our Hearts, that desires Wisdom, and constantly calls upon God for the Light and Joy of his Holy Spirit; it is this Temper alone that can preserve us in any true State of Christian Holiness. There is no Possibility of having our Minds strengthened and fixed in wise and reasonable Judgments, or our Hearts full of good and regular Motions, but by living in such a *way of Life*, as assists and improves our Mind, and prepares and disposes us to receive the Spirit of God. This is as certainly the *one only* way to Holiness, as there is but one God that is Holy. Religion can no more subsist in a trifling vain Spirit, that lives by Humour and Fancy, that is full of Levity and Impertinence, wandering from Passion to Passion, giddy with silly Joys, and burdened with impertinent Cares, it can no more subsist with this State of the Soul, than it can dwell in a Heart *devoted* to Sin.

Any way of Life therefore that darkens our Minds, that misemploys our Understanding, that fills us with a trifling Spirit, that disorders our Passions, that separates us from the Spirit of God, is the same certain Road to Destruction, whether it arises from stupid *Sensuality*, rude *Ignorance*, or polite *Pleasures*. Had anyone therefore the Power of an *Apostle*, or the Tongue of an Angel, he could not employ it better, than in censuring and condemning those ways of Life, which *Wealth, Corruption,* and *Politeness*, have brought among us. We indeed only call them Diversions; but they do the whole Work of *Idolatry* and *Infidelity*, and fill People with so much Blindness and Hardness of Heart, that they neither live by Wisdom, nor feel the want of it, but are content to play away their Lives, as regardless of everything that is wise, and holy, and divine, as if they were mere *Birds*, or *Animals*, and as thoughtless of Death, and Judgment, and Eternity, as if these were Things that had no Relation to human Life.

Now all this Blindness and Hardness of Heart is owing to that way of Life which People of Fortune generally fall into. It is not gross Sins, it is not *Murder*, or *Adultery*, but it is their *Gentility* and *Politeness* that destroys them: It fills them with such Passions and Pleasures, as quite extinguish the gentle Light of Reason and Religion. For if Religion requires a sober Turn of Mind; if we cannot be reasonable, but by subduing and governing our blind Tempers and Passions; if the most necessary Enjoyments of Life require great Caution and Sobriety, that our Souls be not made earthly and sensual by them; what way of Life can so waste and destroy our Souls, so strengthen our Passions, and disorder our Hearts, as a Life of such Diversions, Entertainments, and Pleasures, as are the *Business* of great Part of the World?

If Religion is to reform our Souls, to deliver us from the Corruption of our Nature, to restore the divine Image, and fill us with such Tempers of Purity and Perfection, as may fit us for the Eternal Enjoyment of God, what is the polite Part of the World doing? For how can anyone more resist such a Religion as this; how can more renounce the Grace of God, and hinder the Recovery of the Divine Image, than by living in a Succession of such Enjoyments, as the Generality of People of Fashion are devoted to? For no one who uses the *Stage* has any more Reason to expect to grow in the Grace of God, or to be enlightened and purified by his Holy Spirit, than he that never uses any Devotion. So that it is not to be wondered at, if the Spirit and Power of Religion is wanted, where People so live, as neither to be fit to receive, nor able to co-operate with the Assistance and Light of God's Holy Spirit.

We are taught, that *Charity covereth a multitude of sins;* and that *alms shall purge away sins.* Now let this teach some People how to judge of the Guilt of those Gifts and Contributions, which are given contrary to Charity. I do not mean such Money, as is idly and impertinently squandered away, but such *Gifts* and *Contributions* as are to support People in a wicked Life. For this is so great a Contradiction to Charity, that it must certainly have Effects contrary to it: It must as much cover our *Virtues*, as Charity covers our Sins.

It is no strange Thing, to hear of *Ladies* taking care of a *Benefit-Night* in the Play-House. But surely they never reflect upon what they are doing. For if there is any Blessing that attends Charity, there must as great a Curse attend such Liberalities, as are to reward People for their Wickedness, and make them happy and prosperous in an unchristian Profession. How can they expect the Blessings of God, or to have their Virtues and Charities placed to their Account, when they have blotted them out, by their Contributions and Generosities to the most open Enemies of the Purity and Holiness of Christ's Religion? He that is thus in the Interest of the Play-House, is most openly against God, and is as certainly opposing Religion, as he that rewards those that labour in the Cause of Infidelity.

It is no uncharitable Assertion to affirm, that a Player cannot be a living Member of Christ, or in a true State of Grace, till he renounces his Profession with a sincere and deep Repentance. Christianity no more allows such Plays and Players as ours are, than it allows the grossest Vices. They are Objects of no other Charity or Kindness, than such as may reduce them to a sincere Repentance. What a Guilt therefore do they bring upon themselves, who make Players their Favourites, and public Objects of their Care and Generosity; who cannot be in the Favour of God, till they cease to be such as they encourage them to be, till they renounce that Life for which they esteem and reward them?

When an Object of *Distress* is offered to People, it is common to see them very scrupulous in their Charity; they seem to think there may be such a thing as a blamable Charity; they desire to know whether the Person be worthy, whether his Distress is not owing to his Follies and Extravagances, that they may not relieve such a one as ought to feel the Punishment of his Follies. But what must we say to these things, if those who are thus nice in their *Alms* are yet unreasonable in their *Generosities;* who are afraid of assisting a poor Man, till everything can be said in his Favour, and yet eager to make another rich, who is only recommended by his Follies? What shall we say to these things, if Persons who have so many Rules to govern and restrain their Piety to poor Men, have yet no Rules to govern their Liberalities and Kindness to Libertines, if they should have a *Benefit-Night* upon their hands, not to relieve the Poverty, but to reward the *Merit* of a Player, that he may have the Substance of a *Gentleman* from Christians, for a way of Life that would be a Reproach to a sober Heathen? Shall we reckon this among our small Offences? Is this a pardonable Instance of the Weakness of human Nature? Is it not rather an undeniable Proof, that Christianity has no hold of our Reason and Judgment? And that we must be born again from such a State of Heart as this, before we can enter into the Spirit of Christianity?

I have now only one thing to desire of the Reader, not that he would like and approve of these Reflections, but that he will not suffer himself to dislike or condemn them, till he has put his Arguments into Form, and knows how many Doctrines of Scripture he can bring against those things that I have asserted. So far as he can shew that I have reasoned wrong, or mistook the Doctrine of Scripture, so far he has a Right to censure. But *general Dislikes* are mere *Tempers* as blind as *Passions*, and are always the strongest where Reasons are most wanted. If People will dislike because they will, and condemn Doctrines only because it suits better with their *Tempers* and *Practices*, than to consider and understand them to be true, they act by the same Spirit of *Popery* as is most remarkable in the *lowest Bigots*, who are resolute in a *general Dislike* of all *Protestant* Doctrines, without suffering themselves to consider and understand upon what Truth they are founded.

I can easily imagine that some People will censure these Doctrines, as proceeding from a *rigid, uncharitable* Temper, because they seem to condemn so great a Part of the World. Had I wrote a Treatise against *Covetousness*, or *Intemperance*, it had certainly condemned great Part of the World; but surely he must have strangely forgot himself, that should make that a Reason of accusing me of an uncharitable Temper. Such People should consider also, that a Man cannot assert the Doctrines of Christian *Charity* and *Meekness* themselves, without condemning a very great Part of the World. But would it be an Instance of an uncharitable Spirit; to preach up the Necessity of an universal Charity, because it might condemn a very great Part of the World? And if the *Holiness* of Christianity cannot be asserted, without condemning the Pleasures and Entertainments of the fashionable Part of the World, is there any more Uncharitableness in this, than in asserting the Doctrine of universal Love? Does this any more shew an *unchristian rigid* Spirit, than when the beloved Apostle said, *All that is in the World, the Lust of the Flesh, the Lust of the Eyes, and the Pride of Life, is not of the Father, but is of the World?*

But I shall not now consider any more Objections, but leave all that I have said to the Conscience and Reason of every Person. Let him but make Reason and Religion the Measure of his Judgment, and then he is as favourable to me as I desire him to be.

It is very common and natural for People to struggle hard, and be loath to own anything to be wrong that they have long practised. Many People will see so much Truth in these Arguments against the *Stage*, that they will wish in their own Minds that they had always foreborne it. But then finding that they cannot assent to these Arguments, without taking a great deal of Blame to themselves, they will find strong Inclinations to condemn the plainest Reasonings, rather than condemn themselves. Let but a Person forget that he has any Guilt in relation to the *Stage,* let him but suppose that he has never been there, and that he will go or stay away, just as he finds Reason, when he has examined all that can be said against it, let a Man but put himself in this State of Mind, and then he will see all the Arguments against the Stage as plain and convincing, as any that can be brought against the grossest Vices.

If we could look into the Minds of the several Sorts of Readers, we should see how differently People are affected with Arguments, according to the State that they are in. We should see how they, who have never used the *Stage,* contend with the whole Force of their Minds, and see the Certainty and Plainness of every Argument against it. We should see others struggling and contending against all Conviction, in proportion to the Use that they have made of the *Stage.* They that have been its Friends and Advocates, and constant Admirers, will hate the very Name of a Book that is written against it, and will condemn every Argument, without knowing what it is. They who have used the *Stage* much, though in a less degree than this, will perhaps vouchsafe to read a Book against it; but they will read with Fear, they will strive not to be convinced, and be angry at every Argument, for proving so much as it does. Others, that have used the *Stage* in the most moderate degrees, have yet great Prejudices: They perhaps will own, that the *Stage* is blamable, and that it is very well to persuade People from it: But then, these People will not assent to the whole Truth. They will not condemn the Stage, as they ought, because having been there sometimes themselves, it suits better with their own Practice only to condemn it in the general, than to declare it to be sinful in such a degree, as should condemn those who ever use it.

These are the several Difficulties, which this Treatise has to contend with: It is to oppose an evil Practice, and charge it with *such a Degree* of Guilt, as few can consent to, without taking some Part of that Guilt to themselves.

I have mentioned these several Degrees of Prejudice, to put People upon suspecting themselves, and trying the Stage of their Hearts. For the only way to be wise and reasonable, is to suspect ourselves, and put Questions to ourselves in private, which only our own Hearts can answer. Let anyone who reads this Treatise, ask himself, Whether he reads it, as he reads those things which have no Relation to himself? When he reads a Treatise against *Image Worship,* or Prayers to *Saints,* he knows that he attends to the whole Force of the Arguments; that he desires to see them in their full Strength, and to comprehend every Evil that they charge upon it. Now everyone can tell, whether he reads this Treatise with this Temper, or whether he comes heavily to it, and unwilling to be convinced by it. If this is his State, he ought to charge himself with all that, which he charges upon the most absurd and perverse People in Life. For it is only this Temper, an *Inclination* not to be convinced, that makes People so *positive* and *obstinate* in Ways and Opinions, that appear so shocking to all reasonable Men. It is this Temper, that makes the *Jew*, the *Infidel*, the *Papist*, and the *Fanatic* of every kind. And he that is not reasonable enough to read impartially a Treatise against the *Stage*, has no Reason to think that his Mind is in better Order than their's is, who cannot freely consider a Book that is wrote against the *Worship of Images*, and Prayers to *Saints*.

There is but one Thing for reasonable People to do in this Case, either to answer all the Arguments here produced against the *Stage*, or to yield to the Truth of them, and regulate their Lives according to them. Our Conduct in this Affair is far from being a small Matter. I have produced no Arguments, but such as are taken from the most Essential Parts of Religion: If therefore there is any Truth in them, the Use of the *Stage* is certainly to be reckoned among *great* and *flagrant* Sins.

I have now only to advise those, who are hereby made sensible of the Necessity of renouncing the *Stage*, that they will act in this Case, as they expect that others should act in Cases of the like nature; that they will not think it sufficient to forbear the Stage themselves, but be instrumental as far as they can in keeping others from it; and that they will think it as necessary to make this Amends for their former Compliance, and ill Example, as it is necessary to make *Restitution* in cases of Injury. The Cause of Religion, the Honour of God, the Good of their Neighbour, and the Peace and Satisfaction of their own Minds, necessarily require this at their Hands. For as no one can tell how far his Example may have influenced others, and how many People may have been injured by his means, so it is absolutely necessary, that he do as much good as he can by a better Example, and make his own Change of Life a Means of reducing others to the same State of Amendment.

FINIS.

www.ingramcontent.com/pod-product-compliance
Lightning Source LLC
Chambersburg PA
CBHW051928160426
43198CB00012B/2077